THE DRAGON
AND THE DOVE

The Plays of
Thomas Dekker

JULIA GASPER

D1084272

CLARENDON PRESS · OXFORD
1990

Oxford University Press, Walton Street, Oxford OX2 6DP
Oxford New York Toronto
Delhi Bombay Calcutta Madras Karachi
Petaling Jaya Singapore Hong Kong Tokyo
Nairobi Dar es Salaam Cape Town
Melbourne Auckland
and associated companies in
Berlin Ibadan

Oxford is a trade mark of Oxford University Press

Published in the United States
by Oxford University Press, New York

British Library Cataloguing in Publication Data
Gasper, Julia
The dragon and the dove: the plays of Thomas Dekker.—
(Oxford English Monographs).
1. Drama in English. Dekker, Thomas, ca.1572–ca.1632.
critical studies
I. Title   822'.3
ISBN 0–19–811758–2

Library of Congress Cataloging in Publication Data
Gasper, Julia.
The dragon and the dove: the plays of Thomas Dekker/Julia
Gasper.
p. cm.—(Oxford English Monographs)
Includes bibliographical references.
1. Dekker, Thomas, ca.1572–1632—Criticism and interpretation.
2. Apocalyptic literature—History and criticism. 3. Kings and
rulers in literature. 4. Protestantism and literature. I. Title.
II. Series.
PR2494.G37   1990   822'.3—dc20   2   i   89–48077
ISBN 0–19–811758–2

Typeset by Cambrian Typesetters, Frimley, Surrey
Printed and bound in Great Britain by
Bookcraft Ltd, Midsomer Norton, Bath

THE DRAGON
AND THE DOVE

OXFORD ENGLISH MONOGRAPHS

General Editors
CHRISTOPHER BUTLER   STEPHEN GILL

DOUGLAS GRAY   EMRYS JONES

ROGER LONSDALE

To Marcus

ACKNOWLEDGEMENTS

I am indebted to far more people than I can possibly name for advice, support, and encouragement of every kind. The following list must necessarily be minimal.

My principal thanks go to my supervisor, Professor John Carey. I would also like to thank: Dr Simon L. Adams of Strathclyde University; Ian Archer of Trinity College, Oxford; Professor Fredson Bowers; Susan Brigdon of Lincoln College, Oxford; Julia Briggs of Hertford College, Oxford; the Cambridge University Press for permission to quote from *The Dramatic Works of Thomas Dekker* ed. Fredson Bowers; Michael Dewar of Keble College, Oxford; Katherine Duncan-Jones of Somerville College, Oxford; Dr Lewis S. Feuer; Dr Martin Garrett; Donald Gasper of Glasgow University; Dr Richard Hamer of Christ Church, Oxford; Dr Jennifer Johnson of Hertford College, Oxford; Professor Emrys Jones; the librarians of the Bodleian Library; the librarians of the British Library, and of the Ashmolean Museum, Oxford, the English Faculty and the History Faculty Libraries, Oxford, the libraries of All Souls College, the Blackfriars, Christ Church, Corpus Christi College, Exeter College, Merton College, Queens College, Trinity College, and Wadham College, Oxford, and those of Emmanuel College, Peterhouse, St John's College, Sidney Sussex College, Trinity College, and Trinity Hall, Cambridge, the Cambridge University Library, the Glasgow University Library, the Cathedral Library, Lincoln, and the library of Dulwich College, London; Carolyn Lyle of Reading University; Dr David Norbrook of Magdalen College, Oxford; Miss Daphne Park and the Fellows and librarians of Somerville College, Oxford; Dr R. W. Scribner of Clare College, Cambridge; Professor Robert Smallwood of the Shakespeare Institute, Birmingham; Dr Blair Worden of St Edmund Hall, Oxford; and Lynn Young of Brasenose College, Oxford, who advised me on atrocities.

CONTENTS

LIST OF ILLUSTRATIONS

Photographs are by courtesy of the Bodleian Library, fol. θ 346,
Rawl. 4° 205, F. 31 Th.

ABBREVIATIONS

Very few abbreviations have been used, apart from a few obvious and familiar ones:

BH	*Britannia's Honor*
Cal. State Pap. Dom.	*Calendar of State Papers, Domestic series, reigns of Elizabeth I and James I*
CUP	Cambridge University Press
DNB	*Dictionary of National Biography*
2 HW	*The Honest Whore, Part Two*
ITBNAGP	*If This Be Not A Good Play, the Devil Is In It*
LT	*London's Tempe*
ME	*The Magnificent Entertainment*
MML	*Match Me In London*
N & Q	*Notes and Queries*
NSS	*The Noble Spanish Soldier*
OED	*Oxford English Dictionary*
OF	*Old Fortunatus*
OUP	Oxford University Press
Sat.	*Satiromastix*
SD	*The Sun's Darling*
SH	*The Shoemakers' Holiday*
STW	*Sir Thomas Wyatt*
TLS	*Times Literary Supplement*
VM	*The Virgin Martyr*
WB	*The Whore of Babylon*
WBW	*Women Beware Women* (by Middleton)

All quotations from Dekker's plays are from *The Dramatic Works of Thomas Dekker*, edited by Fredson Bowers.

INTRODUCTION

THIS study concentrates on the religious-political aspect of Dekker's work for the theatre. There have been two prevalent critical views of Dekker in the twentieth century. One is that his work is an expression of nascent bourgeois capitalism. That is an anachronistic view, even by Marxist standards, and its weaknesses are discussed in detail in Chapter 1. The second view is even more hostile, because it is patronizing: the idea that Dekker is gentle and tolerant, but naïve and simple, a sort of good-natured village idiot grinning on a wall. In a rather hasty essay of 1936, which attributed to Dekker passages (in *Patient Grissil*) that are very probably by Chettle, Una Ellis-Fermor accused Dekker of lacking 'a reasoned and coherent group of principles either moral or aesthetic'.[1] It is strange that a writer of Dekker's homiletic tendency should be called unprincipled. Yet the influence of this view has been very extensive, and it has never really been refuted.

M.-T. Jones-Davies's immense and scholarly study, *Un peintre de la vie londonienne: Thomas Dekker*, appears to seek unity in the subject-matter of Dekker's work rather than in his use of that subject-matter. While saying much about his passion for justice, she defines his political beliefs as conservative, nationalistic, and insular.[2] In G. R. Price's book, *Thomas Dekker*, we get a condescending picture. He says that Dekker addresses the individual conscience only, and is not interested in social reform; also that he is 'tolerant' and has no sense of irony.[3] In the recent apparatus to the Cambridge edition of Dekker's collected plays, Cyrus Hoy takes Ellis-Fermor's view to a hostile extreme. He presents Dekker as a completely unprincipled author, willing to write on the Protestant or the Catholic side, and imitating whatever

---

[1] Una Ellis-Fermor, *The Jacobean Drama: An Interpretation* (Methuen and Co.: London, 1936), 119–22.

[2] M.-T. Jones-Davies, *Un peintre de la vie londonienne: Thomas Dekker* (2 vols; Collection des Études Anglaises; Librairie Marcel Didier: Paris, 1958), ii. 400–1.

[3] G. R. Price, *Thomas Dekker* (Twayne's English Authors Series, 71; Twayne Publishers Inc.: New York, 1969), 158, 141–2, 153.

genre, style, or ideas happened to be in vogue. Hoy devotes a great deal of space to Dekker's borrowings, proven or hypothetical, from other works, while saying nothing about other writers' possible indebtedness to Dekker, though the latter group includes Webster and Donne.[4] In both respects Hoy is extremely biased. The influence of Ellis-Fermor can again be seen in M. C. Bradbrook's essay on Dekker in her widely used book *The Growth and Structure of Elizabethan Comedy*. Bradbrook follows Ellis-Fermor in attacking *Patient Grissil* and while one can understand their dislike of the Griselda tradition, they are quite wrong to blame this ancient commonplace on Dekker or even on Chettle.[5] It is frequently found in Shakespeare, and countless other authors. Dekker was actually among the first writers to attack the sexual double standard—in *The Honest Whore, Part Two*—and anticipated Puritan theologians in this respect.

As a playwright, Dekker most certainly had principles, and their imprint is to be found throughout his work, even in the plays he wrote in collaboration. The terms I have used for them most often are ungainly but precise, and may need some explanation. The first is 'religious-political'. In the Reformation era, religion and politics were inseparable, and many, such as Dekker, regarded their separation as not only difficult but undesirable.

The second term is 'militant Protestant'. This refers to those Protestants who were determined to defend the Reformation and made this their highest political priority. They regarded the Reformed Church as the only True Church, and conceived of it as a single, international body. They emphasized its common beliefs, whether Lutheran or Calvinist, and thought that a unified, active defence was necessary in order to survive in the struggle against their great adversary, Rome. In practical terms this meant seeking alliances with Protestant powers abroad, such as the United Provinces, the Scandinavian kingdoms, and the Evangelical

---

[4] Philip Dust, 'A Source for John Donne's Seventeenth Meditation in Rowley, Dekker and Ford's *The Witch of Edmonton*', *N & Q* CCXXIX (June 1984), 231–2. To be fair, this article did not appear until after Hoy's apparatus. For other influences, see below.

[5] M. C. Bradbrook, *The Growth and Structure of Elizabethan Comedy* (Chatto and Windus: London, 1955), 122–31.

Union, as well as welcoming Protestant refugees in England. Military intervention on behalf of other Protestant groups under Catholic attack, such as the Huguenots or the Dutch, was seen as imperative. It was both a religious duty and a form of extended self-preservation. Alliances with Roman Catholic powers, however advantageous they might appear, were to be distrusted and shunned, and economic interests to be, if necessary, sacrificed in the pursuit of this one overriding aim, the preservation of the Reformed Church.

Militant Protestants were deeply influenced by apocalyptic theology; this led them to envisage the world as a dualistic struggle, whose ultimate outcome must be the triumph of the True Church. In England the works of John Foxe, which were placed in every church in the land during Queen Elizabeth's reign, did much to propagate these beliefs. Foxe, whose works provided a comprehensive and coherent interpretation of known history, can be seen as a key figure in the militant Protestant tradition in England. The idea (popularized by Haller) that Foxe's work was nationalistic has already been rejected by several scholars, and the belief that he exalted the authority of the Crown also needs to be re-examined. Foxe exalted the royal authority—and that of Queen Elizabeth in particular—so long as it served the True Church. But when it did not, his attitude to it is highly ambivalent. Throughout Foxe's work there is an identification of the roles of tyrant and persecutor. Almost all of Foxe's thousands of martyrs across the ages were rebels against the authority of their time, whether emperors, popes, or kings. Calvin had taught that this persecution was ordained and was a sign by which the elect could be recognized. Yet while accepting this, Foxe consistently presents the rebels, and not the civil authority, as having moral and religious right on their side. In places, he goes further, and justifies the religious war of the Hussites in fifteenth-century Bohemia against their imperial and monarchical rulers.

This judgement was not good news for absolute monarchs. Foxe by implication did more to encourage rebellion against any future tyrant and persecutor than he did resignation. He, more than any other writer, taught subjects to criticize and judge their rulers, to approve them as saints and martyrs like

King John, or to condemn them as Bloody Marys, Neros, and Antichrists. This was not the blind obedience demanded by the catechism. In fact it was an inherently unstable basis for authority, a compromise that postponed crisis.

The fusion of religion and politics is always a powerful, indeed a momentous, force. This is one reason why both Queen Elizabeth and King James distrusted militant Protestantism. While it usually professed ardent support for the monarchy, its support was of a suspect kind. Not only did militant Protestants feel solidarity with the martyr-rebels of the past, but they were keen to take up arms for persecuted saints abroad in their own day. By absolutist standards, many of these fellow-Protestants were rebels against their lawful sovereign, and this dilemma is a highly significant one that recurs throughout Dekker's career. Both Elizabeth and James realized that militant Protestantism, if taken far enough, was as much a threat to monarchical principle as the notorious teachings of the Jesuits. The Protestant George Buchanan, tutor to King James, had taught in his *De Iure Regni Apud Scotos* (1579) that rebellion against tyrants was obedience to God, and advocated that monarchs could be deposed or legally executed.[6] James was as fond of Buchanan as Nero was of Seneca, and in his *Basilicon Doron* advised Prince Henry to have Buchanan's 'infamovs' works suppressed if any survived into the next reign.[7] Dekker is less certain to have read Buchanan than he is to have read Foxe, and militant Protestants in England were reluctant to adopt, or at least to profess, Buchanan's position. Yet it tended to slip out in their attitude to foreign affairs, and almost any principle held passionately enough must clash with absolutism sooner or later; militant Protestantism, with its dualistic vision of the world and conviction of its own divine right, was not designed for compromise.

Militant Protestantism was confined to no rank, high or low, courtier or citizen, educated or uneducated. It included apprentices as well as peers, bishops as well as soldiers,

---

[6] G. Buchanan, *The Powers of the Crown in Scotland*, trans. C. F. Arrowood (University of Texas Press: Austin, 1949), 143–5.

[7] *The Basilicon Doron of King James VI*, ed. J. Craigie (Scottish Text Society, 3rd series, vol. 16; Edinburgh, 1944), 148.

women as well as men. Its leaders were drawn, however, from the highest rank. When it could not get the sort of committed leadership it wanted from the monarch, it turned to such unofficial leaders as the Earl of Leicester, the Earl of Essex, Prince Henry, and, later, the King and Queen of Bohemia. S. L. Adams has used the term 'political Puritan', or simply 'Puritan', to denote those who held views like Foxe and Dekker, but there are many reasons which make an alternative term desirable.[8] Not only was the term 'Puritan' almost as pejorative in Dekker's time as now (when it has become a term of ignorant abuse), but it was so loosely applied that it could mean anyone from King James to the Anabaptists.[9] Even when used in a neutral and a precise sense, it has many connotations that are inappropriate for militant Protestants, and for Dekker in particular.

If 'Puritan' is taken to mean those who wished for some further reform in the English Church, there were some militant Protestants who did so, but they regarded such issues as secondary. Dekker never attacks the Prayer Book or the office of bishop. In later life he seems to have written a poem, *Paul His Temple Triumphant*, rejoicing in the restoration of London's cathedral.[10] While Dekker was no philistine Roundhead soldier, he did believe in some fundamental reforms, such as the abolition of pluralism, and he may also have had some sympathy for Sabbatarianism, to judge from *If This Be Not A Good Play*.

If we take 'Puritan' to mean separatist, it is even less applicable. Dekker disliked breakaway sects, and when he used the term 'Puritan' himself—in for instance *The Seuen Deadly Sinnes of London* or *If This Be Not A Good Play*—it was to satirize such groups. Memories of the Anabaptist rule in Münster still lingered, and Dekker often suspects separatists

[8] See his articles quoted throughout, and also S. L. Adams, 'The Protestant Cause: Religious Alliance with the European Calvinist Communities as a Political Issue in England, 1585–1630', D.Phil. thesis (Oxford, 1972), esp. pp. 1–5. Many critics have classified Dekker as a Puritan, since Mary Grace Adkins, 'Puritanism in the Plays and Pamphlets of Thomas Dekker', *University of Texas Studies in English* (8 July 1939), 87.

[9] Christopher Hill, *Society and Puritanism in Pre-Revolutionary England* (Martin Secker and Warburg: London, 1964), ch. 1, 'The Definition of a Puritan', 13–29.

[10] Discovered and edited by F. David Hoeniger, *Renaissance News*, XVI (1963), 181–200.

of immorality or hypocrisy.[11] He would have regarded Milton's non-attendance at church with deep suspicion, as weakening the unity of the Reformed Church.

'Puritan' can mean simply Calvinist, but Calvinism was common and indeed semi-official in the Elizabethan Church of England. Of course it dithered and wavered about this, as about most other things in the course of its history. Among the Thirty-nine Articles drawn up by the Elizabethan Church in 1562, number seventeen runs:

XVII. Of Predestination and Election.

Predestination to Life is the everlasting purpose of God, whereby (before the foundations of the world were laid) he hath constantly decreed by his counsel secret to us, to deliver from curse and damnation those whom he hath chosen in Christ to everlasting salvation.

Below this we find:

. . . So, for curious and carnal persons, lacking the spirit of Christ, to have continually before their eyes the sentence of God's Predestination, is a most dangerous downfal, whereby the Devil doth thrust them either into desperation, or into wretchlessness of most unclean living, no less perilous than desperation.[12]

It starts by suggesting optimistically that all are predestined to salvation, then implies that only some are so chosen, and goes on to warn that this is a pernicious doctrine. If it is dangerous, then why put it into the Articles of Religion? Are some souls predestined to hell or not? The Archbishop of Canterbury from 1611, George Abbott, was a convinced Calvinist, and his political views were those of a militant Protestant. The occupant of the See of Canterbury can hardly be classified as a Puritan.

---

[11] *The Non-Dramatic Works of Thomas Dekker*, ed. Revd A. B. Grosart (5 vols.; The Huth Library: Aylesbury, 1884–5), ii. 21. Also *ITBNAGP*, V. iv. 261, and *The Dramatic Works of Thomas Dekker*, ed. F. Bowers (4 vols.; CUP: Cambridge, 1953–61), iii. 210.

[12] 'ARTICLES agreed upon by the Archbishops and Bishops of both Provinces and the whole Clergy in the Convocation holden at *London* in the Year 1562, for the Avoiding of Diversities of Opinions and for the establishing of Consent touching True Religion', *The Book of Common Prayer . . . according to the Use of the Church of England* (Cambridge University Press, n.d., printed by John Clay, MA).

While militant Protestants in England were Calvinist, the difference between Catholic and Protestant was far more important to them than the difference between Calvinist and Lutheran or even Sub-Utraquist. Dekker, who was probably the offspring of refugees from Catholic persecution in the Netherlands, must have been a Calvinist, but it is difficult to find any explicit statement of this in his writings.

In his poem *Dekker His Dreame*, Dekker describes a vision of the Last Judgement. Two 'huge bookes' are opened in which everything past and present is written.[13] The margin gives the source-text as Rev. 20: 12, which says that 'the dead were judged out of those things which were written in the books, according to their works.' We may identify this with the 'book of life of the Lamb slain from the foundation of the world' mentioned earlier in Rev. 13: 8. The first text was often taken as evidence for predestination, but Dekker's preference for the second text may be significant.

Dekker never seems to use the word 'elect', but in his book of prayers, *Foure Birds of Noahs Arke*, he includes a prayer for the Church, and a prayer in time of persecution. The former asks that only 'thy chosen flocke' and not 'the reprobate' should feed in the Temple, while the latter uses the gospel metaphor of the wolves attacking the sheep, which had acquired Calvinist overtones, and links it to the prayer for the Church.[14] Only these few words indicate that Dekker accepted the doctrine of predestination, though entire plays testify to his belief in Protestant solidarity.

To call militant Protestants 'Anglican' would be equally misleading, though not because the term 'Anglican' post-dates the Elizabethan age—an objection put forward by Patrick Collinson.[15] On the same grounds we would have to rule out such terms as 'the Plague bacillus' or 'the Thirty Years' War', or 'inflation' or 'the last decade of Queen Elizabeth's reign': in fact, historians and critics would need to write entirely in Elizabethan English. The real problem with

---

[13] Grosart, iii. 25–6.

[14] *Foure Birds of Noahs Arke*, ed. F. P. Wilson (Basil Blackwell: Oxford, 1924), 117–18, 150.

[15] Patrick Collinson, *The Elizabethan Puritan Movement* (Jonathan Cape: London, 1967), 13.

'Anglican' is that it suggests both Arminianism and insularity. Militant Protestants saw themselves as members of an international Church, whereas Anglo-Catholics who disliked Calvinism also tended to disclaim militant Protestant views on foreign policy. The latter were trying to separate religion from politics, which is precisely what militant Protestants refused to do.

The belief that the typical Elizabethan was chauvinistic is related to the somewhat outdated elect-nation interpretation of Foxe. Dekker clearly renounces this kind of attitude: 'Can the father of the world measure out his loue so vnequally, that one people (like to a mans yongest child) should be more made of than all the rest, being more vnruly than all the rest?' he wrote in *The Seuen Deadly Sinnes*.[16] In the same work he said that there was cruelty in England to compare with the Spanish Inquisition, and accused London of bowing down to the seven-headed beast of corruption.[17] There was patriotic feeling in Elizabethan minds, of course, even some nationalism in times of war, but to militant Protestants there were higher principles. The experience of the Marian exiles and the refugee communities had given them a sense of wider loyalties.

The term 'Protestant' is one that people are curiously reluctant to use. Irving Ribner follows a mass of reference books in calling Dekker 'anti-Catholic', and this kind of negative and prejudicial terminology is typical.[18] David Bevington again calls *The Whore of Babylon* 'anti-Catholic'. He also misleadingly terms Dekker 'Anglican' and 'conservative'.[19] The latter term can only be confusing applied to an era when every political group sought justification in archaism or primitive right, and condemned its opponents as innovators.

Margot Heinemann's controversial book on Middleton employs, from first to last, such terms as 'anti-Catholic', 'anti-Spanish', 'popular anti-Popish feeling'. She also defines

---

[16] Grosart, ii. 10.   [17] Ibid. ii. 75, 79.

[18] Irving Ribner, *The English History Play in the Age of Shakespeare* (Methuen and Co: London, 1957; rev. edn. 1965), 286.

[19] David Bevington, *Tudor Drama and Politics: A Critical Approach to Topical Meaning* (Harvard University Press: Cambridge, Mass., 1968), 292.

Middleton as a Puritan, although he was further from being one in any sense than Dekker was, and Heinemann herself has to admit that 'Middleton never uses the word Puritan in a favourable sense'.[20] A recent article listed among the causes of the Civil War 'a kind of public anti-Popery paranoia'—one of the oddest names for the Reformation I have heard.[21] Yet while such derogatory expressions are rife, nobody refers to the Vatican as 'anti-Protestant'. Dekker's work has certainly suffered from being assessed in these negative terms, and the term 'militant Protestant' is more neutral and more precise than any of these. It is also free from confusing associations with the Civil War era.

Dekker was not the only militant Protestant playwright of his generation. Marlowe, Chapman, Heywood, Webster, Fletcher, and Massinger were all involved with the cause from time to time. But Dekker's commitment to it was stronger and more lasting than any other writer's, and he was the author of *The Whore of Babylon*, which can be called the definitive militant Protestant play. When in his later career Dekker collaborated with younger writers such as Massinger and Ford, the results are still consistent with his own previous work.

Dekker had a great admiration for Spenser. In *A Knight's Conjuring* Dekker places Spenser beside Chaucer in the Elysian grove of poets, and imagines him reciting to his heavenly audience the six remaining books of his unfinished *Faerie Queene*.[22] King James took grave offence at *The Faerie Queene*, because of its defamation of his mother, and attempted to have Spenser brought to trial for it in 1596.[23] This politically sensitive element in the book, particularly the portrayal of Una and Duessa, is the part of *The Faerie Queene* that reveals the influence of Foxe and militant Protestantism most clearly. The fact that militant Protestant

---

[20] Margot Heinemann, *Puritanism and Theatre: Thomas Middleton and Opposition Drama under the Early Stuarts* (CUP: Cambridge 1980), 2, 151, 203, etc.; p. 77.

[21] S. A. Burrell, review of L. L. Peck's biography of Northampton, *Renaissance Quarterly*, XXXVII, no. 3 (Autumn 1984), 455.

[22] *A Knight's Conjuring, Done in Earnest: Discovered in Jest*, ed. E. F. Rimbault (Percy Society Reprints, vol. V, 1842), 75.

[23] D. H. Willson, *King James VI and I* (Jonathan Cape: London, 1956; rpt. 1971), 139.

views were widespread did not make them inoffensive or safe, and Essex did end up on the scaffold.

Dekker's career as a playwright was a reckless one, because he could not depart from his principles. Not only do his plays provide an extensive commentary on the acts of three successive monarchs during a quarter of a century: they participate energetically in religious-political affairs, attacking, defending, or satirizing, and always stirring up support for the Protestant cause at home and abroad. It is extraordinary that Dekker has such a reputation for gentleness and tolerance when he was a life-long supporter of what could be called the war-party.

The theatre's active involvement in religious-political affairs was of course illegal, but it was also characteristic of the age. Censorship does not seem to have dampened the creativity of the Elizabethan dramatists: where it did not persuade them to seek general themes, it certainly sharpened their wits and stretched their ingenuity. Of course militant Protestants in power imposed censorship on their opponents as assiduously as they evaded it themselves. They did not wish, like Milton, to remove censorship, though they often disagreed with the authorities about what should be censored. The existence of this censorship poses problems for interpretation which can be enlightened by consulting the censors themselves: when works of fiction or drama were examined by the Master of Revels or by the Privy Council, they supposed that an author used, and perhaps habitually used, two voices, one direct, and the other indirect.[24] The indirect voice could be understood by the audience because it generally made use of consistent strategies; but this is not to say that the direct voice always lies. They seem, in Dekker's case, to complement each other in interesting ways. To ignore this second voice, or to dismiss it as topical or commercial, is to dismiss a whole tradition of English writing that runs from Spenser to Dryden (at the very least).

We can get a useful insight into Dekker's religious-political views by looking at the prayers he wrote for the royal family in *Foure Birds of Noahs Arke* (1609). Queen Elizabeth is

---

[24] See examples discussed below, e.g. that of John Hayward.

referred to as 'the vertuous and renowned Queene ELIZABETH, of most happie memorie' and a prayer attributed to her is included.[25] The prayer for Prince Henry provides a very militant Protestant vision of his future:

Let Religion be the columne upon which hee shall alwayes stand, zeale the pillow upon which hee shall kneele, and the quarrel of the Gospel, for which he shall goe to warre: knit therfore (O Lord) strength to his right arme, and when a good cause calles him (at his manly state) into the field, gird thou about his loines the sword of victory.[26]

Most interestingly, the prayer for King James begins:

Kings are gods upon earth, yet (O Lord) they are but thy servants; they rule Kingdomes, yet the chariot of their Empire turnes over and over, unlesse thou teach their hands how to hold the bridle. More then men they are amongst men, yet lesse they are then themselves, if they break thy lawes: for sithence they are thy Stewards, and are trusted with much, it is a great reckoning to which they must answere . . .[27]

'Stewards' is a pun on the name Stuart, or Stewart as it had been spelt until Mary Queen of Scots gave it a more refined form. She did not wish the name of a household servant to impair her royal dignity, but Dekker is deliberately reviving it here in an iconoclastic way: the King has a family name like any other man, and can be compared to a servant: the same pun occurs in the prayer for Prince Henry.

'Kings are gods upon earth' is a quotation from King James's *Trve Lawe of Free Monarchies*, and this prayer indicates how troubled militant Protestants were by King James's statements on kingship. Whether King James did put forward any novel theories, and whether he actually governed in an absolutist fashion, would require a book in itself, and it is not my concern here. What matters is that many of his subjects believed that he did, and found evidence for it in his printed works as they interpreted them. In this prayer Dekker tries to arbitrate between those perceived theories and the higher principles of religion.

The Essex rebellion was a critical juncture for militant

[25] F. P. Wilson, pp. 98–100.   [26] Ibid. 110.   [27] Ibid. 101.

Protestantism, and it is probably no coincidence that in 1601 Dekker clashed in the war of the theatres with Ben Jonson, who did not share Dekker's views on religious-political issues. *Poetaster* was written in the spring of that year, very close in date to the execution itself, and *Satiromastix*, Dekker's reply, was performed in October 1601, making it one of the very earliest examples of tragi-comedy to appear on the English stage.[28] While neither play is explicitly concerned with contemporary politics, the friction between the authors was probably aggravated by their opposed convictions: it could hardly be otherwise.

The same is very likely true of the war of the theatres which has been continued by their critics ever since. It is traditional for admirers of Jonson to disparage Dekker, and though Dekker has a loyal following (his plays have received several first-class productions in recent years, for instance by the RSC and the National Theatre, and he is usually named in lists of the half-dozen best playwrights of his age) he has been unpopular with the Cambridge school of critics influenced by T. S. Eliot. Eliot regarded Dekker as almost beneath his august attention. In his *Elizabethan Essays* he confuses *The Witch of Edmonton* with Middleton's *The Witch*, and twice refers to them as if they are the same play, attributing to Middleton lines in the former which happens to be by Dekker, Ford, and Rowley.[29] Eliot's review of F. P. Wilson's edition of Dekker's plague pamphlets states that Dekker shows no sense of the Plague as a divine visitation, a claim that can be refuted from almost every page of the book. Eliot quotes a passage from one of the pamphlets and finds no more to say about it than: 'It appeared a hundred and twenty years before the work of Defoe,'[30] which demonstrates Eliot's ability to count.

Dekker was maligned in countless languages by Germaine Greer in *The Female Eunuch*. She attributed to him an anti-feminist work, *The Batchelar's Banquet*, which is taken from

---

[28] Jones-Davies, ii. 357.

[29] T. S. Eliot, *Elizabethan Essays* (Faber and Faber: London, 1927; rpt. in *Selected Essays*, 1932, etc.), 155, 158. This has also been noted by Mark Eccles, 'Thomas Dekker (or rather Heywood) and Eliot's "Rhapsody on a Windy Night" ', *N & Q* CCXXVI (June 1981), 435.

[30] T. S. Eliot, 'Plague Pamphlets', TLS, 5 Aug. 1926, 522.

a French original. But this book (which is no 'circumstantial account' of marriage, let alone a 'heart-felt cry', as Greer calls it, but a cunning parody of devotional treatises) is not by Dekker. It was printed anonymously, and there never was any evidence for the attribution. F. P. Wilson rejected it in 1929, and every Dekker scholar since has agreed with him, so the sources Greer is relying on must be very out-of-date. Later in the same work, Greer confuses Dekker with Thomas Deloney, which at least makes a change from Middleton.[31]

Of course not everything that has been said against Dekker is wrong. Dekker is an infuriatingly uneven writer, who often concentrates more into one page than into whole scenes that surround it. The most prevalent objection to his work is one that has never been made openly, but often implied: that Dekker is vulgar. And there is some truth in this. But there are worse things than vulgarity, and writing that is vulgar in some respects is not necessarily naïve or uninteresting. Dekker is often at his best when ridiculing forms of refinement that he found pretentious, such as the behaviour of the gallants in *The Gvls Horne-booke*, or Ben Jonson's pedantic tendencies.

The Gvls Horne-booke is usually regarded as a genial piece of satire, but there is indignation and disdain, too, concealed in the playfulness. The Gull is advised,

If you be a soldier, talk how often you have been in action; as the Portingale voyage, Cales voyage, the Island voyage; besides some eight or nine employments in Ireland, and the Low Countries; then you may discourse how honourably your Grave used you (observe that you call your Grave Maurice 'your Grave') . . .[32]

The campaigns listed are the voyages of the Earl of Essex, battles fought for the Protestant cause all over Europe and the New World. The Grave Maurice is Maurice of Nassau, ruler of the Dutch United Provinces, who had just (in 1609, the year of *The Gvls Horne-booke*) been forced to make a truce with Spain because the English King would not support his

---

[31] Germaine Greer, *The Female Eunuch* (MacGibbon and Kee Ltd.: London, 1970; rpt. Paladin Books, Granada Publishing Ltd.: London, 1979), 210, 348. Jones-Davies, ii. 351.   [32] Grosart, ii. 238–9.

cause. Dekker is indignant that these butterflies of the Jacobean Court claim credit not only for daring but for principles that in reality mean nothing to them. The same gallant has difficulty in merely spelling through the epitaph on the tomb of Sir Philip Sidney, who died for the Protestant cause at Zutphen.[33] *The Gvls Horne-booke* shows times, and men, in decline.

The feeling that Dekker is vulgar, or 'popular' to use the usual patronizing term, often goes with the assumption that his writings have no solid basis in culture, and appeal only to an ignorant mob. That is far from being the case. As the following chapters attempt to show, Dekker's plays draw on a broad spectrum of culture, learned and unlearned, making them catholic in the true sense.[34] The militant Protestant tradition possessed an elaborate and highly developed world-view, which was shared by co-religionists all over Europe. It is surprising how many critics (including Dekker's editor, Hoy) have an implicit assumption that Protestant culture is inferior and that it would be very much to Dekker's credit to have written at least one Roman Catholic play, even at the expense of his integrity.[35] Anybody who holds such views must soon reach the conclusion that the whole of Elizabethan drama, and most Elizabethan poetry too, is greatly overrated. What is felt to be vulgar in Dekker is often the product of his era rather than of Protestantism, and if Rubens's Marie de Medicis cycle deserves to occupy an entire room at the Louvre, we can fearlessly acknowledge *The Whore of Babylon* as among the most remarkable products of Elizabethan drama.

At the risk of stating the obvious, I will add that I have argued that Dekker's works are fundamentally consistent with each other, and with what is known about his life. This is not true of every writer, and tends to involve some circularity of argument. But it is generally more true of those who hold

[33] Grosart, ii. 236.
[34] Suzanne K. Blow, *Rhetoric in the Plays of Thomas Dekker* (Jacobean Drama Studies, III; Dr James Hogg Institute, University of Salzburg, Austria, 1972), has demonstrated amply Dekker's mastery of Renaissance poetic techniques.
[35] Cyrus Hoy, *Introductions, Notes, and Commentaries to Texts in 'The Dramatic Works of Thomas Dekker'* (4 vols.; CUP: Cambridge, 1980–1), iii. 197–8.

beliefs of a certain kind, and it is definitely true in Dekker's case. This is why his plays are better understood when considered as a whole corpus than in isolation. This book considers them in chronological order, and includes examples of every genre Dekker worked in: comedy, tragedy, history, tragi-comedy, *comoedia apocalyptica*, city pageant, and one masque.

1

The Anglo-Dutch Alliance in Dekker's Early Works

A. *The Shoemakers' Holy-Day*

Dekker's militant Protestant convictions are discernible in his earliest surviving work, *The Shoemakers' Holiday*, or *Holy-Day*, as the second Quarto, of 1610, entitled it. It was written and performed in 1599.

The Shoemakers' Holiday is an intensely topical play. David Novarr has shown that it not only dramatizes elements of a story about a contemporary Lord Mayor of London, Sir John Spencer, but also refers to the military activities in London the previous year. In Act I soldiers are being pressed in London for a war in France. Lacey and his cousin Askew are officers, and the shoemaker, Rafe, is a conscript. In Act III Rafe's wife Jane is persuaded from a list of casualties to believe that Rafe is dead. In 1598 the Earl of Essex had levied an army in London and elsewhere to serve in his Irish campaign. Rumours of the casualties in that campaign were reaching London in July 1599, about the time Dekker was writing the play.[1] Earlier, in 1591–2, Essex had taken a leading role in the English expedition to support Henri IV against the Catholic League in France. These contemporary campaigns on behalf of the Protestant cause provide part of the assumed background of the play. Only this can explain why the war in *The Shoemakers' Holiday*, despite its evils, is still accepted stoically by the Londoners. While the play creates concern for the casualties of war such as Rafe—a concern that runs throughout Dekker's work—the King nevertheless concludes the play by insisting that the war must go on. This resolution, evidently not a facile one, can only be

---

[1] David Novarr, 'Dekker's Gentle Craft and the Lord Mayor of London', *Modern Philology*, LVII (1960), 234.

understood in the light of the Protestant–Catholic struggle that is fundamental to Dekker's world-view. L. D. Timms has pointed out the double significance of St Hugh, the patron saint of shoemakers. In the play, the apprentices' feast falls on Shrove Tuesday, but it is called 'St. Hugh's Holiday'. November 17, St Hugh's Day in the old Catholic calendar, was also Queen Elizabeth's accession day, and was celebrated as a Protestant national holiday.[2] Much literature and pageantry had already risen around this holiday, which emphasized the Protestantization of pre-Reformation traditions. Maurice Kyffin wrote (in a poem dedicated to Essex):

> Adore Nouembers sacred Sev'nteenth Day,
> Wherein our Second Sunne began her Shine:[3]

The same reforming process is visible in Dekker's source-material, and in the way he used it. Two out of the three stories in Deloney's *Gentle Craft* are saints' stories, and *The Shoemakers' Holiday* is one of several plays in the Dekker canon which take old hagiographical material and make it serve the Protestant cause. In fact, the attraction Deloney's stories had for an English readership in the 1590s probably owes less to their traditionalism than to their suitability as tales of Protestant martyrdom. All three stories are set in England, albeit in ancient England, and the gruesome death of St Winifred and St Hugh, or the persecution of Sts Crispin and Crispianus, would have reminded English readers of the Marian persecutions chronicled by John Foxe. The martyrdom of Sts Winifred and Hugh has a pronounced resemblance to the double execution of Lady Jane Grey and her husband, described by Foxe and dramatized by Dekker and Webster in *Sir Thomas Wyatt*. It is also comparable in some respects to the story of St Dorothea used by Dekker and Massinger in *The Virgin Martyr*.

But while Deloney's stories can be related to this Foxean tradition, his work shows much more nationalistic than

---

[2] L. D. Timms, Dekker's *Shoemakers' Holiday* and Queen Elizabeth's Accession Day', N & Q XXXII, no. 1 (Mar. 1985), 58.

[3] Maurice Kyffin, *The Blessedness of Britain or a Celebration of the Queenes Holyday* (1587), B2ᵛ.

Protestant feeling. Indeed the last story in *The Gentle Craft*, the one about Simon Eyre, is both secular and chauvinistic. It has an extensive sub-plot concerning Simon Eyre's three journeymen: Haunce the Dutchman, John the Frenchman, and Nicholas, an Englishman. These three are rivals for the Eyres' maid, Florence, who is also English. Haunce uses trickery and deceit to win Florence's affections away from John. John and Nicholas then play a cruel practical joke on Haunce to prevent Florence from marrying him, but John double-crosses Nicholas and gets him arrested. Florence is about to become the bride of John when his French wife turns up, newly disembarked in London. Reflecting that Haunce may also have a wife in Flanders, Florence decides to marry Nicholas instead, who is a native Englishman and not a 'stranger'.[4] The slant of this story is distinctly xenophobic; it suggests that foreigners are malicious, deceitful, or even bigamous, and so a sensible girl is better off choosing an English husband.

Deloney's hostility towards immigrants was typical of one section of the London public. The nationalities he picks in the story, Dutch and French, are those of the Protestant refugee communities who had fled to London from religious persecution on the Continent. These 'strangers' were granted asylum and religious freedom by the government, but they were resented by many English people: those who cared less about Protestant solidarity than about trade rivalry (the foreigners were often more skilled than the English), or about the sheer fact of their foreignness. The guilds in London and elsewhere sought to exclude the strangers from employment, and there were complaints to the government about their numbers and status.[5] There were anti-immigrant riots in London in 1593 and 1596, libels being posted in the street and on the walls of the Dutch church of the Austin Friars. One of these accused the 'beastly brutes, the *Belgians*, or rather Drunken Drones, and faint-hearted Flemings' of using 'a feigned Hypocrisy, and counterfeit shew of Religion', in order to establish

[4] *The Gentle Craft*, in *The Novels of Thomas Deloney*, ed. Merrit E. Lawlis (Indiana University Press: Bloomington, 1961), 150–66.

[5] William Cunningham, *The Growth of English Industry and Commerce* (CUP: Cambridge, 1882; 2nd edn. 1938), Part II, i. 36–7, 81.

themselves in England.[6] The same kind of intolerance found a more ingenious expression in John Eliot's *Ortho-epia Gallica* (1593).[7]

In taking over Deloney's stories and making them into a single plot Dekker alters this slant significantly, replacing xenophobia with Protestant fraternity. In *The Shoemakers' Holiday* Lacey disguises himself as a Dutchman in order to seek work in London, and arrives early one morning at Simon Eyre's shop. At first, Eyre responds gruffly to his request for work and tries to turn him away. But Hodge and Firk, Eyre's foreman and journeyman, take the stranger's part and actually threaten to leave if he is not taken on:

HODGE. Fore God a proper man, and I warrant a fine workman: maister farewell, dame adew, if such a man as he cannot find worke, *Hodge* is not for you.[8]

So Eyre reluctantly employs him. This surely is didactic: it shows how the Dutchman ought to be received, not how he probably would have been received in Elizabethan London. Despite his strange speech and appearance, inside he is just the same as an Englishman: very much so, since in this case he is, of course, an Englishman in disguise.

The way Dekker assembles his material confirms his religious motive. In one of Deloney's stories Sts Crispin and Crispianus, two Christian princes, take refuge from persecution by hiding in the household of a shoemaker.[9] Haunce the Dutchman appeared in a different story. By combining them, Dekker reminds his audience that the Dutch immigrants in contemporary London are also to be seen as refugees from religious persecution.

The hospitality shown by Simon Eyre's household towards the Dutchman is handsomely rewarded. Hans soon tells Simon Eyre about the cargo of wares that gains him the basis of his future fortune, and the cargo is obtained from a Dutch

---

[6] A. W. Pollard (ed.), *Shakespeare's Hand in 'Sir Thomas More'* (CUP: Cambridge, 1923), 39.

[7] John Eliot, *Ortho-epia Gallica: Eliot's Frvits for the French* (London, Printed by Iohn Wolfe, 1593). Frances A. Yates, *A Study of Love's Labour's Lost* (CUP, Cambridge, 1936), 42.

[8] *SH*, I. iv. 54–6.   [9] Lawlis, 115–18.

skipper Hans has met in London docks. This time it is a genuine Dutchman who is involved, and he makes a brief appearance in Act II, when he visits Simon Eyre's shop in Tower Street. In Deloney's story the vendor was a Greek captain, not a Dutch skipper, and the news about the cargo was passed on to Simon Eyre by John Denevale, the Frenchman.[10] Dekker has altered both in order to make a point about Anglo-Dutch friendship. The wealth that comes to the Eyre household is a reward for their act of hospitality. To take in a stranger is a Christian act, and the gospel teaching has been given a Reformation stamp: it is a specifically Protestant act too.

Jones-Davies thinks that Deloney's story reflects the contemporary expulsion of the foreign merchants from the Stillyard, when their hasty departure enabled London merchants to buy their goods at profitable prices. This may be true of Deloney, but the story of Simon Eyre long pre-dated *The Gentle Craft* and these Elizabethan events. In the play, we are never told why the captain of the ship from 'Candia' dare not show his head in London, and he appears to be quite a singular case. Dekker's Simon Eyre is a subtly different entity from the Eyre found either in Deloney or in Stowe's *Annales*. The play's economic details are deliberately vague, and the weight of emphasis falls on the friendliness of the Dutch towards the English.

Dekker was probably of Dutch parentage himself, though born in London.[11] But his attitude on this issue was not merely subjective; it was consistent with an entire religious-political outlook. Solidarity with other Reformed Churches was fundamental to militant Protestantism all over Europe, and this is where Dekker differs from the nationalistic Deloney.

In the opening scene of *The Shoemakers' Holiday* we are told how and where Lacey has learnt his craft of shoemaking. His uncle wanted him to travel to Italy, but instead he stopped in Germany:

---

[10] Lawlis, 141.

[11] Jones-Davies, i. 29–30. The name Dekker is still common in the Amsterdam area, and Eduard Douwes Dekker was the real name of the distinguished Dutch novelist who wrote under the pseudonym 'Multatuli' in the 19th century.

LINCOLN. Asham'd to shew his bankerupt presence here,
Became a Shoomaker in *Wittenberg*,
A goodly science for a gentleman
Of such discent.[12]

When donning his disguise, Lacey says:

I know the trade,
I learn't it when I was in *Wittenberge*.[13]

There was no mention of Wittenberg in *The Gentle Craft*, but by adding these allusions to it, Dekker gives Lacey and his trade the right Protestant resonance from the start. Wittenberg was the cradle of the Reformation. It was here that Luther and Melanchthon taught, and it was on the door of Wittenberg Castle church that Luther in 1517 had pinned his ninety-five Articles. Saxony had become and remained a Protestant stronghold.

Anglo-Dutch solidarity was an important issue for foreign as well as home policy. In 1599 England was still at war with Spain, and had been since Leicester's campaign in the Netherlands in 1585. At the time of the Armada, the United Provinces had aided England by blockading Parma's naval force in Dutch harbours.[14] Essex's expeditions had continued the war, and when in 1598 Queen Elizabeth considered making peace with Spain, it was Essex who dissuaded her. He circulated a letter explaining the militant Protestant position; it was published posthumously in 1603, entitled *An Apologie of the Earle of Essex*. In it Essex explains how every military campaign of his career has had the same ultimate objective: from his 'father-in-lawes', i.e. Leicester's, campaign in the Netherlands, to the Cadiz and Azores voyages, they have all aimed to oppose the power of Spain. Spain is 'a general Enimye to all Christendome', and it regards England's religion as 'heresie'.[15]

Essex argues that England must continue giving military

---

[12] *SH*, I. i. 28–31. [13] *SH*, I. iii. 21.
[14] George Edmundson, *Anglo-Dutch Rivalry 1600–1653* (Clarendon Press, 1911), 14.
[15] Robert Devereux, 2nd Earl of Essex, *An Apologie of the Earle of Essex . . . Penned by himself in Anno 1598* (Imprinted at London, by Richard Bradocke, 1603), A4–A4ᵛ, F2ᵛ.

support to the Protestant Netherlanders, since they are not strong enough to resist Spain on their own. He describes them as 'our confederates of the Lowe Countries (who, beeing firmely knitte vnto vs, are of more vse then all the friendes in Christendome, that we euer had or can haue).' As to how the war should be financed, he writes:

> Did the godly Kings and religious people, which wee reade of in the old Testament, to maintaine the warres against the enemies of God, sell the ornaments of the Temple and things consecrated to holy vses? and shall wee, that haue as holy a warre, spare those thinges that wee haue dedicated to our idle and sensuall pleasures?[16]

In a letter of 1597, Essex advised Queen Elizabeth that she could be 'commandresse of the seas' if she would buy ships for the English navy from the Netherlands: 'Your confederates of the low countries will furnish you with better ships of warr then any the king of Spain can hire or draw . . . for the low country ships are better of saile, nimbler and carry as good peeces.'[17] Essex's letter suggests that the Dutch and English fleet together should conduct a trade war against Spain. Two years before, in 1595, a Dutch squadron had accompanied Essex on his Cadiz expedition.[18] So Dekker's Dutch skipper in *The Shoemakers' Holiday* is to be seen not only as a bringer of good luck, but as a confederate and a potential military ally as well.

There is a prevalent view that *The Shoemakers' Holiday* can only be understood in terms of commercial values. This is discernible in such articles as 'Virtue's Holiday: Thomas Dekker and Simon Eyre', by Joel H. Caplan,[19] 'The Economics of Joy in *The Shoemakers' Holiday*', by Peter Mortensen,[20] and others which attempt to prove that the names in the play are numismatic puns.[21] Theses on Dekker

---

[16] Essex, sig. E3ᵛ–E4.

[17] British Library Hulton MS (BM Loan 23 [i] J21 c), fo. 150ᵛ.

[18] Edmundson, p. 15.

[19] Joel H. Caplan, 'Virtue's Holiday: Thomas Dekker and Simon Eyre', *Renaissance Drama*, NS 2 (1969), 103–22.

[20] Peter Mortensen, 'The Economics of Joy in *The Shoemakers' Holiday*', *Studies in English Literature*, 16 (1976), 241–52.

[21] Gilian West, 'Firk's Numismatic Joke', *N & Q* CCXXVI (Apr. 1981), 147, and 'Some Word-Play in Dekker's *Shoemakers' Holiday*', *N & Q* CCXXVII (Apr. 1982), 135.

often have titles like 'The Bourgeois Consciousness of Thomas Dekker',[22] and 'The Cash-Nexus'.[23] E. D. Pendry wrote, 'For Dekker, morality is largely a function of money,'[24] and Harry Levin is quoted as saying that Simon Eyre seemed to him to be 'Shylock masquerading as Falstaff'.[25] In a more recent book the same view has been argued yet again by G. K. Hunter, who makes a most unconvincing comparison between this play and *The Merry Wives of Windsor*. He uses the familiar terms 'bourgeois', 'capitalism', and 'citizen comedy', even admitting this is a 'stereotype'.[26] The influence of this kind of view was noticeable in the 1981 production of *The Shoemakers' Holiday* at the National Theatre, in which Simon Eyre was acted by Alfred Lynch as a surly tycoon.

The more extreme and hostile expressions of this view are not very factually reliable. The names and puns in the play are not numismatic, but are better explained in other ways.[27] Mortensen's article contains various misreadings: for instance, when he says 'Dekker removes the incident of Eyre's masquerade,' he has not looked very closely at Act II, scene iii.[28] His description of Shrove Tuesday as a harvest of Pan is absurd.[29] And the basis of his argument is an equation of what he finds in the play with the views of the economist Thomas Mun, as expressed in *England's Treasure by Forraign Trade* (1664), written at the earliest about thirty years after *The Shoemakers' Holiday*.

Mun's book is in essence an attack on the Dutch, whom he saw as trade rivals of the English. He had put the same view,

[22] E. M. Moseley, 'The Bourgeois Consciousness of Thomas Dekker', Ph.D. thesis (Syracuse University, 1947), esp. p. 151.

[23] L. D. Clark, 'The Cash-Nexus', Ph.D. thesis (University of Missouri, 1979).

[24] Introduction to *Selected Prose Works of Thomas Dekker*, ed. E. D. Pendry (Stratford-upon-Avon Library, 4; Edward Arnold: London, 1967), 13.

[25] Jonas Barish, *Ben Jonson and the Language of Prose Comedy* (Harvard University Press: Cambridge, Mass., 1960), 282.

[26] G. K. Hunter, 'Bourgeois Comedy: Shakespeare and Dekker', in *Shakespeare and His Contemporaries: Essays in Comparison*, ed. E. A. J. Honigman (The Revels Plays Companion Library; Manchester University Press: Manchester, 1986), 1–16, esp. 2, 10.

[27] See my article 'Dekker's Word-Play in *The Shoemakers' Holiday*', *N & Q* XXXII, no. 1 (Mar. 1985), 58–9.

[28] Mortensen, p. 248.   [29] Ibid. 249.

the view of the merchants of London, in an earlier book, *A Discovrse of Trade, from England vnto the East-Indies*, written in 1621, before the Amboyna incident. Both these books point out with alarm the growing prosperity of the Dutch, from fishing, trade, and shipbuilding, and argue that this prosperity is being won at the expense of the English;

It concerneth vs, especially to obserue the diligences and practises of the *Dutch*; who with more gladnesse would vndertake the whole Trade to the *East Indies*, then with any reason we can abandon that part thereof, which we now enjoy; neither can our restraint from the Indies keepe our Siluer from thence, as long as the *Dutch* go thither: for we know, that deuices want not to furnish such dessignes; and when their Ships returne from India, shall not our Siluer out againe to helpe to pay a double price, or what they please, for all those wares which we shall want for our necessitie? Thus should the Dutch increase their honour, wealth and strength, whilest we abate, grow poore and weake at Sea for want of Trade; and call you this a Remedie; no, rather tearme it Ruine, Destruction . . .[30]

This is a far cry from Essex's confederacy. And other economists more contemporary with Dekker took exactly the same line: *John Keymor's Observation Made upon the Dutch Fishing about the Year 1601*, Tobias Gentleman's *England's Way to Win Wealth* (1614), and *The Trades Increase* by I. R. (1615) are all vociferous in their hostility towards the Dutch, who they say are taking the fish from English waters and the business from English merchants everywhere.

Keymor complains that Holland has more ships than 'England, France, Spain, Portugall, Italy, Scotland, Denmark, Polland, Sweethen and Rushea have all put together: and builds every year 1000 new ships'.[31] The Dutch fleet, according to Keymor, sells in English ports fish caught in English waters, and takes all the English gold out of the country, 'a great hurt to the Wealth and Strength of our Land'. Moreover, 'The Hollanders have made a Law in their own Countrey, that we shall sell no White Herrings nor other

---

[30] Thomas Mun, *A Discovrse of Trade, from England vnto the East-Indies* (1621), 48–9.

[31] *John Keymor's Observation Made upon the Dutch Fishing about the Year 1601* (Printed 1664), 1.

fish there,' which was quite true. 'In short time they will be able to eat all our shipping out at Sea . . .'[32]

The same complaint is taken up by Gentleman, who writes that 'the Inestimable summes of money taken yearely for fish and herrings out of his Maiesties Seas by strangers'—a sum he calculates at one million pounds a year—is causing the shortage of gold in England. He regrets that the English cannot compete with the Dutch in this industry, and would like the Dutch trade to be forbidden.[33] The author of *The Trades Increase* goes even further. It is not only the Dutch fishing which is ruining England and should be prohibited: the Dutch have outstripped the English in trade to Muscovy, Turkey, Italy, Danske, Melain, and New England. They have even taken over the English salt trade with France. 'And to conclude this poynt without loue or anger, but with admiration of our neighbours the now *Sea-herrs*, . . . that haue deuanced vs so farre in shipping . . . the chiefest matters they do lade outward, bee English Commodities.'[34] The superiority Essex noted in Dutch shipping was seen with resentment and alarm by the merchants of London, who had to compete with the Dutch *fluyts* for cargo.

Early in his reign, King James came under pressure to exclude Dutch fishing-boats from English waters, and this he did by proclamation in 1609. The result was a crisis in Anglo-Dutch diplomatic relations.[35]

The issue of Anglo-Dutch policy provides an acid test of Dekker's priorities. There were two opposite views. Those to whom money was the highest consideration saw the Dutch as a greater enemy than Spain; but to the militant Protestants, who put religion first, the Dutch were England's friends and confederates. Even Essex in his *Apologie* admits that his policy has been criticized as being bad for England's trade.[36]

In this critical choice, Dekker puts religion first, and so it is quite inaccurate to equate his views with those of Mun, or of a mercantile class. Two of the least attractive characters in *The Shoemakers' Holiday*, Sir Roger Otley and Hammon, are rich

---

[32] Ibid. 3–4.

[33] *England's Way to Win Wealth*, by Tobias Gentleman, Fisherman and Marriner (1614), 4–8, 11.   [34] I. R., *The Trades Increase* (1615), 7, 4–10.

[35] Edmundson, p. 19.   [36] Essex, sig. A3.

merchants of London, and their class of 'penny-pinching fathers', as Simon Eyre calls them, is in no way shielded from criticism.[37] In Dekker's *Old Fortunatus*, which was performed at Court in 1599, Fortune concludes the play by pronouncing to the King of England (in hearing of the contemporary Queen):

> *England* shall ne're be poore, if *England* striue,
> Rather by vertue, then by wealth to thriue.[38]

And in the Prologue to that play, one of the two pilgrims going to visit the shrine of Eliza is an Englishman, while the other is not. The Englishman says:

> Her sacred hand hath euermore beene knowne,
> As soone held out to straungers as her owne.[39]

The virtue of international solidarity is what Protestant England should strive for.

Mortensen's belief in what could be called the unacceptable face of shoemaking derives from L. C. Knights, whom Mortensen quotes at the outset of his article. Knights's aggressive and inaccurate attack on Dekker in the 1930s offered a kind of pseudo-Marxist interpretation. Purporting to compare Dekker to Jonson in terms of class-struggle, bourgeois capitalism, and so on, he applied these terms in a quite anachronistic and non-Marxist way.[40] That of course made them none the less fashionable. But Marx and Engels did not believe that the capitalist system yet existed in Elizabethan England, and their analysis concluded that the significant class-struggle of this epoch lay in the events of the Reformation, Luther fighting the first battle and Calvin the second.

It is certainly Protestantism that provides the driving force in Dekker's plays, and this raises the question of whether *The*

---

[37] *SH*, V. iv. 8.
[38] *OF*, V. ii. 259–60; Bowers, i. 194.   [39] Ibid. i. 114.
[40] L. C. Knights, *Drama and Society in the Age of Jonson* (Chatto and Windus: London, 1937), 236–40. In *The Shoemakers' Holiday by Thomas Dekker*, ed. Paul C. Davies (Oliver & Boyd: Edinburgh, 1968), 5–6, 9, Davies points out some of Knights's oversights. Another critic who has shown Knights's view to be a superficial one is A. Harbage, 'The Mystery of Perkin Warbeck', in *Studies in English Renaissance Drama*, ed. J. W. Bennet et al. (Peter Owen: London, 1959).

Shoemakers' Holiday reveals what Engels defined as Calvinist economics:

But where Luther failed, Calvin won the day. His predestination doctrine was the religious expression of the fact that in the commercial world of competition, success or failure does not depend on a man's activity or cleverness, but upon circumstances uncontrollable by him ... unknown superior economic powers; and this was especially true at a period of economic revolution, when all old commercial routes and centres were replaced by new ones, when India and America were opened to the world, and when even the most sacred economic articles of faith—the value of gold and silver—began to totter and break down.[41]

If Engels is right, and if Dekker is a Calvinist, then it ought to be true that wealth and success in *The Shoemakers' Holiday* are distributed at random, to the stupid and lazy as well as to the active and clever. Yet the more closely we look, the more we find that factual and ethical uncertainty clouds any reading of the play as a fiscal statement.

In the play's romantic plot, Lacey takes the part of hero, and is finally married to Rose, but he is a very strange hero: a deserter, who bribes his own way out of the army in order to pursue a wife, yet refuses to grant the recently married Rafe his legal exemption. Lacey must take the blame for Rafe's disablement, and for all the distress that results to him and Jane. Although it is true that the whole world loves a lover, many critics and reviewers have found Lacey a puzzling, unacceptable hero. F. M. Burelbach, in an essay sympathetic to the play, calls Lacey 'a rather unpleasant young man', and tries to excuse him by saying that he is more agreeable in his role as Hans.[42]

But Lacey's ambivalent status is surely deliberate. The name Lacey suggests 'lazy', that is, both an idle gentleman and a deserter. W. K. Chandler objected that this was not the real family name of the Earls of Lincoln; in fact it is a deliberate choice of Dekker's.[43] When he goes to work in

---

[41] F. Engels, 'On Historical Materialism', in *Marx and Engels: Basic Writings on Politics and Philosophy*, ed. Lewis S. Feuer (Fontana Classics of History and Thought; Anchor Books: NY 1959; rpt. Fontana Books: Glasgow, 1976), 96.

[42] F. M. Burelbach, 'War and Peace in *The Shoemakers' Holiday*', *Tennessee Studies in Literature*, 13 (1968), 104.   [43] P. Davies, p. 3.

Simon Eyre's shop, Lacey puts aside this aristocratic name, then resumes it once more in Act v. The name Hans suggests 'hands' for working. It is Lacey/Hans who teaches Simon Eyre how to become rich, but while he may be lazy in some respects, he is obviously not stupid. He is used for a didactic purpose when posing as a Dutchman, a pose that is distinctly at odds with his other self. Certainly Dekker meant Lincoln's speech (quoted above) on the shame of a gentleman practising a craft, to be deeply ironic. Lacey commands most respect when he is least a member of his 'lacie' family. He is ennobled by the gentle craft.

When in the final scene of the play Simon Eyre begs the King for clemency towards Lacey and his desertion, this is meant to remind us of the opening scene in which it was Simon Eyre who begged Lacey for leniency towards Rafe. The symmetry sets up a measure-for-measure situation: in Christian terms, Lacey should receive as much mercy as he showed to Rafe. But the outcome obeys no such rules and the happy ending is very unfair. Lacey gets not only clemency but a shower of favour. The King first sets him free then knights him into the bargain. The noble deserter gets honoured while the common soldier, crippled for life, is ignored. Instead of all the labourers in the vineyard getting the same reward, those who do least get the most.

There is one way out of this bitterly ironic conclusion. Lacey could yet redeem himself, in both social and spiritual terms, by going to fight in the war at the end of the play. If he did so, he would be doing exactly what he once required of Rafe, since it would mean leaving his newly won bride Rose, just as Rafe had to leave his newly married Jane. The King actually tells Lacey that recruitment is starting up again:

> With the olde troupe which there we keepe in pay,
> We wil incorporate a new supply:
> Before one summer more passe ore my head,
> *France* shal repent *England* was iniured.[44]

But Lacey does not say whether or not he will go. Nor does anybody else, and this leaves an important decision to the director. Is it carelessness that Dekker has not answered this

---

[44] *SH*, V. v. 137–40

question, just as Shakespeare does not tell us whether Isabella marries the Duke of Vienna? Most commentators on the play are sure of one conclusion or another. Mortensen writes twice that 'Lacey will have to leave his bride to accompany the King.'[45] But the point is that we don't know. Lacey may redeem himself or not; the choice is now up to him. There is no sense of the door being shut as yet, nor need we assume that the judgements of the last Act anticipate in every detail those of heaven. If we did so, the conclusion would be sour: does heaven, like a jovial myopic king, hand out rewards at random to those predestined by their privilege of birth, while overlooking the greatest efforts of those like Rafe who simply do not belong to the elect élite? This grim suspicion is deeply written into the structure of the play. Dekker's affable monarch is far less just than Shakespeare's Vincentio. Nevertheless the choice Lacey still has to make is his own, not the decree of a mysterious Providence. And a sense of incomplete knowledge prevents the dark suspicions of the play from hardening into conclusions.

A similar set of doubts surrounds Simon Eyre and his rise to wealth. Eyre himself helps us see the political point when in Act v he says: 'Why my sweete lady *Madgy*, thincke you *Simon Eyre* can forget his fine dutch Iourneyman? No vah. Fie I scorne it, it shall neuer be cast in my teeth, that I was vnthankeful.'[46] In Deloney, the shoemaker who shelters Crispin and Crispianus is not Simon Eyre, nor does he get any richer. But in Dekker's play, Simon Eyre takes in a Dutchman and is rewarded with wealth and prosperity for his Christian act. Dekker has put the material together into an immemorial pattern. The Eyre household could even be compared to Philemon and Baucis, who sheltered the disguised Zeus and Hermes, and were rewarded by the transformation of their cottage into a shining temple. When Lacey becomes a shoemaker, he actually compares himself to a god in disguise:

> How many shapes haue gods and Kings deuisde,
> Thereby to compasse their desired loues?[47]

[45] Mortensen, pp. 249, 252.   [46] *SH*, V. i. 11–13.   [47] *SH*, I. iii. 1–2.

The classical story and the Christian morality follow the same pattern. The good deed of taking in a stranger is followed by an unexpected reward. So in one sense it is easy to see that Simon Eyre's wealth and success are not awarded at random (as Engels thought they should be). He and his household deserve them, first for their generosity and then for the supportive, fraternal way they receive Rafe back after he has become a cripple:

HODGE. Limbs? hast thou not hands man? thou shalt neuer see a shoomaker want bread, though he haue but three fingers on a hand.[48]

This again is ideal and didactic. The Protestant refugee communities in London took care of their old and disabled members by communal systems, which were eventually imitated by the English Friendly Societies.[49] The prosperity earned by the Eyre household is shared by the whole household, nor does Eyre's generosity stop there. His Shrove Tuesday feast, to which high and low are invited alike, becomes a comic vision of the future heavenly feast. The conclusion of *The Shoemakers' Holiday* certainly assumes that wealth rightly used is a desirable thing, particularly when its benefits are spread around. The only people likely to carp are professors whose own modest competency far exceeds the Elizabethans' visions of wealth.

This does not mean that Eyre and his wife are idealized figures, who can do no wrong: far from it. The comical and vulgar aspects of social climbing are broadly satirized in Dame Margery, whose ever-increasing finery and pretentious manners are ridiculed by Firk and make good stage comedy. Meanwhile Jane is allowed to drift away from the household uncared-for, a serious form of negligence in such a society. Not until she is reunited with Rafe and invited to the feast can we regard the fault as atoned for.

Most difficult of all is the problem of Eyre's masquerade. In Act II Simon Eyre sets off to meet the Dutch captain who

---

[48] *SH*, III. ii. 76.
[49] William Cunningham, DD, *Alien Immigrants to England* (Social England Series, ed. K. D. Cotes; Swan Sonnenschein & Co.: London, 1897), 187.

is selling the valuable cargo. Before he goes, he puts on a velvet coat, a seal ring, and an alderman's red gown:

> [*Enter the boy with a veluet coate, and an Aldermans gowne*, Ayre
> *puts it on.*
> EYRE. Peace *Firk*, silence tittle tattle: *Hodge*, Ile go through with it,
> heers a seale ring, and I haue sent for a garded gown, and a
> damask Casock, see where it comes . . .[50]

A modern audience may not notice anything odd about this in performance. But an Elizabethan audience might well have done so, and asked themselves whether Simon Eyre is entitled to wear an alderman's gown. Nothing has been said yet about him becoming an alderman, so early in the play. He becomes sheriff of London in Act III, scene ii, and Lord Mayor in Act IV, scene iii. Before becoming Lord Mayor, a man has to have been both sheriff and alderman, but a sheriff does not necessarily have to be an alderman already. Some are, some aren't. So when exactly does Simon Eyre become an alderman? We are never told, and the result is a crucial ambiguity. Nor is this wholly explained by looking at the source.

In Deloney's story, Simon Eyre is not an alderman, but he is advised by his crafty wife to dress up as one in order to impress the Greek captain. In this way he obtains a large amount of credit. This ruse, which puts him on the road to wealth, is presented as a huge joke, to be admired like the tricks of unfaithful wives in the *Decameron*.[51] Smallwood and Wells write that Dekker would have done better to remove from the play any 'relic' of his source here, because 'in a play which is to be concerned with the proper use of wealth, Dekker may have preferred to avoid any suggestion of impropriety in its original acquisition.'[52] Dekker may, on the other hand, have wished to include it. Elsewhere, Wells calls Simon Eyre 'the shoemaker who during the play's action becomes successively alderman, sheriff, and Lord Mayor'.[53]

---

[50] *SH*, II. iii. 93–7.
[51] Lawlis, pp. 142–5.
[52] *The Shoemaker's* [sic] *Holiday*, ed. Robert Smallwood and Stanley Wells (Manchester University Press: Manchester, 1979), Introduction, 21.
[53] S. Wells, 'Mixed humour', Review of *SH* at Olivier Theatre, TLS, 26 June 1981, 727.

But does he do so in that order? Jones-Davies thinks he becomes sheriff first and then alderman.[54] The uncertainty here, as with Lacey's recommission, is deliberate. If Dekker had wanted to leave out the disguise, he could have left it out entirely. When Elizabethan comedy retains a 'relic' of this kind, it does so for a purpose, usually to stimulate some healthy discomfort. (Valentine's offer of Silvia to Proteus is likewise a 'relic' of its source.) If we wish to assume the best, and take it that Simon Eyre is already an alderman when he first dresses up as one, then all is well with the moral. But if we question this, and wonder why nothing is said about him becoming an alderman, in contrast to the fuss made about his election as sheriff, this casts a shadow of doubt over the whole play. We can hardly regard impersonation as a prank, yet it is something of a jolt to consider Simon Eyre as a confidence trickster. Falstaff masquerading as Shylock?

In a later play, *If This Be Not A Good Play*, Dekker takes as his villain Bartervile, a city merchant and money-lender of diabolical cunning. Bartervile tricks his creditors by disguising himself as a Turk and posing as executor of his own will.[55] Comparing this with Simon Eyre's masquerade gives some idea of the seriousness of the doubt which Dekker has concealed just beneath the comedy surface of *The Shoemakers' Holiday*. Can wealth as great as Simon Eyre's really be acquired completely innocently? What has been taken for Dekker's carelessness here is skill, and the skill lies in controlling the order in which we perceive the various layers of meaning.

If we wish, we can find in this ambiguity a well-observed truth about the business world. When he is dressed in his garded gown, Simon Eyre is told by Hodge, 'Why now you looke like your self master, I warrant you.'[56] If Eyre poses as an alderman, he is taken for one, and so eventually becomes a real one. You are what you can persuade people you are. Credit is credit.

The third problematical figure in the play is Hammon. He

[54] Jones-Davies, i. 211.
[55] *ITBNAGP*, IV. i.
[56] *SH*, II. iii. 104

is the only main character who is not present at the great Guildhall feast, and his exclusion is consistent with the way he has been presented from the start. The name Hammon could suggest 'Mammon' and in the Lacey–Rose plot this is what Hammon stands for: mercenary marriage without the bride's consent, a practice condemned by Protestant theologians (and quite a lot of brides). Hammon's name could also suggest 'Haman', the evil minister of Ahasuerus who tried to exterminate the Jews.[57] Haman was an enemy of the chosen people, and Hammon seems to be an outsider, a villain from the start.

He is never a particularly likeable figure. When he first woos Rose, we see him in the position of rejected suitor. But Rose is already in love with Lacey, and there is no doubt that her father's choice of Hammon is a purely mercenary one:

> OTLEY.   There came of late,
> A proper Gentleman of faire reuenewes,
> Whom gladly I would call sonne in law.[58]

The curious stichomythic verse in which Hammon woos both Rose and Jane is not only archaic but alien and slightly sinister:

> HAM. A deere, more deere is found within this place.
> ROSE. But not the deere (sir) which you had in chace.
> HAM. I chac'd the deere, but this deere chaceth me.
> ROSE. The strangest hunting that euer I see.[59]

It produces an air of tension and insincerity. To find a future wife out hunting is an old folklore motif which presages sorrow and misfortune for the wife.[60] This suggestion of ill-luck, of something ominous, always surrounds Hammon.

When Hammon woos Jane in exactly the same terms as he has just been wooing Rose, his insincerity is proved. He actually asks to buy Jane first, before asking her to marry him:

> All cheape, how sell you then this hand?[61]

---

[57] Esther 3–7.   [58] *SH*, III. iii. 32–4.   [59] *SH*, II. ii. 30–3.
[60] See e.g. the story of Geraint in the *Mabinogion*, trans. Lady Charlotte Guest (Everyman's Library, J. M. Dent & Sons: London, 1906; rpt. 1924), 219–62. There are many others.

The threat of sale, of loss of integrity, hangs over this scene. It is the danger of prostitution: the phrase 'as stale as an Exchange Sempster' was a stock one and appears in *Westward Ho!*[62] So Hammon is Mammon to Jane here, but he is also the Devil trying to buy her soul. Is the appearance of Rafe's name on the list of the dead a mistake, or a forgery?

Hammon damns himself most deeply when he offers, on the steps of St Faith's church, to buy Jane from Rafe, her returning husband:

> Marke what I offer thee: here in faire gold
> Is twentie pound, Ile giue it for thy *Iane*,
> If this content thee not, thou shalt haue more.[63]

At this point the morality is most certain: Hammon is Mammon, using his wealth to corrupt what should be non-commercial, treating both Rafe and Jane with thick-skinned arrogance.

Yet Hammon is allowed to make certain appeals for our sympathy. When Rose rejects him, he says,

> I am not growne so fond, to fond my loue
> On any that shall quit it with disdaine,
> .   .   .   .
> Enforced loue is worse then hate to me.[64]

Before he approaches Jane, he soliloquizes,

> I am infortunate,
> I stil loue one, yet no body loues me,
> I muse in other men what women see,
> That I so want?[65]

Why is he so excluded, so rejected from the outset? Was Hammon even invited to the feast? His attempt to buy love could seem pathetic as well as repugnant. Love cannot be bought, any more than salvation can. Only the Whore of Babylon pretends to sell that commodity.

The concept of hypocrisy has a special significance in

---

[62] *SH*, I. ii. 95–6. Pointed out by Smallwood and Wells, p. 149.
[63] *SH*, V. ii. 75–7.   [64] *SH*, III. i. 24–5, 50.
[65] *SH*, III. iv. 6–9.

Calvinist theology. It provides the clue to what is disturbing about Hammon, as about the villain of another much later Calvinistic story, Henry Crawford in *Mansfield Park*. Like Hammon, Henry Crawford reveals his insincerity by pursuing one woman after another in quick succession. His wealth poses the threat of mercenary marriage for the heroine, of corruption by Mammon. He is insincere even when reading the Bible, and like Hammon he is revealed in his true colours at last, just in time to save the heroine from him. The wicked can pretend to be good, but if they do they only become guilty of the further sin of hypocrisy. They cannot change their essential badness, their exclusion from grace. But what if the bad sincerely want to change? In *Mansfield Park*, it begins to seem as if Henry Crawford genuinely wishes to do so. But Calvinism cannot really entertain this possibility. If the bad really are the bad, they cannot be sincere about anything. In *The Shoemakers' Holiday*, there is something not fully human about Hammon, and Dekker conveys this by means of the highly conventionalized verse-forms and word-play associated with him. The play's strength is that it does arouse uneasiness about this, a sort of uneasiness we never feel about, for instance, Bartervile or about Don John in *Much Ado About Nothing*. It is a little too much like Noah's ark: the door is shut.

Having said so much about the play's dark side, it may seem surprising to reassert that it has any other, but *The Shoemakers' Holiday* is a very complex play. The joyous and ebullient face that we see first is not the only one. If we look at it in another way we discover a second far less optimistic face. This duality, which has been either overlooked or regarded as a sign of failure, should surely be regarded as a virtue. Elizabethan comedy at its best not only combines an extraordinary range of religious, mythical, political, romantic, and comic elements, but by accommodating doubt and conflict enriches itself still further. The exuberance, bawdy humour, and vitality praised by all sensible critics of *The Shoemakers' Holiday* are all there; so are the charity and fraternity which Jones-Davies picks as the play's key qualities. All these facets co-exist.

B. *Getting the Ear of the King*

Dekker's support for the Anglo-Dutch alliance is discernible again in his section of *The Magnificent Entertainment Giuen to King James*. Dekker was commissioned to collaborate with Ben Jonson on this pageant given by the City of London to welcome the newly crowned King on 15 March 1603/4. But the cantankerous Jonson and the intransigent Dekker were still at daggers drawn from the War of the Theatres. So the work was split up and each poet wrote the descriptions and orations for part of the *Entertainment*, publishing his contribution separately.

An account of this pageant is given by David M. Bergeron in *English Civic Pageantry, 1558–1642*. He quotes the Venetian ambassador Giustinian, who in 1607 referred to 'These Progresses, which were started with the object of studying and alleviating the needs of the subjects . . .'.[66] Whether given on a progress or in the City, entertainments were an opportunity for the subjects to address the monarch. In 1595 the Earl of Essex had, with Francis Bacon, written and staged an entertainment, addressed to Queen Elizabeth, for one of her accession-day tilts.[67] In Scotland King James and his mother before him had been greeted with vigorously Protestant tableaux when they made their royal entries into Edinburgh in 1561 and 1579.[68]

Bergeron says that the second and third arches in the *Entertainment* were 'erected by the Italian and Dutch merchants of London', but these 'Strangers', as they were called in the paratitle, were not just merchants in residence.[69] They were Protestant refugee communities, established first in the time of Edward VI, then re-established under Queen Elizabeth. They had their own churches, which followed reformed principles, and were free from supervision by English bishops. Collinson has called them a 'Trojan horse,

---

[66] David M. Bergeron, *English Civic Pageantry, 1558–1642* (Edward Arnold Ltd.: London, 1971), 65.

[67] Discussed in Roy Strong, *The Cult of Elizabeth: Elizabethan Portraiture and Pageantry* (Thames and Hudson: London, 1977), 141.

[68] Bergeron, p. 67.   [69] Ibid. 71.

bringing Reformed worship and discipline fully armed into the midst of the Anglican camp'.[70] In protecting them from persecution on the Continent, England was allying herself to the international Reformed Church, and the prominence given to them in the pageant is an ideological statement. In *Basilicon Doron* King James had praised the superior craftsmanship of the strangers in England, while warning his son in the same book against 'Puritanes, verie pestes in the Church'.[71]

Hoy calls them 'the Italians and Dutchmen resident in London' and agrees with Bergeron that Dekker could have had no part in their contributions.[72] But if we reflect that Dekker was an Anglo-Dutchman himself, born into one of these immigrant communities and able to speak Dutch, then there is reason to suppose that he took part in devising the Dutch tableau, if not the Italian one too.[73] What more suitable writer was there for them to call on? Although this cannot be proved, Dekker certainly devotes a generous amount of space to these second and third arches, particularly the Dutch one, and his enthusiasm for the latter is unconcealable. It contrasts with his laconic summary, a few lines long, of the tableau at the seventh arch, the Temple of Janus, which was written by Jonson. Jonson's part of the *Entertainment* contains no reference to the Protestant communities.

The pageant of the Italians is presented in Gracious (i.e. Grace-Church) Street. It includes a representation of the battle of Lepanto, a compliment to King James's poem on the subject.[74] Many of James's writings had been reissued at his accession and scrutinized closely by his new subjects.[75]

There is another allusion to James's writings in the Latin oration which follows the depiction of the battle. It says that James has now fulfilled his own criterion for ideal government, since he is a philosopher-king. It is a routine compliment, and the same speech says that the Italians are 'full of hopes to

[70] Patrick Collinson, *Godly People: Essays on English Protestantism and Puritanism* (The Hambledon Press: London, 1983), 248.

[71] Craigie, xvi. 78, 92.   [72] Hoy, ii. 129.

[73] Jones-Davies, i. 30–2.   [74] *ME*, 394–400; Bowers, ii. 265.

[75] We know that Shakespeare studied them closely: see Ernest Schanzer, 'Justice and King James in *Measure for Measure*', in *Measure for Measure Casebook*, ed. C. K. Stead (Casebook Series, gen. ed. A. E. Dyson; Macmillan: London, 1971), 233–41.

enjoy a felicity vnder your Royall wing'.[76] A request for assurance concerning their own status is sweetened by flattery. The Italians' pageant reminds us that militant Protestantism was a European-wide movement. The Anglo-Dutch alliance was important, but not exclusively important, and Dekker's sense of fraternity with foreign Protestants was not limited to the Dutch.

After the Italian tableau follows 'The Pageant of the Dutchmen, by the Royall Exchange'. This site was not far from the Dutch church of the Augustine Friars in Broad Street, which had been granted to the Protestant refugees in 1550. Its ministers are known to have been in correspondence with Calvin and Heinrich Bullinger.[77] If Dekker was born into this community, this may well have been the church he went to as a child. Here, Dekker writes,

... the *Belgians*, (attired in the costly habits of their own natiue Countrey, without the fantasticke mixtures of other Nations) but more richly furnished with loue, stand ready to receyue his Maiestie ...[78]

An arch displays a frieze and a Latin inscription in gold, greeting the entire royal family. Through the arch is revealed a device which represents the seventeen United Provinces:

17. yong *Damsels*, (all of them sumptuously adorned, after their countrey fashion,) sate as it were in so many Chaires of State, and figuring in their persons, the 17. *Prouinces* of *Belgia*, of which euery one caried in a Scutchion (excellently pencilde) the Armes and Coate of one.[79]

In *The Faerie Queene* Spenser had allegorized the United Provinces as Belge, a widow with seventeen sons, and Prince Arthur's enterprise to save her from the tyrant Geroneo represents Leicester's campaign in the Netherlands.[80] Dekker uses the allegory of the seventeen maidens twice in later

---

[76] *ME*, 421–32. Bowers, ii. 266.

[77] Frederick A. Norwood, 'The Strangers' "Model Churches" in Sixteenth Century England', in *Reformation Studies: Essays in Honor of Roland H. Bainton*, ed. Franklin H. Littell (John Knox Press: Va., 1962), 182–3.

[78] *ME*, 439–42; Bowers, ii. 266.

[79] *ME*, 481–5; Bowers, ii. 268.

[80] *The Poetical Works of Edmund Spenser*, ed. J. C. Smith and E. de Selincourt (OUP, 1912; rpt. 1937), 321; Book V, canto x.

works: once in *The Whore of Babylon*, and again in a prose work he was writing at about the same time, *The Seuen Deadly Sinnes of London* (1606).[81]

This is the section of the Dutch pageant which seems most likely to have been devised by Dekker. Its allegory is clear and lucid, like the tableaux at the fourth, fifth, and sixth arches, which Dekker definitely wrote. The United Provinces are shown both as wealthy allies, and damsels in distress, relying on England for survival in their struggle against Spain.

Beyond this, passing statues of Divine Providence, Fortitude, and Justice, the spectator reaches a courtyard decorated with three life-size friezes. They show the people of the United Provinces at work in their various occupations: it is as if James is being offered a guided tour. This part of the Dutch pageant probably did not need the help of any poet, as it involves neither emblems nor iconography. The first frieze shows,

... the Dutch Countrey people, toyling at their Husbandrie; women carding of their Hemp, the men beating it ... Lift vp your eyes a little aboue them, and beholde their *Exchange*; the countenaunces of the Marchants there being so liuely, that bargaines seeme to come from their lippes.[82]

In the next:

... men, women and children (in Dutch habits) are busie at other workes: the men Weauing, the women Spinning, the children at their Hand-loomes, &c. Aboue whose heads, you may with little labour, walke into the *Mart* where as well the *Froe*, as the *Burger*, are buying and selling ...[83]

This cannot have pleased the merchants of the nearby Royal Exchange, rivals of the Dutch, nor could the next scene which depicts the Dutch fishing and shipping, the much-resented industry which James was so soon to attempt to curtail:

... and directly ouer the Gate, in a large Table, whose feete are fastned to the *Freeze*, is their fishing and shipping liuely and sweetely set downe: The *Skipper* (euen though he be hard tugging at his Net) loudly singing ...[84]

---

[81] Grosart, ii. 9.

[82] *ME*, 570–7; Bowers, ii. 270.

[83] *ME*, 585–9; Bowers, ii. 271.

[84] *ME*, 595–8; Bowers, ii. 271.

He is singing some verses in praise of Dutch enterprise, which sends its merchants all over the world. This was bad news to Keymor, Gentleman, and Mun: and to Sir Roger Otley, or Hammon, probably. But it evidently delights Dekker. The Latin oration at the end of the Dutch pageant asks James for assurance that the refugee communities will be protected by him as they were by Queen Elizabeth:

Wee (the *Belgians*) likewise come, to that intent: a Nation banisht from our owne Cradles; yet nourcde and brought vp in the tender boosome of Princely Mother, *ELIZA*. The *Loue*, which wee once dedicated to her (as a Mother) doubly doe wee vow it to you, our Soueraigne, and Father; intreating wee may be sheltred vnder your winges now, as then vnder hers.[85]

So the citizens of London greeted James with extravagant acclaim and hope, but also with some broad hints on the kind of course they would like him to follow.

Another hint is offered in the Latin oration (not by Dekker) delivered by a St Paul's scholar at the fifth gate. This invites King James to become an honorary member of the Mercers' Company, the premier city guild:

What glorie should thereby rize vp to the City? . . . what honour besides our Souereigne himselfe might acquire . . .[86]

That the honour would be mutual is a bold suggestion showing that some citizens shared the ideals of *The Shoemakers' Holiday*, in which the King comes to dine at the Guildhall. Queen Elizabeth had been a Mercer, and the City thought its dignitaries quite entitled to get the ear of the monarch.

The criticisms of Dekker's part of *The Magnificent Entertainment* made by D. J. Gordon have already been answered by Hoy.[87] Some clumsy misreadings have more recently been put forward by Jonathan Goldberg. It is worth answering these in detail, since to do so sheds light on the whole *Entertainment*. Goldberg picks on Dekker's description of James as London's bridegroom and immediately

---

[85] *ME*, 693–9; Bowers, ii. 274.
[86] *ME*, 1330–3; Bowers, ii. 294.
[87] D. J. Gordon, *The Renaissance Imagination, Essays and Lectures*, ed. Stephen Orgel (University of California Press: Berkeley, 1975), 11–13. Hoy, ii. 133.

twists marriage into rape—'his ravishing entrance'—and rape into murder—'his devastating exit'.[88] As evidence for this homicidal interpretation he cites Dekker's description of the City as a 'Widdow' when James departs.[89] But if the City is a widow, it must be the bridegroom who is dead. If there is any devastation in this encounter (which I doubt) Goldberg has got it the wrong way round.

Goldberg says that 'Dekker's account of the King's progress is told from the king's point of view, for it is only from his eyes that the display takes on life.'[90] In fact, Dekker varies his assumed viewpoint. He includes a description of James as he first appeared to the citizenry, and one of the crowd before the King arrived.[91] He does use expressions such as 'in his sight' (i.e. James), 'The Obiects that there offer themselues before him,' and 'he might behold the Cathedrall Temple of Saint Paule.'[92] But this is not because the royal point of view is the only one that matters. On the contrary, for an author to try to map out the King's point of view could be a very encroaching, presumptuous thing to do. Most significant in this respect is Dekker's inclusion of his own device, of a meeting between Sts George and Andrew and the Genius of the City. This device was actually cancelled, but that does not prevent Dekker from including it at the head of his printed account, entitled 'A DEVICE, that should have serued at his Maiesties first accesse to the Citie'. And at the end, he writes that although many speeches were cancelled and never heard by the King, 'thou doest here receiue them as they should haue bene deliuered, not as they were.'[93] So Dekker's text tells us not what the King saw and heard, but what Thomas Dekker thought the King ought to have seen and heard. Where the King's viewpoint is defective, Dekker does not hesitate to correct it.

Goldberg misquotes Dekker when he writes: 'As Dekker says, the citizens flocked "like so many Roman Aediles",' to watch King James.[94] What does he think *aedile* means? The

---

[88] Jonathan Goldberg, *James I and the Politics of Literature* (Johns Hopkins University Press: Baltimore, 1983), 30.   [89] *ME*, 1550; Bowers, ii. 301.

[90] Goldberg, p. 31.   [91] *ME*, 204–6, 174–89; Bowers, ii. 259, 258.

[92] *ME*, 34, 562, 1228–9; Bowers, ii. 254, 270, 291.

[93] *ME*, 1624–5; Bowers, ii. 303.   [94] Goldberg, p. 43.

passage actually runs: 'a Select number both of Aldermen and Commoners (like so many Romane *Aediles*) were (Communi Consilio) chosen forth, to whose discretion, the *Charge, Contriuings, Projects,* and all other *Dependences,* owing to so troublesome a worke, was intirely, and judicially committed.'[95] The *aediles curules* and *aediles plebeii* were elected magistrates in charge of public buildings, displays, temples, and theatres and there were only four of them, hardly enough to flock if they tried. Since the office was set up in AUC 753, i.e. 366 BC, in the early years of the Republic, this does not support Goldberg's notion of the *Entertainment* as an imperial triumph. Dekker also calls the Aldermen '*Senators*', suggesting the dignity and pride of the City in its system of self-government. He uses similar republican terms in his other city pageants, such as *Britannia's Honor* and *London's Tempe* written twenty-five years later.[96]

Goldberg misrepresents the contributions of Jonson and Harrison as well as of Dekker. He says that the arches of triumph are all Roman arches, a style which is imperial and absolutist.[97] Harrison's arches do employ classical features, but are highly eclectic in their style. Of those Dekker worked on, the fourth is rather Oriental-looking, as befits Nova Felix Arabia: it has a square doorway flanked by two obelisks. The fifth is positively Islamic, while the sixth is medieval, with a square doorway, round bastions, and battlements mixed in with classical decorations. Dekker calls it an 'inchanted Castle'.[98] The last arch, the Temple of Janus, for which Jonson wrote the device, has the silhouette of a baroque, Counter-Reformation church.[99]

In the dialogue the Genius of the City commands Flamen Martialis to replace ancient Roman ritual with Christianity:

> Back, Flamen, with thy superstitious fumes,
> And cense not here; Thy ignorance presumes

---

[95] *ME*, 146–51; Bowers, ii. 257.

[96] *ME*, 123; Bowers, ii. 257; *BH*, 74; Bowers, iv. 84; *LT*, 114; Bowers, iv. 105. Of course, if Goldberg is one of those who believe that history is merely what we construct, then it is impossible to have an inaccurate or distorted view of it. Even to be ignorant of it becomes impossible.   [97] Goldberg, pp. 33–9.

[98] *ME*, 1340; Bowers, ii. 294.   [99] Bergeron, plates V–VIII.

> Too much, in acting any Ethnick rite
> In this translated temple . . .[100]

That is not very compatible with what Goldberg thinks is James's 'Augustan', 'imperial style', particularly in view of his bizarre assertion that both the Genius of the City and Thamesis are 'alter egos' of James.[101] If I have dwelt at length on Goldberg's supposedly sophisticated book, it is in order to controvert his view that *The Magnificent Entertainment*— and indeed the whole of Jacobean literature—is monolithic and absolutist.

King James's response to the *Entertainment* was not auspicious. He was said to have 'endured the day's brunt with patience', even though many of the speeches were cut.[102] He showed no interest in what the occupants of the City might have to say to him, and while he did not go so far as Charles I, who cancelled his coronation pageant after the City had been preparing it for a year, James did turn down the invitation to be enrolled as a Mercer, a refusal which was a snub to the City.[103] And hopes that he would prove to be a militant Protestant monarch received a severe setback when in August 1604 he signed the Treaty of London, making peace with Spain, despite all the efforts of the English and Dutch to dissuade him.

---

[100] Ben Jonson, *Complete Works*, ed. C. H. Herford Percy and E. Simpson (11 vols.; OUP, 1941), vii. 103.
[101] Goldberg, pp. 43, 50, 52.   [102] Bergeron, p. 75.
[103] Bergeron, pp. 106–8. In *Britannia's Honor*, 350–70, Dekker includes a list of the Kings who have accepted membership of the City Companies, perhaps as a reflection on Charles I, who, like his father before him, did not; Bowers, iv. 92.

2
Sir Thomas Wyatt and the Essex Rebellion

NO Elizabethan history play deals with subject-matter more recent or more dangerous than *The Famovs History of Sir Thomas Wyat*, which was printed in 1607 and, according to its title-page, was 'Written by *Thomas Dickers*, and *Iohn Webster*'. Both its overt and covert subjects, the Wyatt rebellion of 1554 and the Essex rebellion, were highly sensitive political issues. It comes closer than any other Elizabethan play, even the censored and abandoned *Sir Thomas More*, to representing the reigning monarch on the stage, and it includes an insurrection of a far more serious nature than the one that offended the censor of *Sir Thomas More*.

The idea that *Sir Thomas Wyatt* is connected with the Essex rebellion has been discussed by several critics. One is David M. Bevington, who wrote in his *Tudor Drama and Politics* that 'Wyatt's noble rebellion against the threat of Spanish rule could scarcely avoid topical application in 1600–1602. The Essex faction openly accused Cecil, Cobham, Ralegh, and others of preparing for an actual landing on English shores of the Spanish Infanta.'[1] Judith D. Spikes mentioned the idea again in an article on the Jacobean history play.[2] She rightly finds significance in the fact that so many Jacobean history plays use John Foxe's *Actes and Monuments* as their source in whole or part, as does *Sir Thomas Wyatt*. But she tries to argue a single, uniform interpretation of all the Jacobean history plays, and bases this on the belief that Elizabethan Protestantism was purely nationalistic. This is not borne out in the case of Dekker.

M. C. Bradbrook does not reject the theory in her book,

[1] Bevington, p. 292.
[2] Judith D. Spikes, 'The Jacobean History Play and the Myth of the Elect Nation', *Renaissance Drama*, NS 8 (1977), 131.

John Webster, Citizen and Dramatist, but she treats both the idea and the play as unimportant.[3] Part of the reason for this is that Webster may have had only a small part in the collaboration. *Sir Thomas Wyatt* is usually identified, convincingly, with the following entry in Henslowe's diary:

Lent vnto John thare 15 of octob₃ 1602 to geue vnto harey chettell Thomas deckers thomas hewode & mr smythe & mr webster in earneste of A playe called Ladey Jane the some of . . .l.s.[4]

Since Lady Jane Grey and her nine days' reign have a major part in the plot, it is reasonable to regard this as *Sir Thomas Wyatt*: all the more so since the play's title-page says it has been acted 'by the Queens Maiesties Seruants', formerly Lord Worcester's Men, for whom Henslowe commissioned the *Lady Jane* play. The picture is further complicated by another entry in Henslowe's diary:

Lent vnto John ducke the 27 of octob₃ 1602 to geue vnto thomas deckers in earneste of the 2 pte of Lady Jane the some of . . . v.s.[5]

We have no way of knowing whether this second entry only twelve days later refers to an extension of the original play, or to a sequel, and whether this sequel was ever written. The difficulty of apportioning a play between five authors is aggravated further by the fact that the text of *Sir Thomas Wyatt* printed in 1607 is a very bad quarto. Much of the verse is metrically deficient and the text is very short. Fredson Bowers judges it to be 'a corrupt memorial reconstruction'.[6] So most of the usual tests of authorship cannot be applied.

Very little is known about Chettle and Smith, but what is known about Heywood and Webster makes it quite believable that either of them should have collaborated in a militant Protestant play. Webster was a very inexperienced dramatist in 1602, and *Lady Jane* is only the second play he is recorded as collaborating on. There is no sign of his mature style anywhere in *Sir Thomas Wyatt*, though one editor has compared the structure of Jane and Guildford's death to the

[3] M. C. Bradbrook, *John Webster, Citizen and Dramatist* (Weidenfeld and Nicolson: London, 1980), 100.
[4] *Henslowe's Diary*, ed. R. A. Foakes and R. T. Rickert (CUP: Cambridge, 1961), 218.   [5] Ibid. 219.
[6] Bowers, i. 399.

deaths of the pairs of lovers in *The Duchess of Malfi* and *The White Devil.*[7] There is also some resemblance between the part played by the Bishop of Winchester at Lady Jane's trial, and the part played by the Cardinal in the examination of the Duchess of Malfi. But as Spikes points out, Stephen Gardiner, Bishop of Winchester, appears in an unfavourable light in almost every one of the Jacobean history plays because of his part in the Marian persecution.[8] Most critics have seen more of Dekker's style in the second half of the play, particularly Act IV, scenes i–iii, in which Wyatt's rebellion actually takes place.[9] I think that his style can also be traced in III. i. and v. ii. 1–38, in the first of which Wyatt argues with Queen Mary and in the second of which he is led to execution in the Tower of London. This suggests that his main concern was with the Wyatt plot. It is possible that the 1607 play was an abridgement by Dekker and Webster of the original plays: since Wyatt's rebellion chronologically followed the reign of Lady Jane Grey, it may be that only the second play, the sequel, was concerned with Sir Thomas Wyatt.[10] We know that Dekker took a leading part in the sequel, all the more so because on 2 November 1602 Henslowe lent Heywood and Webster £3 for another play. Evidently they were attracted by another more lucrative contract.[11] Despite its origins, the play as it stands is perfectly intelligible, united by its concern with the problems of succession and the crime of treason.

Bevington is right that a date of October to November 1602 for the original Lady Jane plays would have made a topical application hard to ignore. A German visitor to London at this time, eighteen months after the execution, found the people singing ballads about the heroic earl all over the town. He was shown the spot in Tower precinct where Essex had been beheaded, and the earl's tilting-trophies, still hanging in Whitehall.[12] To write a play which mirrored and commented on such recent events was extremely dangerous, but irresistible to a militant Protestant.

---

[7] M. F. Martin, 'A Critical Edition of *The Famous History of Sir Thomas Wyatt*', Ph.D. thesis (University of London, 1930), 38.   [8] Spikes, p. 133.
[9] Hoy, i. 318.   [10] Hoy, i. 311–12; Jones-Davies, ii. 362.
[11] Foakes and Rickert, p. 219.
[12] J. E. Neale, *Queen Elizabeth* (Jonathan Cape: London, 1934), 379–80.

When *Sir Thomas Wyatt* was printed in 1607, it was not registered, and this, together with the poor state of the text, suggests that it may have been pirated. Bradbrook thinks the play was acted again in 1604, but it is very unlikely that Dekker or Webster chose to print a play of such a nature even in 1607, and Bradbrook is misleading when she writes that 'after the succession of James I, who looked on Essex as a martyr for his own cause, the theme of Sir Thomas Wyatt's rebellion would have been quite acceptable.'[13] James's sympathy for Essex's cause is easy to exaggerate: he would probably not have turned down the throne but, after his legal accession, any suggestion of his possible association with an illegal attempt may well have grown more and not less sensitive. Certainly the subject of the rebellion remained a highly seditious one in James's reign and an object of vigilant censorship. It is true that in the early years of King James's reign a cluster of plays and poems appeared which are related in some way, avowed or suspected, to the Essex rebellion. In the period immediately following the Gunpowder Plot, militant Protestantism was particularly bold in its expression. But this does not mean that the authorities regarded references to the Essex rebellion as acceptable.

Robert Prickett was one of those who made the same mistake. His poem, *Honors Fame in Trivmph Riding, or, the Life and Death of the Late Honorable Earle of Essex*, appeared in 1604. It is a panegyric of Essex, and gives a militant Protestant account of his career including his service under 'Lester' and his expedition to 'fruitfull *Portingale* for to inthroane a mournefull bannisht king'.[14] When he comes to the Irish campaign, Prickett suggests that Essex had powerful enemies at Court who sabotaged his plans: 'Enuie . . . that winkt but neuer slept', '. . . an undermining wit'.[15] Either Robert Cecil or Sir Walter Raleigh could be intended by this. Essex himself thought that the Irish council had deliberately hindered his expedition by not supplying it properly, and this belief is endorsed by at least one modern historian.[16]

[13] Bradbrook, *John Webster*, p. 100.
[14] Prickett, *Honors Fame in Trivmph Riding, or, the Life and Death of the Late Honorable Earle of Essex*, sig. A4ʳ.   [15] Ibid. sigs. Bᵛ, B2ᵛ.
[16] J. B. Black, *The Reign of Elizabeth, 1558–1603* (OUP, 1959), 430.

Prickett defends Essex's rebellion as warmly as everything else in his career, insisting that the object of the rebellion was not to kill the Queen but to 'remoue his setled foes', and that 'He always stood for this approu'd Succession.'[17] Prickett insists that Essex was not a traitor,

> Intent and purpose in the act,
> Is that which makes a Traytors fact.[18]

This is certainly the view that emerges from *Sir Thomas Wyatt*, for Wyatt to the end denies that he is guilty of treason. As soon as Prickett's poem appeared, it was suppressed and he was examined by the Privy Council on the charge of seeking to 'extenuate an offence'.[19] And similar treatment was given to other works which were only suspected of alluding to Essex.

In 1605 Samuel Daniel's play *Philotas* fell foul of the censors on suspicion of expressing sympathy for Essex. Although the play, which concerns a rebellion against Alexander the Great, had been largely written in 1600, Daniel appeared before the Council to defend it.[20] And as late as 1608, Chapman's *Conspiracie and Tragedy of Byron*, whose subject had close parallels with Essex throughout, was also censored. It is thought to have originally contained a scene in Act IV in which Queen Elizabeth points out the mouldering head of the Earl of Essex to Marechal Biron, who himself later rebelled against Henri IV and was executed. But the subject was so sensitive that the entire Act was lopped from the play: it is known only by contemporary reports and its place is supplied by a speech reporting Biron's visit to England.[21] This was in spite of the fact that Chapman was patronized by Prince Henry. Neither Dekker nor Webster benefited from such exalted patronage.

Both Bradbrook and Spikes based their argument that *Sir Thomas Wyatt* is concerned with the Essex rebellion on the resemblances between Wyatt's rebellion in 1554 and Essex's in 1601. But, as in the case of Chapman's Byron plays, the

---

[17] Prickett, sigs. B4ᵛ, C2ᵛ.   [18] Ibid. sig. C.
[19] *DNB* entry for Prickett.   [20] *DNB* entry for Daniel.
[21] *The Tragedies of George Chapman*, ed. T. M. Parrott (Routledge and Sons: London, 1910), 591–2.

problem is that the coincidental likenesses between the two cases was so great already as to provide the authors with an excellent defence if they had needed it. Not that the subject of Wyatt's rebellion was a safe one in itself. That Wyatt's rebellion might have been in favour of the monarch still on the throne in 1602 complicated the issue but did not defuse it. Wyatt had been suspected of trying to place the then Princess Elizabeth on the throne, and marry her to Edward Courtenay.[22] When the rebellion failed, he denied strenuously and gallantly that Elizabeth 'knew any thyng of my rising', and this denial, though it might not have been true, undoubtedly helped to save the life of Elizabeth, who was then imprisoned in the Tower.[23]

Later, in a speech to Parliament in 1566, Elizabeth made it clear that she had known something about the rising, though she referred to it in a disapproving way.[24] Few of her subjects would have known about that, but many of them would be aware that she had some connection with the rebellion because these events had been covered in detail by several contemporary histories: Holinshed's *Chronicles*, Stowe's *Annales*, and Foxe's *Actes and Monuments*, the two latter being the sources of the play. Elizabeth's possible involvement with Wyatt's then treasonable plot, coupled with the evident similarities of that plot to Essex's rebellion against Elizabeth, together produced a powerful irony. In condemning Essex, Elizabeth could be accused of condemning herself.

The events of 1553–4 were of renewed interest in the closing years of Elizabeth's reign, when anxiety about the problem of succession had been growing for some time. To settle the succession in favour of a Protestant candidate had been one of the avowed aims of Essex's rebellion. Elizabeth's refusal to name an heir made people fear a repeat of what had happened at the death of Edward VI: civil war, rebellion, and a possible Roman Catholic monarch. Another reason for intense interest in that period of history was that all claims to the English succession had to be considered in the light of

---

[22] Antony Fletcher, *Tudor Rebellions* (Seminar Studies in History, 3; Longmans: London, 1968), 78.

[23] John Foxe, *Actes and Monuments of Matters Most Speciall and Memorable, Happenyng in the Church*, 4th edn. (1583), ii. 1469.   [24] Fletcher, p. 84.

Henry VIII's Will, mentioned in the play by Sir Thomas Wyatt (III. i. 141), a Will which excluded James VI of Scotland and so increased the likelihood of a Catholic succeeding to the throne. All these matters being of such pressing interest in 1602, when *Sir Thomas Wyatt* was written, the subject might well have attracted the dramatists even without the remarkable resemblance between Wyatt's rebellion and Essex's.

When Dr John Hayward was questioned by the Privy Council about his *First Part of the Life and Reign of King Henry IV*, which he dedicated to Essex in 1599, before the rebellion, what the Council particularly sought to prove was that Hayward had tampered with history in order to suggest a parallel between Bolingbroke and the Earl of Essex. There were obvious likenesses: for instance, Bolingbroke had a long list of grievances against Richard II which attracted sympathizers to his cause; Essex, for the same reasons, had become a magnet for the disaffected. But the Privy Council took a great interest in minor alterations, for instance in whether Hayward had any historical source for his description of Bolingbroke as extremely civil and courteous to all ranks of men, high and low—as was Essex.[25]

The Council's principles were perfectly logical, and the same procedure ought to be applied to the case of *Sir Thomas Wyatt*. Large general likenesses are certainly there, but do not in themselves constitute proof. We need to bear in mind that we are dealing with not two but three entities: Wyatt's rebellion, Essex's rebellion, and the drama.

The Wyatt of the play is a popular military commander, winning men's loyalty with his courage and eloquence. He is impetuous and slightly foolhardy, which certainly bears a resemblance to Essex. The Earl had been a distinguished land-commander, particularly in France in 1591 and on the Cadiz expedition in 1596. He was made Earl-Marshall of England in 1597, and his power in winning the devotion of those he commanded was one of his greatest assets—or, in the Queen's eyes, liabilities. However, it is also quite accurate as a picture of the historical Wyatt. As a young man in 1543 he served

---

[25] G. B. Harrison, *The Life and Death of Robert Devereux, Earl of Essex* (Cassell and Co.: London, 1937), 266.

under the Earl of Surrey in the war against France and distinguished himself, earning a responsible command. He actually wrote a formal treatise on the militia.[26] In the play, the object of Wyatt's rising is to prevent Queen Mary's marriage to Philip of Spain, an event which threatens foreign rule and the establishment of a Catholic dynasty:

> I graunt, your predecessors oft haue sought
> Their Queene from *France*, and sometimes to from *Spaine*.
> But neuer could I heare that England yet
> Has bin so base, to seeke a King from either:[27]

He reminds Queen Mary of the statute that prohibited Spaniards from the land, and when addressing his troops before battle he appeals to their fear and hatred of the prospect of Spanish rule:

> You free your Countrie from base spanish thrall,
> From Ignominious slauerie.[28]

Captain Brett, the leader of the band of London soldiers that deserts Mary and goes to fight on the side of Wyatt, gives the same reason for the rebellion.

BRETT. *Wyat* is vp to keepe the Spaniards down, to keepe King *Phillip* out, whose comming in will giue the Land such a Phillip, twill make it reele agen.[29]

Not only had Essex's career been devoted to fighting Spain on behalf of Protestantism, but one of the reasons he gave for his rebellion was the idea that the Privy Council was supporting the claim of the Infanta of Spain to the English succession. In 1594 Robert Parsons, SJ, had published (under the pseudonym of R. Doleman) *A Conference abovt the Next Succession to the Crowne of Ingland*. This book, which was for some reason dedicated to Essex, argued that the Infanta, being descended from John of Gaunt, had as good a claim as James VI.[30] The fact that neither Queen Elizabeth nor any of her Council took steps to oppose this claim alarmed militant

---

[26] *DNB* and Fletcher, p. 80.
[27] *STW*, III. i. 132–5.
[28] *STW*, III. i. 141–3, IV. i. 19–20.
[29] *STW*, IV. ii. 44–6.
[30] Robert Parsons, SJ, *A Conference abovt the Next Succession to the Crowne of Ingland* (1594), 150–3.

Protestants, and Essex feared that even Robert Cecil supported it. He said this both to his followers and to the people of London at the time of his rising, and this was one of the charges against him at his trial.[31]

Nevertheless, the play is quite accurate to the facts of Wyatt's rebellion here. He stated his motive as opposition to foreign rule first and foremost. The proclamation he issued at Maidstone to attract followers to his rebellion said that its aim was 'to defend the realme in danger to be brought in thraldome unto strangers'. He repeated this when met by representatives of Queen Mary on his way to London.[32]

In the play, Wyatt brings his army to London, and arrives at Ludgate. There he is met by the troops of Queen Mary led by the Earl of Pembroke and they deny him entry. When Essex in 1601 brought his armed band to London, he also found Ludgate shut against him and manned by the Queen's forces, but Essex was on the inside, trying to retreat when he had found his support insufficient.[33] The scene in the play could thus be regarded as an ingenious dramatic pun, recalling to the audience an event which many of them might have seen.

Nevertheless, this is based on what happened to the historical Wyatt in 1554. Starting out from Kent, he first tried to approach London from the south at London Bridge, but failing there he crossed the river upstream at Kingston and approached from the north. The Queen's army scattered his men and Ludgate was shut against him.[34]

Wyatt in the play denies that he is a traitor. So did the Earl of Essex. But so also did the historical Wyatt insist that he was no traitor, and that his aim had been to change the Queen's counsellors and not to kill her.[35] That did not

---

[31] Harrison, pp. 276–7, 288, 307. Also Edward P. Cheyney, *A History of England from the Defeat of the Armada to the Death of Elizabeth* (2 vols.; Longmans, Green & Co.: London, 1926), ii. 530. And Francis Bacon, *A Declaration of the Practices and Treasons Attempted and Committed by Robert, Late Earle of Essex, and His Complices* (1601), sigs. G4ᵛ, H.

[32] R. Holinshed, *Chronicles of England, Scotland and Ireland*, augmented edn. (4 vols.; 1587), iv. 1093–6. Also John Stowe's *Annales of England . . . until 1601*, augmented edn. (1601), 1045–6.   [33] Harrison, p. 290.

[34] Holinshed, iv. 1098; Stowe, pp. 1045–6.

[35] *STW*, IV. iv. 34; Holinshed, iv. 1096, 1099.

prevent him from being convicted, and beheaded in Tower precinct, as happens to the Wyatt in the play, and as happened to Essex.

All this unanimity as yet provides no evidence which could prove that the dramatists set out to write a play about the Essex rebellion, rather than about a rebellion which happened to resemble Essex's. If they had been content to leave it there, they might have had a cast-iron defence. In fact, had they ever been charged in the same way that Hayward was, they could even have pointed to further accidental resemblances between the two rebellions, which the play does not include. By an odd coincidence, Wyatt brought his followers to Ludgate on 8 February 1554—the same date that Essex chose in 1601. The dramatists might have found this fact in Holinshed although they do not mention it in the existing text.[36]

Proof, however, is to be found, because the playwrights could not resist improving on the resemblances they found, in two or three crucial ways, and these really clinch the case.

The historical Wyatt was never in the Privy Council, either under Edward VI or Queen Mary. He was a military gentleman, not a statesman, and the sources all make this quite clear. But the Wyatt of the play is a Privy Councillor, the only one who at the start of the play has refused to sign the Will of Edward VI, drawn up by the scheming Duke of Northumberland. He retains this position after the coronation of Queen Mary, and behaves with the most reckless outspokenness to the monarch's very face when her marriage treaty with Philip of Spain is announced.[37] His long tirade and his boldness are not merely dramatic licence for the expression of the dramatists' views: they are deliberate characterization, as the reactions of the other characters indicate. Winchester says, '*Wyat* you are too hot,' and Mary,

> But that wee knowe thee *Wyat* to be true
> Vnto the Crowne of *England* and to vs,
> Thy ouer-boldnesse should bee payde with death.
> But cease, for feare your liberall tongue offend.[38]

[36] Holinshed, iv. 1098.
[37] *STW*, III. i. 80–145.
[38] *STW*, III. i. 93, 146–9.

The Earl of Essex was a Privy Councillor. He had been made one in February 1592/3, and he had consistently used this position to press the militant Protestant cause to the Queen. In 1596 he had urged her to send a force to the defence of Calais, but she hesitated and it fell to Spain.[39] Essex had offended Elizabeth with his liberal tongue on many occasions. In 1598 he quarrelled with her at a Privy Council meeting over Irish policy, and behaved so disrespectfully that Elizabeth descended to boxing his ears.[40] The incident caused a great scandal, and various versions of it were spread. Much of the sympathy went to Essex, whose humiliation was considered to be unjust in respect of his rank and services. On another occasion, Essex had openly brandished one of the Marprelate tracts, a banned work, at Court.[41]

Act III, scene i of the play recalls anecdotes of this kind about Essex. It is meant to give a heroic picture of Essex in Council, representing the views of militant Protestants with courage and indeed with recklessness. It cannot possibly portray the historical Wyatt. When his rebellion has turned out a failure, Wyatt in the play reproaches London for deserting him:

O *London, London*, thou perfidious Town,
Why hast thou broke, thy promise to thy friend?
That for thy sake, and for the generall sake,
Hath thrust my selfe into the mouth of danger?
March backe to Fleet-streete, if that *Wyat* die,
London vniustlie, buy thy treacherie.[42]

The band of Londoners under Captain Brett creep away from him here like cowards, and this incident has been moved from its place in the sources which state that the London whitecoats left Wyatt before he reached Ludgate.[43] The historical Wyatt hoped of course to gain the support of London, as any rising must, but there is no hint in the sources that he had any promise of help from the city, nor that it was

---

[39] Harrison, pp. 75, 96–100.
[40] Ibid., pp. 194–5; Robert Lacey, *Robert, Earl of Essex: An Elizabethan Icarus* (Weidenfeld and Nicolson: London, 1971), 211–12.
[41] *DNB* entry for Devereux.
[42] *STW*, IV. iii. 44–9.   [43] Stowe, p. 1048; Hoy, i. 344.

in some way his special friend. In fact, he was not well known there, and it was a total surprise when, while he was still in Kent, the band of Londoners defected from Queen Mary's troops to his own.

It was Essex who could well have called London his friend, and reproached it for treachery, after the many signs of support he had received from it over the previous years. When he set out from London on his Irish campaign the crowds had followed him four miles out of the city, and when in 1600 he was seriously ill, the clergy in London led public prayers for him, despite the fact that he was in disgrace at Court.[44] At the time of the rebellion, he was told by his followers that he could expect support from an alderman of London, Sheriff Smyth, who was known to be an admirer of Essex's and who could by virtue of his office call on a thousand armed men. But when Essex arrived at Smyth's house in Fenchurch Street on the day of the rebellion, he found that the report was all an exaggeration. Essex spent two hours at the house, and was seen pleading with Smyth in the street, but to no avail.[45]

This public and ignominious disappointment fits in well with Wyatt's accusation in the play about the perfidy of London, and his insistence that it is not he but London which is guilty of treachery. The cowardice attributed to Captain Brett and his band when they all 'steale away from Wyat and leaue him alone' is a judgement on the way that London treated Essex. There is no major battle in the play, nor was there at the time of the Essex rebellion: only the skirmish at Ludgate when a few shots were fired. This is not true of the historical Wyatt, who faced the Earl of Pembroke's troops in battle north of London on 7 February.[46] These surreptitious alterations establish beyond doubt that *Sir Thomas Wyatt* was intended to represent the Essex rebellion.

Dekker's interest in the Wyatt plot is supported by external evidence. A passage in his *Seuen Deadly Sinnes of London*, printed in 1606 (about the time when the abridgement of the *Lady Jane* plays was probably made), mentions the name of Wyatt.[47]

[44] Harrison, pp. 216, 256. [45] Ibid. 283, 287–8; Lacey, p. 290.
[46] Holinshed, iv. 1098. [47] Grosart, ii. 63; Hoy, i. 344.

Sir Thomas Wyatt is concerned both with Essex's uprising, and about the definition of treason in general. Its aim is indubitably to 'extenuate an offence' because in contrast to the many cases of treason and treachery in the play, Wyatt is shown as innocent. He is allowed to put up the most spirited defence of his rebellion to the end, and he dies not as a traitor in our eyes but as a martyr for his country and faith, standing in opposition to the Catholic Bishop of Winchester:

> Traitor and *Wyats* name,
> Differ as farre as *Winchester* and honor.
> .   .   .   .
> When that houre comes, wherein my blood is spilt,
> My crosse will looke as bright as yours twice guilt.[48]

Winchester, who supported Queen Mary in creating so many Protestant martyrs, is a hated figure in Jacobean history plays. In the sources, the historical Wyatt made the equivalent of this speech to Sir Philip Denie, his captor, not to the bishop: 'Thou art more traitor than I.'[49] This alteration turns the scene into a religious confrontation and implies that Wyatt is a Protestant martyr as well as a patriot.

The same impression is created by the scene in which the newly crowned Mary (who has appeared earlier in the costume of a nun) addresses her Council and announces her marriage. She starts by telling them that she plans to restore the Church:

> The ancient honours due vnto the Church,
> Buried within the Ruind Monastaries,
> Shall lift their stately heads, and rise againe
> To astonish the destroyers wandring eyes.
> Zeale shall be deckt in golde . . .[50]

It is at this point that Wyatt changes his allegiance and opposes Queen Mary for the first time. By these means the dramatists subtly suggest the inseparability of religious and political issues. Religion was officially a topic not permitted on the stage, but the intention is clear. Mary is actually

---

[48] *STW*, V. ii. 14–15, 23–4.
[49] Holinshed, iv. 1099; Stowe, p. 1051; Hoy, i. 346.
[50] *STW*, III. i. 7–11.

referred to when she first appears as 'the catholicke Queene', and no English audience could think of this period of history without being acutely aware of the religious demarcation.[51]

Lady Jane Grey and her husband Guildford Dudley are represented as virtual martyrs in the play. Although they were convicted and executed as traitors, this was a widespread attitude to them. Drayton's *Heroicall Epistles* (1619), which includes one from Jane Grey to Guildford and a reply from him to her, describes their death as 'Martyrdome'.[52] The source for this belief, and for the Jane Grey plot, was *Actes and Monuments*, which does not state precisely that Jane Grey was a martyr, since she was never offered her life in return for renouncing her Protestant faith. But it does make clear that she had the calibre of a martyr, and resisted all attempts to convert her. Foxe reproduces her long and learned disputation with Feckenham on the morning of her execution, and various letters concerning doctrine.[53]

It is clear that Jane and Guildford are quite innocent of the charge of treason, because as Guildford says they were simply used to further the stratagems of their fathers, the Dukes of Suffolk and Northumberland: 'And will you count such forcement treacherie?'[54] Winchester presides over their trial, and in reply to Guildford's pleas he brings a conclusive charge: 'They are Heritickes.'[55] The religious and the political are shown as inextricable. Jane and Guildford's pathetic and horrible death becomes not only a martyrdom; but also a proof of how right Wyatt is to rise against the Catholic Queen.

Bevington tries to insist that, in opposing Queen Mary's marriage, Wyatt is somehow not opposing absolutism.[56] But any such distinction is quite impossible, both from a practical point of view for Wyatt himself, and for us in the view of the inseparability of religion from politics in this period. To oppose enforced Catholicism was to oppose the Spanish marriage, and to oppose the Spanish marriage involved defying the hereditary monarch in one crucial, unavoidable way. Even to replace one

[51] *STW*, I. iii. 21.

[52] *The Works of Michael Drayton*, ed. J. William Hebel (5 vols.; The Shakespeare Head Press; Basil Blackwell: Oxford, 1961), ii. 299.   [53] Foxe, ii. 1419–20.

[54] *STW*, V. i. 72–6.   [55] *STW*, V. i. 111.   [56] Bevington, p. 293.

absolute monarch with another more acceptable absolutist is, in a sense, to oppose absolutism, or at any rate to undermine it. Militant Protestants must, sooner or later, part company with royal absolutism, yet until the concept of a legitimate opposition was accepted, the only alternative was regicide. Buchanan's *De Iure Regni Apud Scotos* had quoted with approval examples of kings and tyrants who had been forced to abdicate, and defended the killing of James III of Scotland, which he said had been carried out 'with due regard to legal form'.[57] While this ideal differed from the notions of assassination advocated by the Jesuit Mariana, it was far from absolutist.

Since the Essex rebellion failed, Essex and his followers never had to face the problem of what they would have done if Elizabeth had refused to give in to their demands and change her councillors, or ratify the Protestant succession. The example of Mary, Queen of Scots taught that a deposed monarch caused endless problems so long as she or he were allowed to live. But this is a decision that militant Protestants in Dekker's generation never had to make. The problem is raised, and left unresolved.

Two suggestions have been made about a further contemporary parallelism intended by the dramatists when they chose the subject of Lady Jane Grey. Spikes put forward the idea that she is meant to represent King James's cousin, Lady Arbella Stuart, while Bradbrook suggests that she represents the young Elizabeth.[58] Interesting though they are, neither suggestion stands up to the kind of rigorous examination that can be applied to the Essex theory.

Arbella Stuart, the daughter of Charles Stuart, Earl of Lennox, was a Protestant, although there is a prevalent misunderstanding about this. Many modern writers refer to her as a Roman Catholic, a confusion which has probably arisen because of her association with the plot of Lord Cobham, a Catholic, in 1603.[59] The problem has been aggravated by the fact that neither the entry in the *DNB* nor

[57] Buchanan, p. 124.
[58] Spikes, p. 131; Bradbrook, *John Webster*, p. 100.
[59] e.g. Frank R. Ardolino, ' "In St. Iagoes Park": Iago as Catholic Machiavell in Dekker's *Whore of Babylon*', *Names*, 30 (1982), 4.

the nineteenth-century biography by Elizabeth Cooper make any statement on the subject, probably assuming that her Protestant status was well known. But Arbella's most recent biographer, David M. Durant, makes it clear that she was born and brought up a Protestant. Her education included 'a good dose of Protestant reading', even the works of Calvin.[60] The Venetian ambassador reported that her upbringing was 'Puritan', and Durant says that in her maturity 'If anything, Arbella's beliefs now bordered on Puritanism.'[61] He also thinks that she may have been an admirer of the Earl of Essex's career, although she never met Essex.[62] Women as well as men supported militant Protestantism, and when permitted to do so, some of them became active in the cause: for example Lucy Harington, Countess of Bedford, and King James's daughter, the Queen of Bohemia, in the next generation.

Arbella's royal blood attracted many marriage-overtures from those who sought to use her as a route to the throne—a fate she shared with Jane Grey. In 1594 Parsons's book on the succession drew public attention to Arbella's claim, even suggesting that it was superior in some respects to that of James VI because Arbella had been born on English soil (in Hackney, to be precise).[63] So there may have been some public interest in Arbella Stuart when the first *Lady Jane* plays were written.

But Essex never supported Arbella's claim, and so the two allusions together would not be very consistent. And it was not until 1603, after the original play was written, that Arbella became a serious contender for the throne. Soon after King James arrived in England, Arbella was unwittingly involved in the two plots against him organized by the circle of Lord Cobham (known as the Main Plot and the Bye Plot, as if one of them were written in verse). Not all the conspirators were Catholics, and needing a candidate for the throne they planned to use Arbella and marry her to Lord Grey of Wilton.[64] However, the dramatists have not in any way

[60] David M. Durant, *Arbella Stuart: A Rival to the Queen* (Weidenfeld and Nicolson: London, 1978), 69.

[61] Ibid. 107, 173.   [62] Ibid. 89, 111.

[63] Parsons, p. 124.   [64] Durant, p. 127.

increased the fortuitous likeness between Arbella and her elder cousin Jane Grey, so it looks as if life imitated art here, and not the other way around.

Bradbrook's suggestion that the playwrights intended Jane Grey to remind the audience of the young Princess Elizabeth has some plausibility since the historical Wyatt planned to marry Elizabeth to Courtenay and put them on the throne if necessary.

Such a conjecture might receive indirect support by comparing *Sir Thomas Wyatt* to Tennyson's *Queen Mary* (1875).[65] Tennyson's play has so much resemblance to *Sir Thomas Wyatt* as to suggest that he was actually trying to re-create the fragmented Tudor drama. Wyatt is its hero, and many of the same characters appear, including Captain Brett. But in *Queen Mary*, Jane Grey makes no appearance; instead, the Princess Elizabeth has an important part. Perhaps Tennyson felt that there was some danger of dramatic duplication if he included both in the same play.

Elizabeth, however, was neither married nor martyred, and she conformed to Catholicism during her sister's reign. The dramatists never suggest any connection between Wyatt's second rising and Lady Jane's claim. They boldly depart from history in making Wyatt lead the campaign that brings Mary to the throne in the first part of the play, but do nothing to increase the resemblance between Lady Jane and Lady Elizabeth. Perhaps they simply took an interest in Jane Grey.

If we are meant to see Essex in Wyatt, this suggests a surprising comparison between Queen Elizabeth and Queen Mary rather than Jane Grey. The comparison is an extreme one, but some degree of it is inevitable once the Essex analogy is established. Queen Mary was certainly the most hated monarch in English history at this time, and Foxe had compared the 'bloody times, horrible troubles and great persecution' of her reign to the persecutions of the early Church, even on the title-page of *Acts and Monuments*.

Such a comparison does not indicate the dramatists' attitude to Queen Elizabeth's reign in the aggregate.[66] It is an

---

[65] This comparison was made by Jones-Davies, ii. 295.

[66] Dekker of course wrote a panegyric of Elizabeth after her death in *The Wonderfull Yeare* (Grosart, i. 85–94).

exceptional reaction to one event, the execution of Essex, and it reveals both the strength of the public reaction to this execution, and the place Essex held in their minds as a Protestant leader. On the day of Essex's execution, Derrick, the public executioner, narrowly escaped lynching at the hands of the furious London mob.[67] Prickett describes the execution, and its effect on Londoners: 'The most and best of all sorts wept.'[68] Elizabeth, whose subjects cast her as a Protestant heroine, now with this harsh act seemed to have forsaken Protestant ideals and played the role of her hated sister Mary. It clouded her popularity in her last years.

The parallel between Wyatt and Essex places the Essex rebellion in a long-term historical context. In the play, Wyatt is accredited with more religious motivation than the historical figure actually had, so that his dilemma between the demands of sovereign authority and the demands of religion anticipated that of Dekker's own generation. His difficult decision to sacrifice the first to the second anticipates the long-term outcome of their struggle. These dilemmas of the Reformation era were never fully resolved until the Act of Settlement of 1701. Only after one regicide and one forced abdication, could Parliament finally exclude Catholics from succeeding to the Crown, which was by then a constitutional monarchy. Militant Protestants in Dekker's time could not yet envisage such a solution, but *Sir Thomas Wyatt* reveals the direction in which their principles were leading them.

[67] Neale, p. 378.   [68] Prickett, sig. C2.

3
The Whore of Babylon

A. *The Play as a* Comoedia Apocalyptica

Dekker's *Whore of Babylon* (1605) can be regarded as the definitive militant Protestant play. Although it was written shortly after the Gunpowder Plot, it would be a mistake to see it and its view of events in too narrow a context.[1] While portraying recent events in England, it depicts the struggle between the True Church and her enemy, Rome, in international and apocalyptic terms. Like *Sir Thomas Wyatt*, it has a connection with the Essex rebellion.

The Whore of Babylon belongs to a rare genre which may be called the *comoedia apocalyptica*, to borrow a term from the subtitle of one of the most important examples, John Foxe's *Christvs Triumphans* (1556). In his preface, Dekker warns that his play will be misunderstood if we take it for a straightforward history play: 'I write as a poet, not as an historian . . . and these two do not liue under one law.'[2] The idea that *The Whore of Babylon* is a history play has led to many puzzled or hostile responses, one of the most aggressive being that of Irving Ribner. Even M. G. Riely, who is more sympathetic to the play, complains that it 'violates chronology'.[3]

While it is not uncommon for Elizabethan history plays to violate chronology, the *comoedia apocalyptica* differs from the history play since it aims to interpret events in terms of Protestant historiography derived from the Book of Revelation and other biblical texts. It organizes events by means of

[1] Daniel B. Dobson, 'Allusions to the Gunpowder Plot in Dekker's *Whore of Babylon*', N & Q VI (1959), 257, shows that the play must have been written after Jan. 1606. It was printed in 1607. Further allusions to the Plot occur at *WB*, I. i. 113 and I. ii. 277–80. Hoy sees the play as merely a product of 'revulsion' after the Plot.

[2] Bowers, ii. 497.

[3] Ribner, pp. 283–7. *The Whore of Babylon by Thomas Dekker*, ed. M. G. Riely (Renaissance Drama: A Collection of Critical Editions, ed. Stephen Orgel; Garland Publishing Inc.: NY, 1980), 78.

allegory, and has as its fundamental theme the struggle of the True Church against the Antichrist. In the Prologue, Dekker says 'wee present Matter above the vulgar Argument' for the play will 'lay the Dragon at a Doues soft feete', the Dragon being the Beast of Revelation, and the Dove the True Church inspired by the Holy Ghost.[4]

The place of Spenser in this tradition has already been recognized.[5] Dekker declared his obligation to Spenser by using such names as Faerie Land, Florimell, and Paridell, and there are passages in the play which quote or come close to quoting from Spenser. The statement about poets and historians in the preface echoes one made by Spenser in the letter to Raleigh which he appended to *The Faerie Queene*.[6] But it is not true to say, as Hoy does, that the play's 'mythology ... is freely borrowed from Spenser.'[7] The relationship between the two works is more complex since they both draw on the same Protestant tradition in which Foxe is a crucial influence.

The Protestant apocalyptic tradition goes back to the Reformation and has roots in even earlier biblical exegesis. For centuries theologians had sought a key to church history in the apocalyptic texts of the Bible, such as the Book of Revelation and other sources for a doctrine of the Antichrist. This was done by the orthodox as well as Joachimites, Lollards, and Anabaptists. Wyclif identified the Papacy with the Antichrist in his *De Papa* in 1379.[8] Luther agreed, and his *De Antichristo* (1521) was translated into English by the Lollard John Frith in 1529 as *The Revelation of Antichrist*. Luther was slower to make use of the Book of Revelation in his theology, and said in his 1522 preface to Revelation that its meaning and its apostolic status were uncertain.[9] But he soon changed his views, and in 1528 he published a Lollard

---

[4] Bowers, ii. 499.

[5] Florence Sadler, '*The Faerie Queene*, An Elizabethan Apocalypse', in *The Apocalypse in English Renaissance Thought and Literature*, ed. C. A. Patrides and J. Wittreich (Manchester University Press: Manchester, 1984), 148–74.

[6] Smith and Selincourt, p. 408.   [7] Hoy, ii. 302.

[8] Katherine Robbins Firth, *The Apocalyptic Tradition in Reformation Britain 1530–1645* (Oxford Historical Monographs; OUP, 1979), 7.

[9] Richard Bauckham, *Tudor Apocalypse* (The Courtenay Library of Reformation Classics, 8; The Sutton Courtenay Press: Oxford, 1978), 42.

commentary on Revelation dating from 1390. In his 1530 translation of the Bible he gave Revelation a new preface in which he wrote that it was prophetic of the history of the Church.[10]

Calvin also identified the Papacy with the Antichrist. Although he wrote no commentary on Revelation and doubted its apostolic status, his commentaries on the apocalyptic passages in the New Testament epistles make this teaching quite clear. One of these passages, in 2 Thess. 2: 3–12, predicts the reign of 'the mystery of iniquity', and Calvin's gloss on it, published in 1540, runs:

It was said of Nero that he was taken up from the world and would return again to persecute the Church by his tyranny. This was nothing but an old wife's fable, and yet the minds of the ancients were so bewitched that they believed that Nero would be Antichrist. Paul, however, is not speaking of one individual, but of a kingdom that was to be seized by Satan, for the purpose of setting a seat of abomination in the midst of God's temple. This we see accomplished in popery.[11]

Calvin's commentary on 1 John 2, published in 1551, has the following gloss on the passage which runs 'And as ye have heard that antichrist shall come, even now are there many antichrists':

The papists have imagined an antichrist who is to harrass the Church for three and a half years. All the marks by which the Spirit of God has pointed out antichrist appear clearly in the Pope: but their triennial antichrist has such a hold on the foolish Papists that seeing they do not see.[12]

This belief was not only spread by the written word. Despite its preface, Luther's New Testament of September 1522 carried the famous woodcut by Lucas Cranach the Elder, showing the Whore of Babylon from Rev. 17 wearing the papal triple tiara (Fig. 1).[13] It was a clear indictment of the

[10] Bauckham, 43.

[11] Calvin's *Commentaries on the New Testament*, ed. D. W. Torrance and T. F. Torrance, various translators (12 vols.; Oliver & Boyd; Edinburgh, 1959–65), iv. 339.   [12] Ibid. iii. 256.

[13] W. Worringer, *Lucas Cranach* (Klassische Illustratoren, III; R. Piper and Co., Verlag: Munich, 1908), plate 44.

1. The Whore of Babylon, from Luther's Translation of the
New Testament (Wittenberg, September 1522)

sale of indulgences by the corrupt papacy. Luther's patron the Elector of Saxony feared this illustration would provoke the Emperor, and so in the December 1522 edition of the same work the tiara was reduced to a coronet, but in subsequent editions such as Luther's 1545 Bible the tiara was restored. Many later sixteenth-century Bibles bore similar illustrations, including some English ones such as the revised Tyndale New Testament of 1552.[14]

The iconographic tradition stemming from Cranach was not restricted to Bibles. Examples of Whore of Babylon figures representing the papacy can be seen in Protestant political pamphlets printed in Germany throughout the sixteenth and seventeenth centuries.[15] Most of these pamphlets were produced in a context of religious war, and the figure of the Whore of Babylon changes little in the course of one and a half centuries. She is always seated on her seven-headed beast and holding the cup of abominations which resembles a chalice for the Mass. In 1588, the year of the Armada, an elaborate example appeared in an English book, Hugh Broughton's *Concent of Scripture* (Fig. 2).[16] In 1587 the Dutch struck a medallion showing Elizabeth and Leicester with the apocalyptic beast at their feet, and some engravings of the period actually depict Elizabeth as the Woman Clothed with the Sun.[17] Certain late paintings of Queen Elizabeth are open to the same interpretation, for instance the portrait at Montacute House attributed to John Bettes, and the celebrated Rainbow portrait with its motto '*Non sine sole Iris*', i.e. no rainbow without the Sun, or, no peace without the victory of the True Church.[18] Both portraits depict Elizabeth with

[14] Illustrated in Bauckham, p. 244, no. 4.

[15] R. W. Scribner, *For the Sake of Simple Folk* (Cambridge Studies in Oral and Literate Culture, 2; CUP: Cambridge, 1981), 161, 173, 213.

[16] Hugh Broughton, *A Concent of Scripture* (1590 edn.), last page, unnumbered.

[17] Roy C. Strong, *Portraits of Queen Elizabeth I* (OUP, 1963), 138. Frances A. Yates reproduces an engraving after Hilliard of Elizabeth as the Woman Clothed with the Sun in *Astraea: The Imperial Theme in the Sixteenth Century* (Routledge and Kegan Paul: London, 1975), plate 9b.

[18] Strong, ibid. paintings no. 55 and 100. Strong, whose conception of Elizabethan mythography is essentially secular, nevertheless says that the Rainbow portrait alludes to Elizabeth as the Sun (p. 86) and in a later article, 'Icons of Power and Prophecy: Portraits of Elizabeth I', in *Queen Elizabeth I: Most Politick Princess*, ed. S. Adams (A History Today Production, series editor Juliet Gardiner, 1984), 14, he calls the same painting 'almost apocalyptic'.

The empire of Rome, that crucified our Lorde and
serueth Satan in might and hypocrisy, is pictured
thus in Gods worde.

2. The Whore of Babylon, from Hugh Broughton's *Concent of Scripture*
(1590 Edition)

colouring and attributes suggestive of the Woman Clothed with the Sun.

A series of illustrations derived from those of Cranach, including one of the Whore of Babylon, appeared in John Bale's *Ymage of Both Chvrches* (1545), the first Protestant Revelation commentary in English. Bale's book identified the seven-headed beast of Rev. 13 as 'one vnyuersall antychrist . . . comprehending in him so wel Mahomyte as the Pope'.[19] Bale, whose work strongly influenced Foxe's, also wrote the first English *comoedia apocalyptica*, *King Johan*. This play, written c.1538–40 and revised in 1560, was never printed in its own time and Dekker was probably not aware of it. Nevertheless, it has some distinct family resemblances to *The Whore of Babylon*. Drawing on the work of Tyndale as well as on Bale's own apocalyptic interpretation of the seven ages of history, the play presents King John as an enlightened monarch whose breach with Rome foreshadowed the Reformation.[20] It includes such allegorical figures as Truth, Dissimulation, Treason, and Usurped Power.

King John warns his subjects:

> All Christen people, be ware of trayterouse pristes,
> for of truthe they are, the pernicyouse Antichristes,

and the papacy is identified as the Antichrist throughout. After King John has been murdered by a monk, Verity defends the King's noble memory.[21] In *The Whore of Babylon* we find a similar opposition between the monarch, Titania, and the powers of Rome, erupting into a series of assassination attempts on Titania by Babylon's servants.

King Johan concludes with an extended prophecy of the reign of Queen Elizabeth, written shortly after her accession. Drawing on Revelation and the Book of Daniel, it says that Elizabeth is the Angel who in Revelation marks out the servants of God, the elect or True Church. The Clergy and Nobility pray that she will 'subdewe The great Antichriste'.[22]

---

[19] John Bale, *The Ymage of Both Chvrches after the Moste Wonderful and Heauenly Reuelacion of Sainct John the Evangelist* (1550 edn.), sig. D8.

[20] Firth, p. 38, points out evidence for Tyndale's influence.

[21] John Bale, *King Johan*, ed. J. H. P. Pafford (Malone Society Reprints: OUP, 1931), 103, 110.   [22] Ibid. 133–4.

In *The Whore of Babylon* Dekker does something very similar, by including a prophecy of the reign of the current monarch, King James, and predicting that he will 'shake all Babilon' (III. i. 244). Such prediction is a form of wishful thinking which comes very close to telling the monarch what to do. Bale left an intriguing record of a play with the same title as Dekker's, *The Whore of Babylon*, written by the young King Edward VI himself.[23] It is not extant, but its authorship hardly supports the accusation so often made, that the ideas in Dekker's play are popular in the sense of vulgar, ignorant, or plebeian.

The doctrine that Rome was the Whore of Babylon spread rapidly in England, though its status was always ambiguous. No Church of England Prayer Book or conference ever gave apocalyptic theology official recognition, yet it received marks of approval which came very close to this. Very soon after Elizabeth came to the throne, Heinrich Bullinger's *A Hundred Sermons vp on the Apocalips of Jesu Christe* was printed with the royal permission. This Revelation commentary gives an interpretation which is typical of militant Protestant theology. Bullinger identifies the Woman Clothed with the Sun, of Rev. 12, as the True Church of pure doctrine, supplanted by the Whore of Babylon. The Whore is said by the angel to be 'that great city which reignest over the kings of the earth' and she rides on the beast whose seven heads St John is told are 'seven mountains'.[24] She is naturally interpreted as the 'Romane Empire or the kingedome of the Pope or of Antichrist'.[25] There were many more Revelation commentaries printed during Elizabeth's reign and though they varied in detail this dualistic core of interpretation remained consistent. In it can be recognized the skeletal outline both of Dekker's play and of Book I of *The Faerie Queene*.

The most ambitious and the most influential apocalyptic work of the Elizabethan age was Foxe's *Actes and Monuments*. Foxe was writing a Revelation commentary, *Eicasmi*,

---

[23] F. E. Schelling, *Elizabethan Drama 1558–1642* (2 vols.; Houghton, Mifflin & Co.: Boston and NY, 1908), i. 60.

[24] Heinrich Bullinger, *A Hundred Sermons vpon the Apocalips of Jesu Christe* (1561), 348; Rev. 17: 9, 18.   [25] Bullinger, p. 506.

at the end of his life, and all his work has an apocalyptic basis. Foxe's historical framework in *Actes and Monuments* is derived from the prophecies in Rev. 13 and 20, as he explains in the first volume of the book.[26] This scheme divides time into five great ages, marked by apocalyptically revealed events such as the binding and loosing of Satan. Throughout it runs the dualistic struggle between the True Church and the forces of Antichrist, represented first by pagan and then by papistical Rome.

Foxe not only expounds the doctrine of the Whore of Babylon himself, but also allows many of his martyrs to make use of it in their denunciations of Rome. In the first volume he comments on the passage in Rev. 13 in which the beast with seven heads emerges from the sea:

Because that the same cruell beast which came vp out of the sea, hauing 7. heads, and 10. hornes, to whome there was power geuen ouer euery tribe, people, and toung, and the power geuen for the space of 42 monethes: Thys beast doth note the Romaine Emperors, which most cruelly did persecute the people of God, aswell Christians as Jewes. For when as the condemnation of the great whore sitting vpon the many waters was shewed to John: he saw the same woman sitting vpon the purple coulored beast full of the names of blasphemy, hauing 7. heads, and 10 hornes: and he saw a woman being dronken with the bloud of the Saintes and Martyrs of Jesu. And the angell expounding and telling him the mistery of the woman and the beast that caried her sayde: That 7. heades are 7. hilles, and are 7. kinges: Fiue are fallen, one is, the other is not yet come: & when he shall come, he must reigne a short time. And the 10 hornes whiche thou sawest, are 10. kinges, who haue not yet taken theyr kingdome, but shall receiue theyr power as it were in one hour, vnder the beast. And finally he sayth, ye woman whom thou sawest, is the great Citty, which hath the kingdome ouer the kings of the earth. And it is manifest that the City of Rome, at the time of this prophecy, had the kingdom ouer the kings of the earth. And this City was borne vp & vpholden by her cruell & beastly Emperors.[27]

He goes on to expound the Papal Antichrist doctrine, the Rome of the popes being the successor to imperial Rome. In

---

[26] Foxe, i. 1, 397, 482.   [27] Ibid. i. 482.

the second volume Foxe quotes a letter of Bishop Ridley written shortly before his martyrdom in 1555, in which he says that the Pope is Antichrist, and that the Church of Rome is the Whore of Babylon, quoting Rev. 17 for his authority.[28]

Foxe also quotes a treatise written by Ridley, entitled: *The Whore of Babilon, with her Cup of Abominations, Expounded. Apoc. 17.* This interprets the passage in greater detail, identifying Babylon with Rome and 'the whole trade of the Romish religion'.[29] Later in the same volume Foxe quotes a letter from John Hullier, another of the Protestant martyrs under Queen Mary, in which the Church of Rome is once again identified with the Babylon of Rev. 17.[30] Since *Actes and Monuments* was ordered to be placed in churches and public places, it was certainly the most widely disseminated source of this belief.

Dekker and Spenser were both probably influenced by Foxe's Latin play *Christvs Triumphans*, and some of the resemblance between *The Whore of Babylon* and *The Faerie Queene* may be the result of them drawing on this common source. Foxe's play was printed at Basel in 1556, and again at Nuremberg in 1590, and it was definitely in circulation in England in Dekker's lifetime. A reading of *Christvs Triumphans* was given at Magdalen College, Oxford in 1561, and a performance of it took place at Trinity College, Cambridge in 1562–3.[31] Whether the performers were using imported editions or manuscript copies, the play evidently attracted some interest. The copy now in the Bodleian Library belonged to John Selden, who was a friend of Jonson and Drayton, so although the play was not printed in England until after the date of Dekker's play, there is no doubt that he could have had access to it.

In *Christvs Triumphans* Foxe presents an allegory of the history of the True Church, from the Fall of Man to the Reformation. Central to his plot is Pseudamnus, the Antichrist, who is identified with the papacy. The heroine of the last three acts is Ecclesia, who represents the True Church,

---

[28] Ibid. ii. 1775.   [29] Ibid. ii. 1779.   [30] Ibid. ii. 1908.
[31] *Two Latin Comedies by John Foxe the Martyrologist*, trans. and ed. John Hazell Smith (Cornell University Press: Ithaca, 1973), 215. F. S. Boas, *University Drama in the Tudor Age* (OUP, 1914), 387.

and also corresponds to the Woman Clothed with the Sun, the adversary in Revelation of the Whore of Babylon. The latter is represented by an anti-heroine, Pornapolis. In Act IV Pseudamnus uses Pornapolis to impersonate and supplant Ecclesia, so that he can attain power through her. For a while the plan succeeds, and Pornapolis herself describes how successfully she has passed herself off as Ecclesia in Rome, and has seduced three kings.[32]

While neither Spenser nor Dekker took over Foxe's structures unchanged, many resemblances suggest that Dekker was taking Foxe's play as his starting-point, particularly Acts IV and V in which the allegory alludes more and more closely to the events of the English Reformation. Dekker's Empress of Babylon corresponds to Foxe's Pornapolis, and the title 'Empress' recalls Foxe's theory that imperial power was revived in the Popes. She is opposed by Titania, who represents Queen Elizabeth, the leader of the True Church. The name Titania is derived from Titan, one of the mythological names for the sun, and this suggests that Titania is to be identified with the Woman Clothed with the Sun. The identification is much less clear and explicit than that of the Empress of Babylon, and to suggest that Queen Elizabeth should be seen in such apocalyptic terms was extreme even among militant Protestants. Foxe never considered such a comparison, and though a few writers had done so they did it very discreetly as if verging on the sacrilegious. Edward Hellwys's *Marvell Deciphered*, a commentary on Rev. 12 published soon after the Armada, makes this suggestion throughout but never mentions Queen Elizabeth's name. Its dedicatory epistle gives a Calvinist interpretation of the Armada victory.[33] Spenser's Una can likewise be identified with the Woman Clothed with the Sun.

M. G. Riely has pointed out how frequently Titania is compared to the sun in the play.[34] Of course the comparison between any monarch and the sun is an Elizabethan commonplace, and Dekker is subtly suggesting a further significance for it here without taking it too far. It is not that the

---

[32] J. H. Smith, pp. 313–27.
[33] Hellwys, *A Marvell Deciphered* (1589), 1 and throughout.
[34] Riely, p. 96.

allegorical figure and the historical Elizabeth are to be equated, but Elizabeth as Titania plays a role, that of leader of the True Church, which is to be understood in apocalyptic terms.

There is a second level of allegory in *The Whore of Babylon*, occupied by the figures of Truth and Falsehood who also correspond to the apocalyptic pattern. Truth in the play speaks to other allegorical figures, like Plain-dealing and Time but not to characters who represent individuals. The play opens with a dumb show: Truth, blind and asleep, is awakened at the funeral of a Queen (Mary I) and is embraced by the new Queen (Elizabeth). In the first scene of dialogue, the Empress of Babylon, who combines the functions of Foxe's Pornapolis and Pseudamnus, accuses Truth of being a cunning imposter. Like Pornapolis, the Empress enslaves three Kings, the biblical 'kings of the earth', and these are identified with the contemporary Roman Catholic powers: Spain, France, and the Holy Roman Empire.

The fifth Act of *Christvs Triumphans*, which is concerned with the Reformation era, is the one which Dekker imitated most closely, for instance in the scenes where the Empress complains to her courtiers about her declining power and reputation.[35] The scene in Dekker's play in which the King of Spain disguises himself and his servant in order to win over Campeius seems to be derived from the one in Act V of *Christvs Triumphans*, in which Satan disguises himself and his servants before sending them out into the world to seduce souls.[36]

The *comoedia apocalyptica* was an international tradition, like militant Protestantism itself. *Christvs Triumphans* is thought to have been influenced by Thomas Kirchmeyer's *Pammachius*, which was published at Wittenberg in 1538 and dedicated to Luther.[37] Foxe may also have known Nicholaeus Bartolomaeus's *Christus Xylonicus* (1531) and Francesco Negri's *Libero Arbitrio* (1546), which was translated into English by Henry Cheeke and printed in London in 1589.[38]

---

[35] J. H. Smith, pp. 347, 351, 353.
[36] Ibid. 337–41.   [37] Ibid. 43.
[38] Francesco Negri, *A Certayne Tragedie Wrytten Fyrst in Italian by F. N. B. Entituled, Freewil, and Translated into English by Henry Cheeke* (1589).

Christvs Triumphans itself was translated into French in 1561 by Jean Bienvenu and printed in Geneva in 1562. In 1575 the Huguenot Thrasibule Phenice (Theodore de Beza, whom Collinson calls 'one of Calvin's lieutenants') published his play *Comedie dv Pape malade et tirant a la fin* at Orleans. This allegorical play whose cast includes Satan, the Pope, Truth, the Hungry, and the Church, is certainly a *comoedia apocalyptica*. In it the papacy is identified with Antichrist and its days on earth are found to be nearing their prophesied end, as its punning title implies.[39] In the play, Satan helps the Pope to devise various plots against the godly, and many details of the contemporary persecution of the Protestants in France are introduced, some of the persecutors even being named.[40] The author's preface refers to Rome and its fornications as 'ceste abominable eglise Romaine' and 'la grande paillarde'—the great whore.[41] Although Dekker could not have read Phenice, the two plays are products of the same tradition.

The internationalism of the tradition needs to be emphasized because Dekker and other Protestant writers have often been assumed to be expressing merely nationalistic sentiments. However, Haller's view that Foxe believed England to be an elect nation whose events were fulfilling some unique prophesied role has now declined in favour, and has been rejected by Bauckham, Olsen, Firth, and Sadler.[42] Foxe was writing for an English audience in *Actes and Monuments*, but he still devoted very large sections of the book to religious reform and persecution all over Europe, particularly in the Empire. Where he does not have room for all the details and persecution outside England, he includes lists of the martyrs in sixteenth-century Germany, France, Spain, and Italy.[43] He planned a further volume entitled *Rerum in Ecclesia Gestarum* which was to have chronicled recent martyrs on the Continent in more detail, and in his *Eicasmi* he gives no precedence to English affairs.

---

[39] Thrasibule Phenice, *Comedie dv Pape malade et tirant a la fin* (Glvade d'avgy, Orleans, 1575), 12; Collinson, *Godly People*, p. 249.
[40] Phenice, pp. 50, 57, 60, 65, 66, etc.   [41] Ibid. 5–6.
[42] Bauckham, pp. 86–7, quotes Olsen and Firth as agreeing with him; Sadler, pp. 158–60.   [43] Foxe, ii. 886–942.

In Act v of *Christvs Triumphans* Foxe's allegory does represent in detail events in England: particularly the martyrdom of Cranmer and Latimer under Queen Mary, which had just taken place at the time when he was writing. But he fits this into a larger, universal picture, and this is one of the purposes of *comoedia apocalyptica*: events like persecution and assassination are put into a prophetic context which is ultimately optimistic. Ecclesia has three sons, Europus, Africus, and Asia, and when the latter are not shown, their development is reported.[44] All three are with her at the conclusion of the play, when Ecclesia, dressed as a bride, waits for the coming of her bridegroom, Christ, to end her sufferings.

Dekker's *Whore of Babylon* needs to be seen in the same way. Like *Actes and Monuments*, it was written for an English audience, and it concentrates on English events. But it puts them into the context of an international Reformation, and the concept of the True Church was certainly an international one. *The Whore of Babylon* contains many references to the Church abroad: its audience was expected to be able to pick up allusions not only to the Gunpowder Plot, but also to Henry VIII's campaigns in France, the St Bartholomew's Day massacre, and the seven Electors of Germany.[45]

Foxe leaves the action of *Christvs Triumphans* unresolved because history was unfinished: the Church was still awaiting the fulfilment of the final prophecies, and her victory over her enemies.[46] Likewise, in *The Whore of Babylon*, the Armada victory is not presented as a conclusion but only as the first battle of the great struggle which was yet to take place. Dekker's theology is more militant than Foxe's, and while Ecclesia renounces arms, Titania in Act v leads her force into battle.[47] In this respect, Dekker is closer to the contemporary successors of Foxe whose theology interpreted the Armada battle as a spiritual victory. When Titania in the last line of the play says 'We are neere shore,' she is referring to Protestant historiography once more. According to Foxe's scheme, the

---

[44] J. H. Smith, p. 335.   [45] *WB*, I. ii. 110–13, II. ii. 16–21, V. vi. 129–31.
[46] David Norbrook, *Poetry and Politics in the English Renaissance* (Routledge and Kegan Paul: London, 1984), 38, 265.   [47] J. H. Smith, p. 359.

second great age of persecution of the Church, which had begun at the time of the forerunners of the Reformation, was now nearly over and the defeat of the Antichrist could before too long (on a historical scale) be expected.

Among the writings of Foxe's successors, two works shed further light on *The Whore of Babylon*. Both of them happen to be dedicated to the Earl of Essex, and in unmistakably militant Protestant terms. One is George Giffard's *Sermons Vpon the Whole Booke of the Revelation* (1596). Giffard (or Gifford, 1548–1600) was a Calvinist and a non-conformist who was deprived of his living, but continued to lecture and to publish sermons. He was one of the chaplains present when Sidney died at Zutphen, and is the author of the letter 'The Manner of Sir Philip Sidney's Death'.[48] His Revelation commentary, which emphasizes recent history, incorporating the Armada victory, the emergence of the Catholic League and events in the German empire, demonstrates how militant Protestants were constantly bringing their interpretations up to date after the death of Foxe. It is one of the closest analogues of Dekker's play.

Giffard calls Rev. 17, in which the Whore of Babylon appears, the key that opens the mysteries of the book. He identifies the Whore as the Church of Rome both for its idolatry and because of the sale of indulgences:

No man is able with words sufficiently to express how much and how madly men in the time of popery doted vpon the rotten filthy inuentions of the Pope. How did they drinke vp his pardons and indulgences euen as men drinke vp sweet wine? How ranne they after stockes and stones at his appoyntment?[49]

Giffard, like Dekker, identifies the Whore's purple and scarlet robes with popish vestments, and her seven-headed beast with the Holy Roman Empire, which is represented in the play by one of the vassal kings. Giffard meditates at length on the antithesis between the Whore and the Woman Clothed with the Sun, whom he identifies as 'the Church militant

---

[48] *Miscellaneous Prose of Sir Philip Sidney*, ed. Katherine Duncan-Jones and J. Van Dorsten (Clarendon Press: Oxford, 1973), 161.

[49] George Giffard, *Sermons Vpon the Whole Booke of the Revelation* (1596; rpt. 1599), 324.

vpon earth', 'the Spouse of Christ, the Lambes wife'.[50]
Giffard's account of events amounts to a militant, almost a
military, programme. He refers triumphantly to the Armada
victory and to the attempts by the Roman Catholic powers to
assassinate Elizabeth, the events which provide the material
for the plot of Dekker's play:

The Romish beast & his companie haue espied so much and do
make full account, that all their wars and enterprises against the
Church are to small purpose, vnlesse they could first supplant and
destroy her Maiestie. And to effect this their wicked desire, they
haue inuented all the waies and meanes which possibly they can.
Their Pope (who is the standard-bearer in that apostacie) did long
since excommunicate her Highnesse. He hath from time to time
sent forth his Iesuite Priests & others, to worke all maner of
trecheries, and traiterously to murther her royall Person: wherein
the Lord God hath ofte preuented them miraculously, for which we
are bound most deepely to giue him thanks. The King of Spaine, who
hath giuen his power to the beast, sent his forces Anno 88. for to
inuade her land, and to throw down her excellent Highnesse, from
that sacred authoritie and power in which Almighty God hath
placed her, & miraculously protected her, fighting from heauen
against her enemies, euen to the wonderment of the whole world.
And what shall we thinke, that they haue now done? Naye, looke
how long that great fierie dragon, Sathan, that prince of darkenes
doth burne in hatred against God & his truth, so long Antichrist
and his adherents moued by his instigation, will be restless in
seeking the subuersion of our religion, Queen, and countrie. Then
do we especially and aboue many others, stand in neede of noble
warriors & mighty men.[51]

The mighty men he is thinking of include both Sidney and
Essex. In the latter part of his book Giffard envisages the final
downfall of Rome in a holy war in which the Protestant
powers of England, Scotland, Denmark, and France will be
united and the Earl of Essex will be their general. He grounds
this in the prophecy of Rev. 17: 16 concerning the ten horns
that will make the Whore desolate.[52] Dekker's play contains a
reference to the same prophecy in its concluding lines,
combining it with 2 Kgs. 19: 28, when the second vassal king
vows that he will desert the cause of Babylon.[53]

[50] Ibid. 217.   [51] Ibid. A3–A3ᵛ.
[52] Ibid. 339.   [53] WB, V. vi. 126–31.

The other apocalyptic work could be regarded as the handbook for the Protestant soldiers who were to serve in this holy war. It is *The Sacred Shield of Al Trve Christian Sovldiers* (1599) by John Gibson. This is a manual of devotion designed to be used by the armed forces, containing a detailed exposition of the theology of the just war, and of the apocalyptic prophecies concerning the final confrontation between the True Church and her Babylonian adversary. First it quotes Old Testament precedents for holy wars, then goes on to give a militant Protestant reading of Revelation. The greatest enemy of the True Church is said to be:

... that most bloudy and cruell beast, that Antichrist of Rome, being in these latter dayes the very arch and head enemy, vnder whose banner and conduct they all, whether forraigne or domesticall, as rebels and traytors that are within the profession of Christianity, but in the practise of Antichristianity, do or shall make warre against us ...[54]

This idea of an international Catholic alliance aiming to stamp out Protestantism is seen in Dekker's play. Simon Adams traces it back to the 1570s, and it was shared by Continental Protestants.[55] Gibson goes on to identify Rome as:

... that whore of Babilon, that with her golden cup of abominations, and filthinesse of fornications, hath deceiued the kings and inhabitants of the earth ... all which is nowe come to passe, euen by that septicole, or seuen hilled Citie of Rome, as it is now the seat and place of Antichrist, that is there the worker of all these abominations and bloudshed ... warres, sedition, rebellion, treasons, or most horrible murders, as by close poysoning, or anie violent meanes ...[56]

Gibson goes on to reproduce Foxe's doctrine that the number of the Beast in Revelation, 666, can be interpreted to mean 'Lateinos, & Italica ecclesia'.[57]

A third apocalyptic work of the 1590s, an anonymous

---

[54] John Gibson, *The Sacred Shield of A1 Trve Christian Sovldiers* (1599), 61.

[55] Simon Adams, 'The Queen Embattled: Elizabeth I and the Conduct of Foreign Policy', in *Queen Elizabeth I: Most Politick Princess*, ed. S. Adams (A History Today Production, series editor Juliet Gardiner, 1984), 41.

[56] Gibson, pp. 69–70.

[57] Ibid. 72; Foxe, i. 500. (Other Protestant writers attribute this idea to St Ireneus.)

pamphlet entitled *Babylon is Fallen*, has been suggested by Hoy as a possible source or analogue of the play.[58] It has less in common with the play than Giffard and Gibson do, as it deals principally with prophecies from the Book of Esdras rather than from Revelation. It actually has more relevance to Dekker's later play *The Virgin Martyr* (and it was reprinted in 1619/20), but, like Giffard's and Gibson's books, *Babylon is Fallen* is dedicated to the Earl of Essex, in a long and affectionate epistle which says that the author has served under Essex's command.[59]

Giffard's epistle dedicatory 'To the Right Noble Earle of Essex, his verie good Lord' not only compares Essex to Joshua and other godly leaders in the Old Testament, but actually invites him to take up the role of the White Horseman of the apocalypse in the great battle which is to come:

Put on that fine white linnen and pure, ride vpon that white horse among this blessed company, and follow this high captain: and then shall your H. performe right worthy things to the glorie of God, to the good of his people, and to your owne eternall praise and felicitie.[60]

Gibson's dedication compares Essex to Moses, Joshua, and Baracke, anticipating the time when he will lead the forces of the True Church in the final confrontation with its enemy.[61]

These dedications are a sign of Essex's position as patron and leader of the militant Protestants at the end of Queen Elizabeth's reign. He was their hero, political leader, and military commander. In view of Dekker's prominent involvement in *Sir Thomas Wyatt*, it is not surprising to find such a close correspondence between his view of the events of his own time and those of the professed followers of the Earl of Essex.

Essex himself was a firm believer in the Protestant apocalyptic interpretation of events. In his letter to Queen Elizabeth written on 12 August 1597 during the Azores voyage, Essex outlines his view of the world situation, and the prospects for war or peace between the Protestant and Roman

---

[58] Hoy, ii. 314.
[59] *Babylon is Fallen* (anon., 1594; 2nd edn. 1597), sig. A2.
[60] Giffard, A5ᵛ.   [61] Gibson, A3.

Catholic powers. He gives little hope of peace, and explains his opinion in apocalyptic terms by saying of Elizabeth and the King of Spain:

> But you two are like 2 mightie Champions entred into the lists to fight for the two great generall quarrells of Christendome, Religion and Libertie, hee forcing all to worship the beast, your Ma^{ty} standing for God and his truth, Hee aspiring to an vniuersall Monarchy, Your Ma^{ty} releeuing all the oppressed, and shewing that you are powerfull enough to make him feede w^{th}in his tether.[62]

Here we find the dualistic world-view so typical of militant Protestantism. Queen Elizabeth, like Dekker's Titania, stands for God and his truth, while Spain, like the first King in the play, is the most powerful arm of Babylon, 'forcing all to worship the beast'. By 'releeuing all the oppressed' Essex means that Elizabeth has been giving aid to Protestants abroad, most notably in the Netherlands and in France, to the supporters of Henry IV in 1591.

Essex's position as leader of the militant Protestants was well enough understood abroad for him to be the target of a Jesuit assassination attempt during the Azores voyage, around the time when he wrote this letter. The would-be assassin, Edward Squire, was an Englishman trained abroad, like the Jesuit assassins who appear in the play.[63] Essex remained a figurehead of militant Protestantism in the public mind long after his death, and in 1624 Thomas Scott published a compilation from Essex's *Apologie* as a warning against the Spanish marriage: *Robert, Earle of Essex, His Ghost Sent from Elizian . . . printed in Paradise.*

B. The Play in Relation to the Events of Queen Elizabeth's Reign

In *The Whore of Babylon* Dekker portrays Titania as a militant Protestant leader, much more militant than the historical Queen Elizabeth was ever willing to be. The play is

---

[62] British Library Hulton MS, fo. 149.

[63] *A Letter Written Out of England to an English Gentleman Remaining at Padua, Containing a True Report of a Strange Conspiracie . . .* (anon., printed by Christopher Barker, 1599).

a panegyric of Elizabeth but it is also much more, because idealization is a form of implied criticism, intentionally or otherwise. Where Titania differs from the historical Elizabeth, this is because she approaches more closely to the ideal monarch the militant Protestants would have liked to see. And Essex, the Protestant champion, who appears to be absent from the play, is there as a posthumous presence. The stance that the play takes on specific issues is closer to that of Essex than to that of Queen Elizabeth and her closest advisors, the Cecils.

When Titania comes to the throne, the first decision that she is required to make concerns her marriage. The three Babylonian Kings who come to woo her are identified by Dekker in the margin as Spain, France, and the Holy Roman Empire, all of which did at one time or another make marriage overtures to Elizabeth. When she asks the advice of her councillors, they warn her at some length that if she marries any minion of Babylon, Titania will be involved in a civil war. In essence, their courtly speeches contain a polite threat: marry a Catholic, and we fight.

Resistance to Elizabeth marrying a Catholic was of course bitter, and her negotiations with the Duc d'Alençon in the 1570s met with strong opposition in and out of her Council, particularly from the Earl of Leicester. Sidney opposed it strongly enough to write his 'A Letter . . . to Queen Elizabeth Touching Her Marriage With Monsieur'. The preacher John Stubbes actually had his right hand cut off for opposing the marriage in *The Discoverie of a Gaping Gulf*, a pamphlet of 1579.[64]

In the play Titania gives temporary cause for alarm on this issue, making a speech to her councillors which sounds more like King James, or Queen Mary in *Sir Thomas Wyatt*, than the discreet Elizabeth:

> Stay: Princes are free-borne, and haue free wils,
> *Theis* are to *vs*, as vallies are to hills,
> We may, be counceld by them, not controld:
> Our wordes our Law.[65]

---

[64] Elizabeth Jenkins, *Elizabeth the Great* (Victor Gollancz Ltd.: London, 1958; rpt. Book Club Associates: London, 1971), 225–8.   [65] *WB*, I. ii. 209–12.

This is a tense moment. What will happen if Titania refuses to behave as the ideal Protestant monarch should? But the crisis passes. Titania equivocates with the Kings, telling them she will postpone making a decision until some mysterious time in the future, very much as Queen Elizabeth did. She decides not to marry any of them, and says in the next scene about her councillors:

> Wise Pilots? firmest pillers? how it agrees,
> When Princes heads sleepe on their counsels knees.[66]

This is an ideal sentiment from a militant Protestant point of view: they did not want any headstrong monarchs. But the problem of what Titania's subjects would have done if she had put her absolutist ideas to the test, is shelved rather than resolved.

The second issue that arises is aid to the Protestants in the Netherlands. In Act II an embassy arrives on Titania's shores, 'On Dolphins backes that pittie men distrest', and she is told who has sent them:

> Neighbours: tis the nation,
> With whome our Faries enterchange commerce,
> And by negotiation growne so like vs,
> That halfe of them are Fayries: th'other halfe
> Are hurtfull Spirits, that with sulphurous breath
> Blast their corne feilds, deface their temples, cloth
> Their townes in mourning, poyson hallowed founts,
> And make their goodliest Citties stand (like tombes)
> Full of dead bodies.[67]

The description suggests Alva's Council of Blood in the Netherlands in 1567–72. The United Provinces are allegorized as seventeen maidens threatened with ravishment or death, and this reminds us of *The Magnificent Entertainment*:

> They haue but seuenteen daughters young and faire,
> Vowd to liue vestalls, and not to know the touch
> Of any forced or vnreuerend hand.
>
> .   .   .   .
>
> They pray to haue their virgins wait on you,
> That you would be their mother, and their nurse,

---

[66] *WB*, II. i. 32–3.   [67] *WB*, II. i. 230, 234–41.

Their Guardian and their Gouernour; when Princes
Haue their liues giuen 'em, fine and golden threds
Are drawne and spun (for them) by the good fates,
That they may lift vp others in low states.[68]

When Leicester was entertained at Leiden at the start of his
Netherlands campaign in January 1586, they presented a
device to him in which 'a fair woman—Leiden—was now
assaulted, now liberated by various allegorical characters,
thus enacting the national and local history of the past twelve
years.' Finally she sought refuge with Leicester himself.[69]
Spenser had allegorized Elizabeth's aid to the Low Countries
in the figure of Mercilla in Book v of *The Faerie Queene*, and
Titania's response is even warmer:

Els let our selfe decline; giue them our presence:
In mysery all nations should be kin,
And lend a brothers hand.[70]

The historical Elizabeth was neither so warm nor so
prompt in embracing the principles of international solidarity
and interventionism. The United Provinces did offer her their
crown in 1584 but she twice refused it.[71] She was furious with
Leicester in 1586 when he accepted the title of their
Governor, the title Dekker uses. Essex was acting as one of
Leicester's chief officers on the occasion.[72] Elizabeth considered replacing Leicester as commander altogether when
she found out about this.

Fundamentally Queen Elizabeth preferred a more equivocal
foreign policy to one that was reckless and provocative. While
permitting Leicester's campaign in the Netherlands, she was
simultaneously negotiating with Parma, the Spanish general.
She disliked persecution but did not wish to be trapped into a
military or ideological confrontation, and she had deeply
rooted reservations since the Netherlands were rebels against
their Spanish sovereign.

Essex was the active successor of Leicester in persuading
Elizabeth to continue aiding the Netherlands throughout the

[68] *WB*, II. i. 243–56.
[69] R. C. Strong and J. van Dorsten (eds.), *Leicester's Triumph* (OUP, 1964), 60.
[70] *WB*, II. i. 257–9.   [71] Jenkins, p. 265.
[72] Harrison, pp. 11–15.

1590s, when she and all the rest of her Council were increasingly reluctant to do so. Not only did he serve in Leicester's campaign, but throughout the decade he encouraged pirate warfare with Spanish ships there, and encouraged the Queen to maintain garrisons in the United Provinces. His *Apologie* defended the continuation of this war. Dekker is attributing to Titania the views of Leicester, Sidney, and Essex.

The third issue is that of the Portuguese succession. Immediately after the emissaries of the seventeen maidens have been favourably received, Titania welcomes to her Court an orphan prince whose throne has been usurped: identified in the stage directions as the Prince of Portugal. She offers him aid as readily as she does to the Netherlanders. By making this prince the son of the last King, 'a Prince (made wretched, by his vnhappy father, that lies slaine by barbarous swords', whereas the real Don Antonio was only the natural son of the late King's brother, Dekker gives a definite push in favour of Don Antonio's claim.[73]

Don Antonio of Portugal was very much Essex's protégé, and his cause was favoured by militant Protestants in the 1590s. This is the only instance in which their policies can properly be called anti-Spanish, as Don Antonio was not a Protestant but his rule in Portugal was seen as preferable to that of Philip II. Don Antonio and his son had been in Leicester's entourage, and when an expedition was sent in 1589 to try to put him on the throne of Portugal, Essex joined it in defiance of Queen Elizabeth's orders. After Don Antonio's failure to get the throne, Essex continued to shelter him and his son in London for many years, and went on supporting Don Antonio's cause, mainly through espionage, though the pretender's credibility in the eyes of the world had fallen to virtually nil.[74]

Dekker puts the Portugal and Netherlands episodes into the same scene, though they were divided by several years in reality. This emphasizes their political consistency, and is typical of the way that *comoedia apocalyptica* distorts

---

[73] *WB*, II. i. 264–6.
[74] Harrison, p. 82.

chronology to make its ideas as clear as possible, in this case
the policy of intervention.

In April to May 1601 Dekker had collaborated with
Chettle on a Henslowe play, now lost, called *King Sebastian
of Portugal*. At that time there were sensational rumours that
the last King of Portugal, Sebastian, had survived the battle of
Alcazar and would return to claim the throne. The subject
had an obvious appeal for militant Protestants who had
supported Essex's policy on Portugal.

The fourth issue is that of rebellion in Ireland. In the play
the first Babylonian King, representing Spain, tells us that he
is giving aid to Titania's refractory child:

> You haue a sonne,
> Rebellious, wild, ingratefull, poore
>
> .   .   .   .   .   .
>
> Yet doe we succour him.[75]

In 1599, when Essex led his disastrous expedition to subdue
Ireland, the Irish were getting aid from Spain: Philip II had
provided Tyrone with money as well as a small force. As early
as 1580, Philip had sent reinforcements for the Smerwick
expedition into Ireland, organized by Rome.[76] Their general,
Recalde, was a Spaniard.[77]

Only a fragment remains of Sidney's *Discourse on Irish
Affairs*, but Spenser in *The Faerie Queene* had allegorized the
English struggle to subdue Ireland as the final and greatest
achievement of the just knight Sir Artegall, whose task is left
unfinished.[78] Dekker uses a quite different allegory from
Spenser's to represent Ireland: not a captive maiden but a
rebellious child. He is doing his best to avoid any analogy
between the Irish and the Netherlanders, not only by
referring to them in different scenes but by describing the
Irish as wild and primitive:

> (as men did in the golden Age)
> He liue[s] ith' open fields, hiding his head
> In dampish caues, and woods, (sometimes for feare.)[79]

[75] *WB*, I. ii. 141–53.   [76] Neale, pp. 248–9.   [77] Jenkins, p. 231.
[78] Smith and Selincourt, p. 333; Book V, canto xii. 27.
[79] *WB*, I. ii. 150–2.

This was the usual English view of the Irish at this time. The Netherlanders are described as a much more advanced people, with a flourishing trade, cities, and temples, so that their claim to self-determination is a much stronger one than that of a mere child.

The historical Queen Elizabeth actually felt the analogy between the two cases keenly. She was aware that there was a tit-for-tat element in the foreign policies being pursued by herself and King Philip, and if she had not been aware of it before, Philip himself pointed it out to her in a letter when she protested about his presence in Ireland.[80] To those who saw sovereignty as the paramount issue, the two cases were clearly analogous, but to those, like Dekker, who saw the paramount issue as being religion, they were clean opposite. Titania is determined to subdue her rebellious child, while also intervening in the Netherlands and Portugal.

The fifth key issue is that of the Lopez plot, which is one of several plots to assassinate Titania in the course of the play. Titania's doctor, Ropus, who is identified as Lopez, turns up at the Court of the Empress of Babylon in Act III. Together with Campeius (Edmund Campion) he accepts the Empress's indulgences and bribes to turn against Titania. In Act IV Fideli uncovers Ropus's plot to poison the Queen, and reads out a letter proving his guilt:

> One crowne doe's serue thy tourne, but heere's a theefe,
> That must haue fifty thousand crownes to steale
> Thy life: Here 'tis in blacke and white.[81]

Ropus confesses at once, and Titania is immediately convinced of his guilt.

The historical Lopez never visited Rome, nor was there any letter that could easily persuade Queen Elizabeth of his guilt. These inventions of Dekker's are strong signs of his support for Essex. The Lopez plot (if there was a plot) was Essex's personal discovery. In 1594 he wrote excitedly to Anthony Bacon saying that he had discovered a plot to poison the Queen, by her physician Dr Lopez, who was in the pay of Philip II.[82] But the first investigations found nothing, and

[80] Neale, p. 249.   [81] WB, IV. ii. 113–15.   [82] Harrison, p. 84.

Robert Cecil used this to discredit Essex in the eyes of the Queen, suggesting him to be unreliable. Essex was angry at being made to look a fool, and became determined to prove Lopez's guilt. Lopez was put on the rack, and enough evidence was extracted for a commission to find him guilty of treason. Essex was also on the commission. Elizabeth was still unconvinced of the guilt of her private physician, and ordered the Lieutenant of the Tower not to release Lopez for his execution. Only after two months of pressure on her did Essex succeed in getting Lopez executed, and in vindicating his own pride. Some accounts even suggest that Essex had to have Lopez smuggled out of the Tower.[83]

In his *Apologie*, Essex alludes to 'Emanuell Lewis the Portugal, . . . that brought *Lopus*, and *Stephano Ferrara* assurance for 50000. Crownes to be paid, as soon as their diuelish Conspiracie against the life of our precious Soueraigne, should take effect'.[84] The view of the matter given in the play is thus not only a simplified and fictionalized one, which it is bound to be, but one which takes pains to show that Essex was right, and that Robert Cecil, together with Queen Elizabeth herself, was wrong.

The Armada victory, a triumphant confrontation with the forces of Babylon, provides the climax to the play's action and to its argument. It is out of chronological order, partly for dramatic reasons, and partly because, while the Armada battle was not the final encounter, it is used to prefigure the greater final struggle and to afford a promise of future victory. What makes it a specifically militant Protestant view is that it is presented in apocalyptic terms. It is not simply a national victory, like the battle of Agincourt in *Henry V*, but a spiritual and ideological victory, which is part of an international apocalyptic war. Truth fights on the Protestant side, and Time addresses her in terms that quote the Pauline Epistles.[85] Titania's principal adversary in the battle is not the first King (Spain) but the Empress of Babylon herself, and the other two Kings (France and the Empire) are there on the periphery, making the enemy, like the True Church, an

[83] Neale, pp. 335–6.   [84] Essex, sig. C3.
[85] *WB*, V. iii. 11–19. Riely, p. 260, points out that this derives from Eph. 6: 13–17.

international entity. The model for the battle is Rev. 9: 19–21: 'And I saw the beast, and the kings of the earth, and their armies, gathered together to make war against him that sat on the horse, and against his army. And the beast was taken . . .' In *Sir Thomas Wyatt* Dekker and his collaborators endeavoured to give quite a small-scale national rebellion the maximum militant Protestant significance, but in the Armada battle Dekker found an ideal subject for his purpose. It offers a dualistic confrontation that perfectly suits his symbolic scheme and his world-view.

In Act IV, scene ii Titania signs a death-warrant, and there has been a great deal of speculation about the identity of the person being sentenced. F. G. Fleay thought that the image of 'the Moone' in the opening lines must refer to Mary, Queen of Scots. But he also thought that the rest of the passage had been clumsily altered by somebody other than Dekker, and that the result 'goes on in allusion to Essex quite beyond the scope of the original play. All the he's in this passage have been changed from she's'.[86] This was taken over by M. L. Hunt, and later critics have repeated the theory of alteration.[87] Riely suggests Norfolk rather than Essex, and only W. W. Greg questioned the identification as Mary.[88]

One reason for taking it to be Mary might be that this scene has a distinct resemblance to the passage in Book v of *The Faerie Queene* in which Mercilla, who represents Queen Elizabeth, is persuaded by her councillors to sign the death-warrant of Duessa, who at that point represents Mary, Queen of Scots. Both episodes contain a long deliberation on the subject of mercy before the warrant is signed, and Dekker quotes some phrases from Spenser. Spenser's 'But she, whose Princely breast was touched nere / With piteous ruth',[89] is

[86] Frederick Gard Fleay, *A Biographical Chronicle of the English Drama 1559–1642* (2 vols.; Reeves and Turner: London, 1891) i. 133.

[87] M. L. Hunt, *Thomas Dekker* (Columbia University Press: NY, 1912), 37; Jones-Davies, i. 124; E. K. Chambers, *The Elizabethan Stage* (4 vols.; OUP, 1923, rpt. with corrections, 1951), iii. 296; Hoy, ii. 304.

[88] Riely, p. 216; W. W. Greg, *Henslowe's Diary* (2 vols.; A. H. Bullen: London, 1904–8), ii. 210.

[89] Smith and Selincourt, p. 320; Book V cantos ix–x. It would only cause confusion to enquire whether Spenser meant any ironic pun on 'touched nere' and 'touched ne're'. There is no doubt that militant Protestants approved of the execution of Mary, or at least thought it necessary.

echoed in Titania's phrase, 'children, / Whom we haue nourisht at our princely breast'.[90]

But Dekker is not simply rewriting Spenser, and most of the resemblances between what is said about mercy in these two passages are the result of them drawing on a common source which was well known in the Renaissance, Seneca's essay *De Clementia*. Spenser's Mercilla is reluctant to sign the warrant, but she is urged on by resolute, indeed impassioned, advisors. The moment when by 'Strong constraint' she actually signs the warrant is glossed over and we are only told later that she has given in to the pressure.[91] But Titania, while speaking of regret, sheds no tears and is clearly responsible for the signing of the warrant. Titania is not behaving like Mercilla.

Recently, a new argument has been brought by Hoy for the Mary Queen of Scots case, but it is not convincing. He suggests that the scene dramatizes an incident in Holinshed in which Elizabeth receives a deputation from Parliament with a petition begging her to carry out the sentence on Mary.[92] But in *The Whore of Babylon* it is not a petition or deputation Titania receives: it is the warrant itself, brought by one person, her familiar advisor, Fideli. At line 34 she actually signs the paper, as she has been asked to do, and she could hardly be expected to sign a petition to herself. Mary's execution was a sensitive subject since the accession of King James, and this might be one motive for avoiding the name if it were Mary's, but the suggestion that Dekker may have forgotten that Mary's son now sat on the English throne really cannot be seriously entertained.[93]

Hoy quotes a Parliamentary speech concerned with Mary's execution and reproduced in Holinshed, which resembles a line in the play: 'All mercy in a Prince makes vile the state.'[94] But this is a quotation from Dekker's source for the entire passage, Seneca's essay *De Clementia*, and it was so familiar as to be proverbial. Not only was this essay used by Dekker and Spenser, but it was also drawn on by Shakespeare for

---

[90] *WB*, IV. ii. 10–11.
[91] Smith and Selincourt, pp. 320–1; Book V, canto ix. 47 and Book V, canto x. 4.
[92] Hoy, iii. 301–2.
[93] Ibid. iii. 304.   [94] *WB*, IV. ii. 22; Hoy, iii. 353.

Portia's famous speech on mercy in *The Merchant of Venice*.[95]

With the exception of the gender in Fideli's second speech, all the details in the passage fit the case of the Earl of Essex much better than that of Mary Queen of Scots, and there is no real need to posit revision, authorial or otherwise, because of the change of gender. If Dekker and the other Protestant writers could represent the Popes in a female figure, the Empress of Babylon, he could presumably use a feminine metaphor for a man such as the Earl of Essex.

> TITANIA. What comes this paper for?
> FIDELI.   Your hand.
> TITANIA.   The cause?
> FIDELI. The Moone that from your beames did borrow light,
>   Hath from her siluer bow shot pitchy clowds
>   T'ecclipse your brightnes.[96]

The feminine pronoun relates to the moon, and is being used in a figurative sense, whereas the masculine pronoun in the latter half of the passage is being used in a straightforward sense:

> FLORIMEL. You must not (cause hee's noble) spare his
>   blood.[97]

Some obscurity may be deliberate, because the subject of Essex was still a risky one when the play was written. But it is an intelligible obscurity, not a wild or clumsy alteration. Essex had been tried by jury and convicted of treason in Star Chamber, as Fideli's speech says. And the image of the moon would be far more suitable for him than for Mary. The Elizabethans were quite familiar with the fact that the moon's pale fire was reflected, or borrowed, from the sun. Titania obviously is the sun, but Mary Queen of Scots never derived her greatness from Elizabeth. When she was a Queen in Scotland she owed nothing to Elizabeth, and as a captive in England she had no greatness to owe.

The metaphor is, however, an extremely suitable one for

---

[95] *The Merchant of Venice*, ed. John Russell Brown, The Arden Shakespeare (Methuen: London, 1955; rpt. 1984), 111.

[96] *WB*, IV. ii. 1–4.   [97] *WB*, IV. ii. 15.

Essex, who as a royal favourite owed all his appointments, power, influence, and even his income directly to the Queen. He was reminded of this when in 1600 she took them away from him. Titania says:

> Must we then,
> Strike those whom we haue lou'd? albeit the children,
> Whom we haue nourisht at our princely breast,
> Set daggers to it, we could be content
> To chide.[98]

This could not possibly apply to Mary. Elizabeth did not love her arch-rival; though she pitied her, the two never met, and Elizabeth's letters to Mary are formal, cold, and calculating. The passage does apply very closely to Essex, who was at first like a spoilt favourite son to the ageing Queen. Few other people had been so intimate with her or had been allowed such privileges. The text also tells us that the condemned person is noble, in fact a peer, and that several other nobles are being condemned with him. The only person who fulfils all these conditions, thoughout the passage, is Essex:

> Euery Peeres birth stickes a new starre in heauen,
> But falling by *Luciferan* insolence,
> With him a Constellation drops from thence.[99]

When Titania and Fideli have deliberated at some length on the subject of mercy, Titania sets her hand to the warrant:

> Giue me his Axe—how soon the blow is giuen?
> Witnesse: so little we in blood delight,
> That doing this worke, we wish we could not write.
> Let's walke my Lords.[100]

Her personal responsibility is emphasized by the striking metonomy in 'Axe'. And underlying ironies increase the difference between Titania and Mercilla. Hoy points out that Dekker echoed this passage in a prose work of 1608, *The Dead Tearme*:

And that Mirror of her Sexe, both for magnanimity of minde, (&) inuinciblenesse of Spirit . . . that Goddesse vpon earth whilest she

---

[98] *WB*, IV. ii. 9–13.   [99] *WB*, IV. ii. 31–3.   [100] *WB*, IV. ii. 34–7.

liued ... our *Good Mistris (Eliza)*, when she was to sign any warrant for the death of any Peere, would passionately (yet with a Spirit equal to Caesars) Say thus, *Would to God wee had neuer been taught how to write.*[101]

The speech is italicized, as quotations usually are in the pamphlets, and there is a clue to its source in the reference to the Caesars. In fact, these are some of the most famous words the Emperor Nero ever spoke. They are attributed to Nero by two writers: by Seneca, in *De Clementia*, and by Suetonius in his history of Nero. Suetonius's version of the anecdote is only three lines long,[102] and Dekker was certainly drawing on Seneca since the scene contains other extensive quotations from the same essay. Seneca's essay was highly esteemed in the sixteenth century, and Calvin wrote a commentary on it—the work that first brought him fame as a scholar and teacher.

Seneca's essay is addressed to Nero and is a masterpiece of flattery which tries to manipulate the ruler by presenting him with an attractive self-image. It is also rich in unintentional, historical irony, as Seneca extolls the god-like mercy of the emperor who, not long afterwards, invited his former tutor to take a hot bath.

Dekker has introduced not one but half a dozen quotations from Seneca's essay into the dialogue at this point. Fideli says:

> All mercy [i.e. excessive mercy] in a Prince makes vile the state.[103]

This is the line which Hoy compares to one in Holinshed. But it is derived from a well-known passage in Seneca:

Pardoning ought not to be too common ... for when the distinction between the bad and the good is removed, the result is confusion and an epidemic of vice.[104]

Fideli also says:

> All justice [i.e. excessive punishment] makes euen cowards desperate.[105]

---

[101] *The Dead Tearme* (1608), F2ᵛ; Hoy, iii. 353.

[102] Gaius Suetonius Tranquillus, *The Twelve Caesars*, trans. Robert Graves, The Belle Sauvage Library (Cassell & Co.: London, 1962), 191.

[103] *WB*, IV. ii. 22.

[104] *Moral Essays of Lucius Annaeus Seneca*, trans. John W. Basore, Loeb Classical Library (3 vols.; Heinemann: London, 1928), i. 363.   [105] *WB*, IV, ii. 23.

Seneca writes:

You will more easily reform the culprits themselves by the lighter form of punishment; for he will live more guardedly who has something left to lose. No one is sparing of a ruined reputation; it brings a sort of exemption from punishment to have no room left for punishment.[106]

Titania says:

> In neither of these seas, spread we our sayles,
> But are the impartiall beame between both scales;
> Yet if we needs must bow, we would incline
> To that where mercy lies, that scales's diuine:[107]

Seneca writes:

We should maintain the mean, but since a perfect balance is difficult, if anything is to disturb the equipoise it should turn the scale towards the kindlier side.[108]

Seneca also says several times that mercy is divine:

To spare life is the peculiar privilege of exalted station which . . . has the same power as the gods . . . Let a prince therefore, appropriate himself the spirit of the gods.[109]

Titania says:

> We must the Surgeon play, and let out blood.[110]

Seneca writes:

If there should ever be need to let blood, the hand must be held under control to keep it from cutting deeper than may be necessary.[111]

Not only is this dialogue filled with quotations from Seneca's essay, but the whole scene of the signing of the death-warrant is, in itself, a species of quotation. It dramatizes an incident which Seneca relates in *De Clementia*, an incident which he says inspired the whole essay. It is worth quoting this passage at length so that the similarities to the play, and

---

[106] Basore, i. 419.
[107] *WB*, IV. ii. 24–7.   [108] Basore, i. 365.
[109] Ibid. i. 373. I have altered one word, 'save', to 'spare' for sake of clarity.
[110] *WB*, IV. ii. 30.   [111] Basore, i. 371.

the various layers of irony surrounding Seneca's passage and Dekker's reworking of it, can be appreciated:

> I have been especially induced to write on mercy by a single utterance of yours, Nero Caesar, which I remember, when it was made, I heard not without admiration and afterwards repeated to others—a noble, high-minded utterance, showing great gentleness, which unpremeditated and not intended for other's ears suddenly burst from you, and brought into the open your kind-heartedness chafing against your lot. Burrus, your prefect, a rare man, born to serve a prince like you, was about to execute two brigands, and was bringing pressure apon you to record their names and the reasons why you wished their execution; this, often deferred, he was insisting should at last be done. He was reluctant, you were reluctant, and, when he had produced the paper and was handing it to you, you exclaimed 'Would that I had not learned to write!' ['Vellem litteras nescirem!'] What an utterance! . . . It should have been spoken before a gathering of all mankind, that unto it princes and kings might pledge allegiance. What an utterance! Worthy of the universal innocence of mankind, in favour whereof that long past age should be renewed.[112]

Calvin notes the irony added by history to Seneca's text. His commentary tells us that not only Seneca himself but Afranius Burrus too met his death at Nero's orders. The emperor sent Burrus a remedy for a swollen throat, which proved fatal.[113]

It would be difficult to find anywhere a single sentence more loaded with ironies than this line that Dekker puts into the mouth of Titania. He is being oblique, but not obscure: every Elizabethan schoolboy studied Seneca. The inference is that if Nero could sometimes be merciful, Queen Elizabeth could at times act like a Nero.

In Reformation thinking, Nero was not only the arch-tyrant. (And Seneca says, perhaps significantly for the play, 'It is mercy that makes the difference between a king and a tyrant.'[114]) Nero was also seen as the arch-persecutor of the True Church. Lists of the ten great persecutors of the early Church varied, but they all had one thing in common: they all

---

[112] Basore, i. 432–3.

[113] Calvin's *Commentary on Seneca's 'De Clementia'*, ed. and trans. F. A. Battles and A. M. Hugo (Renaissance Texts Series, 3; Renaissance Society of America: Leiden, 1969), 337.   [114] Basore, i. 393.

start with Nero. Foxe names Nero as the first of the persecutors in *Actes and Monuments*; and again in *Christvs Triumphans*, in which Dioctes, the persecutor, names those who have served him best on earth. Nero is at the head of the list.[115] Protestant pamphlets of the time frequently depicted Nero as the prototype of the persecutors and enemies of the True Church.[116]

There was an even older tradition which identified Nero as the seven-headed beast of Rev. 17 and as the Antichrist himself. Calvin referred to this belief in the excerpt from his commentary on Thessalonians quoted above. Hence the term 'Nero redivivus' was a synonym for the Antichrist. This tradition went back to the third-century commentary of Victorinus. The twelfth-century Joachim of Fiore identified one of the beast's seven heads as being Nero.[117] Bishop John Bale in his Revelation commentary of 1550 agreed that Nero was one of those who had fulfilled the apocalyptic prophecy: 'Muche after this sort, became the Emperour Nero, this beastes image imediatly after Christes asention by the subtil slaights of the spiritual sorcerer Simon Magus, at Rome.'[118] Foxe refers to this belief, although he did not hold it himself:

Likewise Orosius writing of the said *Nero*, saith that he was the first which in Rome did raise up persecution against the Christians, and not onely in Rome but also through all the prouinces therof, thinking to abolish and destroy the whole name of Christians in all places . . . many there were of the Christians in those dayes, which seying the filthy abominations, and intollerable crueltie of Nero, thought that he should be Antichrist.[119]

For Dekker to suggest, even for a moment, that we should see Queen Elizabeth in such a light, is extreme. Of course in a play like *The Whore of Babylon* which is composed of extremes, everything has to be extreme. But the concealed violence of this reaction must also be explained by the position that Essex held as champion of the Protestant cause.

[115] Foxe, i. 31; J. H. Smith, p. 287.

[116] Scribner, p. 114.

[117] Bernard McGinn, *The Calabrian Abbot: Joachim of Fiore in the History of Western Thought* (Collier Macmillan: London, 1985), 80, 159.

[118] Bale, *The Ymage of Both Chvrches*, sig. f. iiii.   [119] Foxe, i. 34.

His execution was a blow to that cause and to the hopes of the True Church, seen by them as verging on an act of religious persecution. Nothing that Queen Elizabeth did in her reign was more profoundly at variance with the role of Protestant figurehead which militant Protestants were allotting her. The result is a scene of complex irony, the expression of a severe dilemma of political judgement.

Dekker's preface to *The Whore of Babylon* begins: 'The Generall scope of this Drammaticall Poem, is to set forth (in Tropicall and shadowed collours) the Greatnes, Magnanimity, Constancy, Clemency, and other the incomparable Heroical vertues of our late Queene.'[120] The play's veiled criticism of Queen Elizabeth does not contradict its overt idealization, but extends it in a necessary and logical way. It is in the service of one consistent ideal that Elizabeth Tudor is mythologized, exploited, and taken to task.

C. *The Play in Relation to the Events of King James's Reign*

Dekker's subtle misrepresentation of Queen Elizabeth as the ideal militant Protestant leader provides a picture of the course that militant Protestants were still hoping King James would take. There is only one overt reference to King James in the play, which is identified as such in the margin. It is the passage that was earlier compared to Bale's prophecy of Queen Elizabeth:

> 1. CARD. Say that *Titania* were now drawing short breath,
> (As that's the Cone and Button that together
> Claspes all our hopes) out of her ashes may
> A second Phoenix rise, of larger wing,
> Of stronger talent, of more dreadfull beake,
> Who swooping through the ayre, may with his beating
> So well commaund the winds, that all those trees
> Where sit birds of our hatching (now fled thither)
> Will tremble . . .
>
> .   .   .   .
>   Yea and perhaps his talent
> May be so bonie and so large of gripe,
> That it may shake all *Babilon*.[121]

---

[120] Bowers, ii. 497.   [121] *WB*, III. i. 232–44.

This picture of a war-like James who will take the offensive against Rome with more resolution than Elizabeth had done, is very different from the prophecy of King James's reign in Shakespeare and Fletcher's *Henry VIII* written half a dozen years later:

> Nor shall this peace sleep with her; but as when
> The bird of wonder dies, the maiden phoenix,
> Her ashes new create another heir
> As great in admiration as herself,
> So shall she leave her blessedness to one—
> When heaven shall call her from this cloud of darkness—
> Who from the sacred ashes of her honour
> Shall star-like rise, as great in fame as she was,
> And so stand fixed. Peace, plenty, love, truth, terror,
> That were the servants to this chosen infant,
> Shall then be his, and like a vine grow to him . . .[122]

This pacific vision of James's reign accords well with the King's own policies, and whether or not Shakespeare and Fletcher had read *The Whore of Babylon*, the hopes and ideals they reveal are very different from those of Dekker's play. To describe James's reign as a blessed peace was to congratulate the King on the path he had chosen. And the words of *Henry VIII* allude to Old Testament prophesies, rejecting apocalyptic ones.

There are other passages in *The Whore of Babylon* which suggest that the figure of Titania is meant to be seen, not only in relation to Queen Elizabeth, but also to King James. There are two very distinct clues in Titania's first scene, in fact in the very first words she speaks, and these are intended to alert us.

> Wee thought the fates would haue closde vp our eyes,
> That wee should nere haue seene this day-starre rise:
> How many plots were laid to barre vs hence,
> (Euen from our Cradle?)[123]

It was James, not Elizabeth, who had been the target of assassination-attempts in his cradle, or, to be precise, shortly before he reached the cradle. The murder of Rizzio in front of

---

[122] *King Henry the Eighth*, ed. J. C. Maxwell (CUP: Cambridge, 1969), V. v. 39–49, pp. 110–11. Compare also to *WB*, I. ii. 187–205.
[123] *WB*, I. ii. 1–4.

Mary Queen of Scots in 1566 was intended to make her miscarry, and prevent her giving Scotland an heir. James was born three months later.[124] There had been several other attempts on his life but Elizabeth had never been the target of an assassin before becoming Queen.

The newly crowned Titania goes on:

> *Truth* be my witnes (whome we haue imployde,
> To purge our Aire that has with plagues destroyed
> Great numbers, shutting them in darksome shades)
> I seeke no fall of hirs[125]

It was in 1603, at the accession of James, not at that of Elizabeth, that London was struck by Plague. Dekker chronicled the event in *The Wonderfull Yeare*. So Titania is meant to be seen in relation to the new King.

In most respects she is a model for him, an ideal of conduct, and this is particularly true of the direction in which Titania develops. Her growing antagonism to Rome by no means resembles the historical Elizabeth. When Titania first comes to the throne, she is pacifist by inclination. She wishes to avoid war at any cost and believes it is possible to be reconciled with Babylon:

> I seeke no fall of hirs, my Spirit wades,
> In Clearer streames; her bloud I would not shed,
> To gaine that triple wreath that binds her head.[126]

This was very much the case with James. Soon after signing the Treaty of London he relaxed the penalties against Roman Catholics in England. There was even some negotiation for Prince Henry to marry a Spanish princess.[127] This was not at all what militant Protestants wanted to see, particularly after the breakdown of the Hampton Court conference in 1604.

But Titania changes drastically in the course of the play. The implacable hostility of Babylon, evinced by a series of attempts on her life, gradually persuades her that a conciliatory stance is unrealistic. She is in effect converted to militant

---

[124] D. H. Willson, p. 16. [125] *WB*, I. ii. 13–16.
[126] *WB*, I. ii. 16–18. [127] D. H. Willson, pp. 221–2.

Protestantism as the play goes on and by Act V has become a dynamic leader willing not only to send aid but to take the offensive. In Act II Paridell, who confesses he has had treasonable intentions, is pardoned by Titania; the result is that he goes on to plot against her again, encouraged of course by an indulgence from Babylon. But the second time Titania is not so merciful.[128] She has learnt the lesson that leniency against the forces of Babylon simply will not work. There is no historical basis for the first interview and pardon.

Nothing would have pleased militant Protestants more than to see King James respond in such a way after the lesson of the Gunpowder Plot. It seemed logical to them that he should respond in this way, almost impossible that he should take any other course, since he had himself put into print views which sounded extraordinarily like those of a militant Protestant.

King James's *Fruitefull Meditation . . . of the 7, 8, 9 and 10 Verses of the 20 Chapter of the Reuelation* was first printed in Edinburgh in 1588 and was reprinted in London in 1603. It is an exposition of the passage in Rev. 20 which describes how the Antichrist, after being bound for a thousand years, is loosed and goes out to deceive the earth. His forces surround the tents of the saints but he is eventually defeated and cast into a lake of fire along with the beast and the false prophet. James's exposition of this is very much in accordance with Protestant tradition. He writes 'of al the Scriptures, the Booke of the *Reuelation* is most meete for this our last age, as a Prophesie of the latter time,' and in the text Satan, the Antichrist, is clearly and repeatedly identified with Rome.[129] The camp of the saints, the 'beloved city' of verse 9, is said to be the Church of the elect, and there is a brief allusion to the 'Woman clad with scarlet', the Whore of Babylon, who is identified with the corrupt antichristian Church.[130] When it comes to the prophesies about this 'false hipocritical Church', James writes:

Now whether the Pope beareth these markes or not, let any indifferent man judge: I thinke surely it expoundes it selfe. Doeth

---

[128] *WB*, II. i. 148–80; V. ii. 159–61.
[129] *A Fruitefull Meditation* (1603), sig. A6.
[130] Ibid. A9ᵛ, B2ᵛ.

he not usurpe Christ his office, calling himselfe vniuersall Bishoppe and head of the Church? Playeth hee not the parte of *Apollyon*, and *Abaddon* the king of the Locustes and destroyer, or Sonne of perdition, in chopping and changing of Soules betwixt heauen, hell, and his fantasticke or imagined purgatory at his pleasure? Blasphemeth he not in denying vs to be saued by the imputation of Christ his righteousnesse? Moreouer hath hee not sent foorth and abused the worlde with innumerable orders of locustes and shauelings: Hath thee not so fullye ruled ouer the world these many hundreth yeeres, as to the fire went he, whosoeuer he was that durst denie any parte of his vsurped supremacie? And hath he not of late dayes seeing his kingdome going to decaye, sent out the Jesuites, his last and most pernitious vermin to stirre up the Princes of the earth his slaues, to gather and league themselues together for his defence, and rooting out of all them that professe Christ truely? And whereas the open enemy of God, the Turke was vnder bloudye warres with him euer before, is there not of late a truce among them, that the faithfull may be the more easily rooted out? And are not the armies presently assembled, yea vpon the very point of their execution in *France* against the Saints there? In *Flaunders* for the like: and in *Germanie*, by whom already the Bishop of *Collein* is displaced? And what is prepared and come forward against this Ile? Doe we not dayly heare, and by all appearance & likly-hood shall shortly see?[131]

The last part of the passage is a reference to the preparations for the Armada invasion in 1588, and King James is interpreting this event in an apocalyptic way. He concludes the book by saying:

All men should be lawfully armed spiritually and bodily to fight against the Antichrist, and his vpholders . . . since with good conscience wee may, beeing in the tents of the Saints and beloued Cittie, stand in our defence: encourage one another to vse lawfull resistance, and concurre or ioyne one with another as warriours in one Campe . . . in defence of our liberties, natiue countrie and liues. For since we see God hath promised not onely in the world to come, but also in this worlde, to giue us victory, let vs in assurance hereof stronglye trust in our God, cease to mistrust his promise, and fall through incredulitie or vnbeliefe.[132]

Those in England who read these fighting words must have had the liveliest hopes that James would pursue a militant

[131] *A Fruitefull Meditation* (1603), sigs. B3ᵛ–B4ᵛ.   [132] Ibid. B7ᵛ–B8.

Protestant policy at home and abroad. And after the Gunpowder Plot, it must have seemed stranger and more frustrating than ever that James persisted in his peaceful and conciliatory policy towards all the powers of Babylon.

Whether James ever believed what was in the tract or whether it was a cunning move to increase his popularity in every quarter is difficult to tell. He referred to the doctrine of the Papal Antichrist in some of his later works too.[133] But even if he did believe it, he was never one to equate religion with politics in practice. Like Elizabeth, or perhaps to an even greater extent, he hated war and believed that a policy of direct confrontation was rash, belligerent, and potentially destabilizing.

While on the throne of England, King James continued to allow many people who were much closer to the Court than Dekker to believe that he subscribed to these apocalyptic views. In 1608 Robert Abbott, bishop of Salisbury (brother of the Archbishop of Canterbury) published his *Antichristi Demonstratio* in which he argued that the papacy was Antichrist.[134] He also identified it with the 'meretrix' of Revelation.[135] This book was dedicated to King James and the Latin text of James's *Fruitefull Meditation* was reprinted at the end of it.

The Archbishop of Canterbury was among many other highly placed people in Jacobean England who not only subscribed to these apocalyptic views but believed that they should be put into practice diplomatically and militarily. Adams quotes a letter which the Archbishop wrote in 1619, commenting on the imminent war between Catholic and Protestant forces in Germany: 'And methinks I do in this, and in that of Hungary, forsee the work of God, that piece by piece, the Kings of the Earth that gave their power unto the Beast (all the word of God must be fulfilled) shall now tear the Whore, and make her desolate, as St. John in his Revelation hath foretold.'[136] Presumably George Abbott would not have expressed his view so warmly if he did not

---

[133] D. H. Willson, pp. 231, 237–8.
[134] Robert Abbott, *Antichristi Demonstratio* (1608), 1.   [135] Ibid. 322.
[136] Bodleian Tanner MS 74, fos. 221–2; quoted in S. L. Adams, 'The Protestant Cause', p. 284.

know it was shared by the recipient of the letter, Sir Robert
Naunton, one of King James's secretaries of State, who had,
as it happens, started his career as one of the Earl of Essex's
agents on the Continent.

Adams also quotes a letter of 1612 written by Sir John
Throckmorton to William Trumbull, King James's ambassador at Brussels, in which the same belief is referred to in
passing, as if taken for granted: 'that whore who hath but too
long occupied that seat of Babylon'.[137] So the views Dekker
was appealing to in his play were widespread in Court circles,
not confined to a mob or to a minority of non-conformists,
preachers, or extremist pamphleteers. And they persisted for
a long time after he wrote *The Whore of Babylon*.[138]

But James still refused to let them influence his policies. In
1611 the Huguenot Philippe du Plessis-Mornay dedicated to
James his book *Le Mystere d'iniqvité*, a history of the
corruptions of the papacy. It takes its title from 2 Thess 2: 7
and from Rev. 17: 5: 'And upon her forehead was a name
written, MYSTERY, BABYLON THE GREAT, THE MOTHER OF
HARLOTS AND ABOMINATIONS OF THE EARTH.' Mornay's book,
whose title-page showed the Tower of Babylon being ignited
from the foundations, invited James to come forward as
Protestant champion in a military offensive against Rome.[139]
Militant Protestants were still looking for a leader to succeed
Essex and if Mornay had judged James by *A Fruitefull
Meditation* he might well have expected the King of England
to adopt this role. But James wrote to Mornay declining the
role, and saying that he could find no basis for such a religious
war either in the Bible or in the teachings of the early
Church.[140] Mornay should have taken warning from *Basilicon
Doron*, which told kings, 'Doe as ye would be done to;
Especially in counting rebellion against any other Prince, a
crime against your selfe because of the praeparitiue. Supplie
therefore nor trust not other Princes Rebelles.'[141] James

---

[137] Adams, 220.
[138] Patrides and Wittreich trace the influence of the tradition through to George
Eliot and Karl Marx.
[139] *Le Mystere d'Iniqvité* (Saumur, 1611), A–A[v]. The same picture appears in the
Latin and English editions.
[140] S. L. Adams, 'Protestant Cause', p. 189.
[141] Craigie, xvi. 98.

would not support Mornay's section of the Huguenot party which was meeting in 1611 at the Assembly of Saumur, since he regarded them as acting in defiance of their own Catholic monarch, Louis XIII. Sovereign authority was at stake.

There are other details in the play which seem to reflect on James in a more personal way. Armed with an indulgence from Babylon, Paridell boasts to his cousin that the assassination he plans will not be a difficult one:

> like the Turke
> Shee walkes not with a *Ianisarie-Guard*,
> Nor (as the Russian) with fowle-big-boand slaues,
> Strutting on each side with the slicing Axe,
> Like to a payre of hangmen: no, alas:
> Her Courts of *Guard* are Ladies, and (sometimes)
> Shee's in the garden with as small a trayne,
> As is the Sun in heauen . . .[142]

It was true that Queen Elizabeth did not usually keep a heavy guard about her person.[143] It was also true that King James did. His early experiences had made him timid, and after the Gunpowder Plot his precautions bordered on the comical. He ate alone, slept in a room padded with mattresses, and had himself guarded by Scots.[144] The passage suggests there is something barbaric or even unchristian about this: unchristian because a Christian king ought to trust in divine protection. Pusillanimity, however rational, was not the most regal quality, and particularly unsuitable in a prospective leader of an apocalyptic war.

Titania of course behaves with superb courage, indeed with complete indifference to danger. She is in a garden when Paridell approaches her, and she dismisses even her ladies:

> How? feare?
> Why should white bosomes feare a Tyrants Arme?
> Tyrants may kill vs, but not doe vs harme.[145]

Titania is so confident of going to heaven that she has no fear of death. Her faith is rewarded by heavenly protection in the strange scene that follows, for Paridell twice tries to kill her

---

[142] *WB*, V. i. 29–35.   [143] Jenkins, pp. 262, 270–1.
[144] D. H. Willson, p. 277.   [145] *WB*, V. ii. 39–41.

but fails. The just and devout monarch need have no fear of
'tyrants' (i.e. one who would seize power). Later in the scene
Titania is reading a book, and her quotation from it is related
to the same theme:

> A tyrants strange but iust end!
> Ran mad for sleepe, and died. Princes that plunge
> Their soules in ranke and godlesse appetites
> Must seeke no rest but in the armes of Sprites.[146]

The tyrant here appears to be identical with the prince, in a
case comparable to Macbeth's: he is an assassin who seizes
power and makes himself a prince, or seizes more power than
is his right.

Paridell is arrested when Titania's courtiers return suddenly
and surprise him. This idea of the good monarch's invulner-
ability poses some problems. If it is true, then when a
monarch like Duncan is killed, must we assume that he was a
tyrant? And why should traitors be condemned to death, if
they were doomed to failure?

At the time the play was written, however, the failure of the
Gunpowder Plot seemed to be a sign that the providence of
God was indeed protecting the King of England and his
family. King James made a speech in Parliament giving heaven
the credit for his personal escape, though he remained as
timorous as ever. But for a time he expressed himself strongly
on the evils of the Catholic doctrine that it was lawful to kill
non-Catholic princes.[147]

This doctrine was attributed to the Jesuits, but it went back
to the Council of Constance (1414–18). The Council had
refused to condemn formally a tract by the Dominican John
of Falkenberg which defended tyrannicide as justifiable in the
case of heretics, or their allies.[148] This was recalled by the
Protestants when, in 1589, Henri III was murdered by a
Dominican. The same doctrine was maintained by Cardinal
(later Saint) Roberto Bellarmine, SJ (1542–1621), against
whom Abbott took up the controversy. In his *Apologie*, the

---

[146] *WB*, V. ii. 125–8.
[147] D. H. Willson, pp. 226–7.
[148] *New Catholic Encyclopaedia* (1967), iv. 222.

Earl of Essex wrote that the Jesuits 'teach desperate con-
spirators, that to murder Princes is the way to Heauen'.[149]
Militant Protestants were very keen to use this means of
manipulating the sovereign in a Protestant direction.
This is what Titania is alluding to when she tells the
Babylonian Kings she will marry among them, but only

> When from yon towers I heare one cry,
> You may kill Princes lawfully,[150]

that is, when Roman Catholic doctrines prevail in England.
The third King, angered by her refusal, threatens to return
and invade, 'With large pattents to kill Kings and Queens'.[151]
He is as good as his word and in the next Act the Empress and
her cardinals expound their regicidal doctrine and strategy.
Having failed to seduce Titania into marriage, they must
assassinate her. Allusions to the Gunpowder plotters and
their hiding places are woven into the instructions the
Empress gives Campeius and Ropus, so that the events of the
present are prophesied by those of the past.[152]

The most detailed discussion of this doctrine of tyrannicide
occurs in Act III when Paridell is already planning to go to
Babylon and get an indulgence so that he can murder Titania
'vnder the seale of Heauen'.[153] He confides his plan to
Palmio, a Jesuit who encourages him and introduces him to
an agent of the Empress called the Albanoys, i.e. the
Scotsman. Jones-Davies discovered that the Albanoys was
based on the Scottish Jesuit William Creitchton, who was
mixed up in the Parry affair, and that Dekker's source for the
scene was a letter from Creitchton, printed in Holinshed, in
which he pleaded his innocence.[154] In *The Double PP* Dekker
warns of the equivocating Jesuit who 'teaches Others to kill
their Soueraignes' and 'subtile threds does weaue'.[155] This is
certainly true of the Jesuit in the play, as Dekker makes sure
with a few discreet alterations to his source.

[149] Essex, sig. C4.   [150] *WB*, I. ii. 239–40.   [151] *WB*, I. ii. 264.
[152] *WB*, III. i. 140–72. Pointed out by Dobson, p. 257.
[153] *WB*, III. ii. 15.
[154] M.-T. Jones-Davies, 'Source du latin scholastique dans *The Whore of Babylon*
de Thomas Dekker', *Études Anglaises* (May 1953), 142–3.
[155] Grosart, ii. 165, 176.

In his letter Creitchton relates how Parry asked him 'if it were leason to kill the queene' and got the reply '*Quod omnino non liceret*': that it is absolutely not permitted.[156] In the play the Albanoys's answer to the same question is '*Quod non omnino Licet*', which Paridell takes to be a definite negative, as it was in the source.[157] But '*non omnino Licet*' means 'not absolutely permitted', that is to say 'not entirely forbidden'. Paridell's innocence creates a dry species of comedy as the Jesuit continues to give these subtly ambiguous answers, and Paridell fails to recognize them as such.

In the letter Creitchton says that he told Parry '*Quod non sunt facienda mala, vt veniant bona*', the reverse of the doctrine usually ascribed to the Jesuits.[158] In *The Trve Lawe of Free Monarchies* King James discusses the question of tyrannicide, and quotes this same teaching: 'First, it is a sure Axiom in Theologie, that euill should not be done, that good may come of it.'[159] But while the Albanoys in the play repeats the Latin correctly, his translation of it is much less clear and accurate than James's. Its word-order is so convoluted that it sounds like two separate sentences:

> For good; (how great soeuer) must be don,
> No ill how small soeuer.[160]

A hearer would naturally take this to mean 'Do good things. Don't do bad things.' And this ambiguity sheds an interesting light on the Albanoys's Latin speech that follows, again quoted inexactly from Creitchton's letter; it makes a distinction between what is '*bonum*' and what is '*legitime*'.[161] Dekker's Jesuit identifies regicide as an act which is '*bonum*', good, though it is not '*legitime*', legal, and so while he does say regicide is forbidden he says so in a very provocative way, increasing the effect with the hint that 'God loves adverbs as much as nouns,' i.e. it's less what you do than how and why you do it that counts.

To complete the picture, Dekker has added a speech at the

[156] Holinshed, iii. 1388.   [157] *WB*, III. ii. 137.
[158] Holinshed, iii. 1388.
[159] *The Trve Lawe of Free Monarchies* (Edinburgh, 1598; 2nd edn. London, 1603), D5ᵛ.
[160] *WB*, III. ii. 149–50.   [161] *WB*, III. ii. 152–6.

end of the dialogue which is not in the source. When Paridell, persisting as doggedly and imperceptively as ever, says that some theologians defend regicide, the Albanoys replies that this is

> on no warrant
> That they can shew me written, but being stird,
> With a humaine compassion to mens liues.[162]

This makes regicide sound like a Christian duty. And the conclusion,

> And lesse you reuelation haue diuine,
> That bids you do, doe not. Thus you haue mine,[163]

is as much as to say, 'If you think you have got divine revelation, go ahead.' It is a hypocritical denial calculated to inflame an idealist or fanatic.

Dekker's depiction of the Jesuit is not altogether unflattering, though of course it was not intended to be favourable. It is a subject that would have appealed to its audience, highly educated or not, on many different levels. Militant Protestants were still hoping that fear of regicide would eventually make the King reverse his lenient and pacific policies towards Rome.

Recently, Frank R. Ardolino has argued that the double reference to 'St. *Iagoes* parke' made by Paridell in Act V may be a cryptic way of saying 'that King James I has become an Iago-like ally of Catholicism in the early years of his reign,' and that Dekker is 'directing James toward more emphatic Protestant policies in the face of the ongoing Spanish threat'.[164] The first part of this is possibly true, particularly as Ardolino links it with Kelsie B. Harder's earlier speculation that 'the great Dego of Diuels' in Dekker's *Newes From Hell* is also an unflattering allusion to James. The pamphlet and the play were written in the same year, and Harder is on strong ground in reading the passage as an attack on James's peace-treaty with Spain. 'Nay since my flag of defiance is hung forth, I will yeelde to no truce.'[165]

---

[162] *WB*, III. ii. 163–5.   [163] *WB*, III. ii. 166–7.
[164] Ardolino, pp. 3–4.
[165] Kelsie B. Harder, 'The Names of Thomas Dekker's Devils', *Names*, 3 (1955), 212.

But Ardolino's second idea is rather curious, as it assumes not only that the King would have seen a play put on at the Red Bull, but also that he would have listened to its advice where he did not take that of his own secretaries and councillors. After Dekker's experience with *The Magnificent Entertainment*, he would have had no illusions of that kind. It is better to see the play as an expression of the political feelings and desires of a certain section of the public, a product perhaps of wishful thinking, or, to put it another way, of political frustration.

4

If This Be Not a Good King

A. *The Devil Is In It*

If King James was the 'Dego of Diuels', Dekker's *If This Be Not A Good Play, The Devil Is In It* (written *c.* 1611, printed 1612) offers some explanation of how that might have come about. The known source-material for this play is rather scant, and its most important source is in contemporary events. Jones-Davies noted that it draws on the old tale of Friar Rush and it may possibly also have been influenced by Machiavelli's story *Belfagor* (or *Belphegor*), which had been translated into English by Barnabe Riche and printed in 1581.[1] But Dekker has extended the idea to cover Court and City as well as Church, and so most of the plot is original.

As well as those stories, Dekker may have read *A Discourse Vpon the Meanes of Wel Governing and Maintaining in Good Peace, a Kingdome or Other Principalitie . . . Against Nicholas Machiavel the Florentine*. This treatise by the French Protestant Innocent Gentillet, originally written in 1576, was printed in an English translation by Simon Patericke in 1602. Several themes and ideas link it with the play. One is its stout defence of parliamentary power to ensure the monarch governs by consent. Gentillet asserts that the French monarchs had always needed to get the assent of a Parlement for any taxation.[2] This was a very topical issue in England and may explain why Patericke's translation was reprinted in 1608. Another theme is that of tyrannicide. In the epilogue to the play, Ravaillac, the murderer of Henri IV, is seen in hell together with Guy Fawkes, suffering torments which suggest that Dekker did not at this date agree with Gentillet's defence of tyrannicide, though he might have read it with great

---

[1] Jones-Davies, i. 113–14, 121; *The Literary Works of Niccolo Machiavelli*, trans. and ed. J. R. Hale (OUP, 1961).

[2] Innocent Gentillet, *A Discourse Vpon the Meanes of Wel Governing . . .*, trans. Simon Patericke (2nd edn. 1608), 15–17. The date of 1602 is in STC.

interest. Gentillet (whose views on this were closer to Mariana's than to Buchanan's) asserted that tyrannicide was 'not onely lawfull, but also honourable and meritorious'; he justified even a vassal in killing a tyrant, though preferring that it should be done by those of high rank.[3]

The opening of Gentillet's book warns how Satan has infiltrated the Courts of rulers and 'with fooles uttering their pleasant jeasts in the Courts and banquets of Kings and princes, laboured to root up all the true principles of Religion and Policie'.[4] This sounds very like what happens at the Court of Naples when the devil Rufman arrives to subvert it. If Dekker had not read Gentillet, it still offers interesting evidence that the minds of militant Protestants were working along similar lines in England and abroad.

Although *If This Be Not A Good Play* is set in Naples, it is really concerned with events in England. The tale of Friar Rush, the devil posing as a monk, could not be set in a Protestant country, and this foreignness provides a necessary disguise for the satire. It also has the effect of preventing the play from becoming too serious. It deals with serious matters in a comedy framework and the result is both odd and idiosyncratic.

The play's central plot concerns Alphonso, King of Naples, who is corrupted by the devil Rufman and leads his kingdom to the brink of disaster. Twice in the course of the play, Alphonso refers to himself as a lion:

> Flying swiftly backward, the kingly Lion quaild.
>
> .   .   .   .
>   If the Lion must fall,
> Fall shall he like a Lion.[5]

The Lion was King James's emblem, and an accumulation of details in the play makes it clear that Alphonso has been designed as a vehicle for criticizing King James. He is not—except in occasional touches—a portrayal of James. At his best he is an exemplary figure, and at his worst he is made up of some rather Jamesian vices. Between these two extremes, there is a varied play of irony.

---

[3] Gentillet, 211–12.   [4] Ibid. sig. ¶ iii.
[5] *ITBNAGP*, V. i. 25; V. iii. 55–6.

Alphonso's first appearance raises fundamental questions. He enters in Act I, scene ii newly crowned and laden with regalia. But when his courtiers kneel to him, he reproves them:

> KING.   None to vs shall bow,
>   Giue God your knees.
> OCT.   Whose owne voice does allow
>   That Subiects should to those who are *Supreme*,
>   Bend, as to God, (all Kings being like to him.)[6]

Octavio, the King's uncle, is putting forward the doctrine of the divine right of kings, as expounded by James in his *Trve Lawe of Free Monarchies*:

... a Monarchie, (which forme of gouernment, as resembling the Diuinitie, approcheth neerest to perfection, as all the learned and wise men from the beginning haue agreed vppon).

Kings are called *Gods* by the Propheticall *King David*, (Psal. 82. 6) because they sit vpon God his throne in the earth, and haue the count of their administration to giue vnto him.[7]

In *Basilicon Doron* James had taught Prince Henry that he was obliged to the Almighty 'for that he made you a little God to sit on his Throne, & rule ouer other men'.[8] But Alphonso, like a model militant Protestant monarch, disclaims this doctrine:

> Pray mocke not mee with such Idolatry,
> Kings, Gods are, (I confesse) but Gods of clay,
> Brittle as you are, you as good as they,
> Onely in weight they differ, (this poore dram)
> Yet all but flesh and bloud; And such I am.
> If such, pray let mee eate, drinke, speake, and walke,
> Not look'd cleane through, with superstitious eyes,
> (Not star'de at like a Comete.)[9]

Obviously, neither James nor militant Protestants considered government to be a secular activity, but these general shared

---

[6] *ITBNAGP*, I. ii. 12–15.
[7] *Trve Lawe*, sigs. B, B3. See also D. H. Willson, p. 226.
[8] Craigie, xvi. 24.
[9] *ITBNAGP*, I. ii. 19–26. The 'poor dram' is presumably the crown, referred to as an 'Idoll' a few lines earlier.

assumptions left plenty of room for disagreement, indeed for warfare in Scotland. To make the King himself denounce James's inflated theories is an ingenious piece of irony.

> ALPH. Pay vnto *Caesar* onely *Caesars* due.[10]

When newly acceded in 1603, James had a medal struck in his own honour which proclaimed him 'Caesar Caesarum'.[11]

Queen Elizabeth had discreetly accepted the cult which surrounded her, realizing that it served many purposes—not necessarily of her own choosing. But when James himself started to put forward such ideas as theories to be taken literally, and regarded as justifying absolutism, he may have provoked a reaction. James had argued that tyranny was lawful, and that the king could break the laws or help himself to his subjects' property without them having any redress. He quoted St Paul, who told the Romans to obey 'Nero that bloody Tirant, an infamy to his age, and a monster to the world, beeing also an idolatrous persecutor'.[12] No arguments could have been better designed to defeat their own purpose. Many who had accepted absolutism before, must have developed grave doubts about it as a result of reading King James's works.

Alphonso proceeds to demonstrate the behaviour of a model king. His first act is one of mercy, but it is more than that. Octavio asks him to sign the death-warrant of those who were involved in a conspiracy in the previous reign:

> Here are the Names of bold conspirators,
> (Yong *Catilines*, and farre more desperate)
> Who in your Fathers dayes kindled the fires
> Of hote Rebellion.[13]

Alphonso pardons them:

> ALPH.   Shall Recordes say
> Being Crownde, he playd the Tyran the first day,
> How should that Chronicler be curs'd? your paper.
> When such a fatall booke comes in my sight,
> Ile with *Vespasian* wish I could not write,

---

[10] *ITBNAGP*, I. ii. 35.   [11] D. H. Willson, p. 168.

[12] *Trve Lawe*, C4ᵛ.   [13] *ITBNAGP*, I. ii. 39–42.

Their bond is canceld. I forgiue the debt,
See that at liberty, they all be set.
OMN. A Princely Act.[14]

Dekker is alluding to his own scene in *The Whore of Babylon* in which Titania signs the death-warrant of the Earl of Essex, quoting the words of Nero as she does so.

When King James came to the throne, he performed the princely act of pardoning those who had been involved in the Essex rebellion. The Earl of Southampton was released from the Tower, and the other conspirators, such as Bedford, Sandys, Mounteagle, and Cromwell had their huge outstanding fines remitted.[15] Dekker's echo of *The Whore of Babylon* confirms the Essex interpretation of that scene, and shows that militant Protestants thought that James had, in that respect, made a good beginning.

The passage is obscured by two jokes, one of a rather private nature. Ben Jonson's play *Catiline His Conspiracy* had come out in 1611, and—unlike *Sir Thomas Wyatt*—it had nothing at all to do with the Essex rebellion. By using the name Catiline to allude to Essex, Dekker could be casting a provocative and undeserved suspicion on Jonson's play. The audience would probably not have noticed this, but a reader of the 1612 Quarto may well have done so.

The second joke lies in the misattribution to Vespasian, and would have been quite clear to the audience: the joke is that nobody dares correct the mistakes of the British Solomon. Dekker's joke has serious overtones even at this stage, and later in the play there is a direct allusion to Nero of a far from comic kind. When totally corrupted by the Devil, Alphonso proclaims that he will become a follower of Nero: 'Midst flames weele dance, and dye a *Nerenist*.'[16] As in *The Whore of Babylon*, Dekker is using the name of Nero here as the epitome of all that is worst in a ruler. When Caesar is given the due of God, Caesar becomes Nero.

However, in Act I Alphonso is still an ideal king, and he starts his reign by making a plan of how he will spend each day of the week. The plan reveals a lot about what militant

---

[14] *ITBNAGP*, I. ii. 48–55.
[15] Lacey, p. 315–16.
[16] *ITBNAGP*, III. iii. 187.

Protestants considered to be the true principles of religion and policy.

King Alphonso's first resolution is Sunday observance:

> sacred is that and hye;
> And who prophanes one houre in that, shall dye.[17]

Spendola comments that not many will be left alive at that rate, and the penalty does sound as if the new King is being over-zealous.

One of the requests of the Millenary Petition in 1604 was for the strict observance of the Sabbath, and so Dekker's stance here does invite comparison to what is loosely termed 'Puritan'. But the Millenary Petition also asked King James to abolish such superstitious symbols as the sign of the Cross, and even the ring given in marriage.[18] There is no evidence that Dekker was hostile to these. Later in the play, the Subprior uses a crucifix to drive away the fiends that are tormenting him, and the same motif occurs in *The Virgin Martyr* in a Dekker scene. In *The Honest Whore, Part Two* Infaelice and Hippolito have exchanged rings when they were married.[19]

King James's laxity in Sunday observance was a conspicuous departure from the practices of Queen Elizabeth. A rule that would have been unrealistic for the poor could easily have been observed at Court, but James ignored it. It was not until 1618 that he issued his Book of Sports, which openly disregarded Sunday observance, but his attitudes had long been clear.[20]

King Alphonso's second resolution concerns the law. He announces that he will stamp out corruption:

> The poore and rich mans cause
> Ile poize alike: It shall be my chiefe care
> That bribes and wrangling be pitch'd o're the barre.[21]

The taking of bribes was officially condoned by no one. But in practice, the system had long functioned through bribery,

---

[17] *ITBNAGP*, I. ii. 70–1.
[18] D. L. Farmer, *Britain and the Stuarts* (G. Bell and Sons Ltd.: London, 1971), 39.   [19] *ITBNAGP*, IV. iv.; *VM*, V. i.; *2 HW*, III. i. 50–1.
[20] D. H. Willson, p. 400–1.   [21] *ITBNAGP*, I. ii. 88–90.

and King James did nothing to discourage this. When Francis Bacon, then Lord Chancellor, was impeached for peculation and disgraced in 1621, he excused himself with the famous words, 'I may be frail and partake of the abuse of the times,' which was no more than the truth.[22]

The third resolution Alphonso announces concerns charitable works. He decides to build hospitals for the sick and poor:

> Churles (with Gods mony) shall not feast, swill wine,
> And fat their rancke gutts whilest poore wretches pine.[23]

The years immediately preceding 1612 had seen dearth in England. Severe inflation and terrible hardship for the poor had led to riots in some areas, described by Dekker in *Work for Armourers* (1609). Rioting was a felony and the culprits were hanged. Against this background the extravagance of the Court seemed particularly indecent.

In Dekker's later play, *The Wonder of A Kingdom*, the plight of the poor and the proper use of wealth are the central concern of the plot. The charitable hospital set up by Gentili, which shelters the poor and nurtures scholars, is contrasted with the meretricious extravagance of the courtier Torrenti, who builds himself a gilded banqueting hall, but will not spare a crumb for his starving brother. Gentili's hospital is a compliment to Edward Alleyn's foundation of Dulwich College and its dependent almshouses, and it is probable that the ostentatious edifice of Torrenti carries some unflattering reflection on the Jacobean Court: Inigo Jones had completed the Royal Banqueting Hall at Whitehall for King James during the same period.[24] There is no architectural resemblance, but such a moralistic antithesis would be typical of Dekker's attacks on the Court, attacks which could be thought, in some respects, vulgar. So, however, could

---

[22] Godfrey Davies, *The Early Stuarts*, Vol. ix of *The Oxford History of England*, gen. ed. Sir George Clark (OUP, 1937; rpt. 1967), 26.

[23] *ITBNAGP*, I. ii. 111–12.

[24] The evidence for the attribution of sections of the play, which was a collaboration with John Day, and for its close connection with Alleyn can be found in my article, 'The *Noble Spanish Soldier*, *The Wonder of A Kingdom*, and *The Parliament of Bees*: The Belated Solution to a Long-standing Dekker Problem', *The Durham University Journal*, LXXIX, no. 2 (June 1987), 223–32.

Torrenti's building, which is a bizarre and showy artefact of Babylon.

To return to the earlier play, Alphonso decides that he will devote Wednesdays to giving audience to foreign ambassadors, and Thursdays to wars: very necessary, if it is a militant Protestant foreign policy he is pursuing with the ambassadors. He launches into a long speech about how badly soldiers are treated, how poorly they are paid, and how callously they are discarded by society afterwards.[25]

This is a frequent concern of Dekker's—best dramatized in the figure of Rafe in *The Shoemakers' Holiday*—as it was to all militant Protestants. The Earl of Essex had been appointed in 1593 almoner of a fund set up by the House of Lords to give assistance to discharged soldiers.[26] After his death in 1601, the Statute of Elizabeth XLIII cap. III was passed, 'An Act for the Necessary Relief of Soldiers and Mariners'. This required each county to provide for ex-servicemen at rates decided by the magistrates.[27] But the law had little effect, and disabled soldiers, without pensions, were still a common sight begging in London. Both compassion and practicality motivate Dekker here. If militant Protestants wanted a policy of continued war, it made sense to take proper care of the troops.

Alphonso's final resolution is a dual one: to promote learning, and to do it by abolishing pluralism.

> . . . none shall hold
> Three or foure Church-liuings (got by *Symonious* gold)
> In them, to fat himselfe as in a stye,
> When greater Schollers languish in beggery:[28]

The abolition of pluralism and non-residence was one of the requests of the Millenary Petition. Whether or not simony was involved, pluralism involved the exploitation of many penurious curates, and many parishes had no preacher. But the awarding of plural livings was a royal prerogative, and King James was very keen on preserving it. It was a way of rewarding those clergy whose views pleased him, and so

---

[25] *ITBNAGP*, I. ii. 123–37.   [26] *DNB* entry under Devereux.
[27] *The Statutes at Large, Edward IV–Elizabeth* (Eyre, Strahan & Co.: London, 1786), ii. 699.   [28] *ITBNAGP*, I. ii. 145–8.

determined was James not to compromise on this issue that later, in 1616, he actually dismissed Chief Justice Coke over a case of *Commendams* involving the Bishop of Lichfield.[29] Coke tried to use common law to challenge the royal prerogative, and for Dekker to criticize pluralism was to criticize the King.

In *The Gvls Horne-booke*, which is not usually thought of as a Puritan text, Dekker suggests to his decadent courtier:

Demand if there be any gentleman, whom any there is acquainted with, that is troubled with two offices, or any vicar with two church-livings; which will politicly insinuate, that your inquiry after them is because you have good means to obtain them.[30]

So far, Alphonso has outlined the course militant Protestants wished their King to follow. But at this point the Devil intervenes. Narcisso announces the arrival of a mysterious stranger at the Court of Naples, Bohor who is really the demon Rufman in disguise. He loses no time before starting to uproot the true principles of religion and policy, and he soon wins Alphonso over with a doctrine of straightforward hedonism. All the new King's good resolutions are forgotten in self-indulgence, and Rufman becomes Alfonso's reigning favourite.

The results of Alphonso's corruption are seen in Acts II and III. Octavio brings Alphonso his own list of good resolutions which he calls 'that booke of statutes, were enacted / In the high Parliament of thy roiall thoughts', but Alphonso has already lost interest in them.[31]

A series of entertainers arrives at his Court, including a group of city water-bearers and one from the Turners Company (there was of course a Turners Company in the City of London). These are followed by a soldier, a scholar, and a mariner. But Alphonso spurns and dismisses them all. King James never saw any reason to be gracious to his subjects, as Queen Elizabeth had done, and disliked face-to-face encounters with them. The gulf that grew up in his reign between courtly entertainments and popular ones can be seen

[29] Farmer, p. 42.
[30] Grosart, ii. 239–40.
[31] *ITBNAGP*, II. i. 3–4.

in the split between the court masque and the civic pageant, both of which derived from the same Elizabethan root, the royal progress.

Rufman suggests 'idle counterfet Sea-fights' and displays of fireworks as suitable amusements for a monarch, and James was actually very fond of both of these.[32] The first idea could be another allusion to Nero. According to Suetonius, Nero made a parade of virtue at the start of his reign, but as he grew to be more of a tyrant, so his taste for extravagant entertainment increased, and he once had a naval battle staged on an artificial lake.[33]

The corruption of Alphonso and his Court is epitomized by his rejection of his bride, Erminhild: like so many Dekker heroines she appears to have a symbolic role, representing the moral and political health of the state. In the middle of the play, Erminhild disappears and is thought to be dead.

In Act III, Octavio brings a petition to King Alphonso: his kingdom is now suffering from poverty, bankruptcy, and desperation. Rich courtiers do not pay their debts and as a result poor tradespeople starve.[34] The corrupt Alphonso has grown indifferent to the economic problems of his kingdom, and proposes to stop the cries of the poor 'With halters'.[35] When Octavio asks Alphonso whether this is in accordance with his book of laws, previously dictated, Alphonso simply replies:

Still brauing me with this? burne it.[36]

This is the logical conclusion of King James's view of the law:

The King is aboue the Law, as both the author, and giuer of strength therto: yet a good King will, not onely delight to rule his subiectes by the Law; but euen will conforme his owne action thervnto . . . yet is he not bound thereto but of his own good wil . . .[37]

If the King can make and unmake the law, what happens when the monarch does not have good will? Gentillet had called his book an anti-Machiavellian treatise because Machiavelli had advised the Prince to make all decisions

[32] *ITBNAGP*, II. i. 189–92; D. H. Willson, p. 286.   [33] Graves, pp. 191–2.
[34] *ITBNAGP*, III. iii. 70–3.   [35] *ITBNAGP*, III. iii. 90.
[36] *ITBNAGP*, III. iii. 93.   [37] *Trve Lawe*, sig. Dᵛ.

alone.[38] Absolutism was thus linked with a name that was tantamount to Satan's.

In 1607 John Cowell's law dictionary, *The Interpreter*, put the view that the king was above the law, and that his prerogative was enough to make laws or to levy subsidies. This so roused the indignation of the 1610 Parliament that it ordered Cowell's book to be burned by the public hangman, and King James assented.[39] This was extraordinarily ironic, since James had put the same view in his own book: of course, nobody asked to burn that. It was not until the Petition of Right in 1628 that a Parliament openly demanded that the King disclaim the right to impose arbitrary taxation, that was, to make and unmake laws.

While Rufman implants the seeds of absolutism in the royal mind, other devils have been at work in City and Church. Bartervile, who represents the City, is described as a merchant, but he is much more than that. He is a usurer, a keeper of brothels (like Henslowe), and a tax-farmer, who profits out of collecting taxes for the Crown. His wickedness so far outreaches that of hell that the devil Lurchall becomes his apprentice, and listens in awe as Bartervile explains the fearful mysteries of the business world. Bartervile wields power over high and low alike: even the King relies on him to raise revenues, furnish loans, and finance his wars. Lurchall describes him as,

> A Master, who more villenie has by hart,
> Then thou by rote; See him but play his owne part,
> And thou doest Hell good seruice.[40]

Very soon, we hear Bartervile computing how much profit he has made by purchasing the right to farm the 'salt tribute'—rather a lot since the amount owing to him is still 'Seuen thousand Crownes':

> Thats well: a sauorie summe:
>
> . . . .
>
> Me thinkes tis fit a subiect should not eate
> But that his Prince from euery dish of meate

---

[38] Patericke, p. 16. The passage referred to seems to be in Niccolo Machiavelli, *The Prince*, trans. W. K. Marriott (Everyman's Library, 280, gen. ed. Ernest Rhys; S. M. Dent and Sons: London, 1908), 185–6.

[39] G. Davies, p. 13.   [40] *ITBNAGP*, II. ii. 12–14.

Should receiue nourishment: for (being the head)
Why should he pine, when all the body is fed?
Besides, it makes vs more to awe a King,
When at each bit we are forc'd to thinke on him.[41]

This can be elucidated by consulting that scandalously neglected text, the 1608 *Book of Rates*. Its table of import duties includes the following entry:

	white or Spanish salt the bushell . . . viij.d.
	white or Spanish salt the Way, cont. forty bushels . . . xxvj.s. viij.d.
Salt.	Bay or French Salt the bushell . . . vj.d.
	Bay or French Salt the Way, cont. forty bushels . . . xx.s.[42]

Not only was there a tax on salt in Jacobean England, but this and all taxes on common foodstuffs aroused deep resentment. So indeed did the whole system of selling the farm of taxes. In itself, farming taxes was not new: in fact, the Earl of Essex had held the farm of sweet wines from 1590 to 1600.[43] It was one thing to make such an award to a popular and impecunious peer (who did nothing to maximize the revenue), but it was another to sell the farms to anybody who could bid for them. In King James's reign there had been an increase both in the levels of taxation and also in the range of things taxed. His first Treasurer, the Earl of Dorset, had been anxious to obtain a reliable income to meet the soaring expenditure of the royal households, and so in 1604 he leased the Great Farm of the Customs to a syndicate for seven years in return for £112,400 per year. These rights were blatantly auctioned and when peace with Spain increased trade, the customs farmers did very well out of the arrangement, arousing resentment in many quarters. Bartervile has got rich by conciliating the powers of Babylon.

But James's debts still continued to mount, and when Robert Cecil, now Earl of Salisbury, took over as Treasurer in

---

[41] *ITBNAGP*, II. ii. 46–53. Hoy, iii. 100, explains this salt tax as a tax on lechery, but I think it makes much more sense to read 'salt' and 'bit', i.e. bite, literally, in this case.

[42] *The Rates of Marchandizes, as They are Set Downe in the Booke of Rates* (n.p., n.d., but opens with a declaration from James R.), sig. E8ᵛ, or K3ᵛ in the edn. of the same date with larger print.   [43] Harrison, p. 45.

1608 he issued a new *Book of Rates* which increased the import duties on a wide range of goods. Not only salt but other foods such as cod, eels, haddocks, and herrings, were taxed, as were spices, currants, prunes, needles, and children's dolls. There was a sizeable increase in the tax on silk of every kind—Granado, Naples, Organzine, etc.—for which Salisbury held the farm of the customs himself.[44] He leased it from the Crown for £8,900 p.a. and sublet it to contractors, making a profit of £7,000 p.a.[45] This helps explain why he was, when he died in May 1612, so rich and so unpopular (though he was only one of many who took advantage of this system). A militant Protestant foreign policy would have meant a loss of profit for the King's ministers—and the Crown itself.

When in Act III Bartervile is struck down in front of the King and appears dead, Spendola (urged on by Rufman) starts begging the office of salt-tax farmer from the King before the merchant can even be carried out. His avidity is rewarded by Alphonso:

> ALPH. The office of this periurde *Bartervile*,
> I frankly giue away, diuiding it
> To the Count *Spendola*, and our worthy friend
> Braue *Bohor* here; farme it to whom you please.
> BOTH. We thanke your Highnes.
> SPEND. Who bids most, he buyes it.[46]

When Bartervile recovers sufficiently to return to the King's presence, the first thing he does is to buy back his office from Spendola and Rufman. The Court is being run like an auction, and the King is at the centre of the corruption. The satire is not merely aimed at one section of society: there is no opposition between Court and City here. Dekker is not (like Jonson) hostile to the City because its power challenges that of the King, and neither is he hostile to King and Court because he is uncritical of what goes on in the City. He is criticizing a whole system in which monarch, noblemen, and money-merchants all participate.

This system of taxation came under severe attack in the

---

[44] *Book of Rates*, sig. F.
[45] Farmer, pp. 30–3.
[46] *ITBNAGP*, III. iii. 54–9.

Parliament of 1610, which held a debate on impositions and the royal prerogative to impose them. The House was almost unanimous against the Crown, and took violent issue over food taxation. One historian writes, 'They were . . . determined that not a penny should be laid upon the food of the people.'[47]

In 1610, a year before the play was written, Parliament was almost persuaded by Salisbury to vote the King £200,000 p.a. in return for a reduction of such impositions, but the bargain failed because at the last moment James asked for £300,000.[48] The same Parliament presented James with a Petition of grievances on 7 July 1610, covering such matters as the restitution of deprived ministers, but James responded in a negative way. In retrospect, it is easy for us to link these two events. Dekker does not make any connection between taxation and representation: he just dislikes the tax, and dislikes the policies of the King.

When Alphonso's policies have led Naples into war, he demands a huge loan from Bartervile in order to finance it. Bartervile consents—he cannot openly refuse—but he soon devises an ingenious method of avoiding lending all his money to the King. It involves spreading the rumour that he is dead, and then arranging to inherit his own fortune under an assumed identity. Forced loans to the Crown were another topical grievance. The government had borrowed £100,000 from the City of London in 1610, and would demand another £116,000 over the next two years. But the repayment was slow or unreliable, so much so that by 1614 the City refused James another loan.[49]

With the profits he makes from farming taxes, Bartervile practises usury, and of course cheats his customers. Lending money at interest was legal in England, and a statute of 1570 fixed the maximum rate at ten per cent.[50] Like prostitution, the practice was disapproved of, but went on everywhere. Religious leaders of every shade of opinion continued to denounce it. The Puritan William Perkins condemned usury in some of his sermons: 'Seeking of abundance is a hazard to

---

[47] Samuel R. Gardiner, *A History of England . . . 1603–1642* (10 vols.; Longmans: London, 1883; rpt. 1890), ii. 82–3.   [48] Farmer, p. 32.
[49] Ibid. 32–3.   [50] *Statutes at Large*, ii. 581–2.

the salvation of the soule by reason of mans corruption.'[51] But in other places he excused limited forms of it, practised with consideration.[52] This had been Calvin's view.

Bishop John Jewell, an orthodox churchman, wrote that usury was,

... filthy gaines and a worke of darkenesse. It is a monster in nature; the overthrow of mighty kingdoms, the destruction of flourishing States, the decay of wealthy Citties, the plagues of the world and the miserie of the people. It is theft, it is the murdering of our brethren.[53]

Bartervile certainly has a philosophy of ruthless individualism. He milks the system while acknowledging loyalty to nobody in it:

Nature sent man into the world, (alone,)
Without all company, but to care for one,
And that ile doe.

The devil Lurchall replies, 'True Citie doctrine sir'.[54]

It would be inexact to describe Bartervile as a capitalist, since he has no stocks and shares, no gilt-edged securities, no limited liability companies, no equities or dividends. In so far as he is an anti-social profiteer, there is no doubt that he is condemned, yet his energy and dynamism endow him with some attractive qualities and, though he does end up in hell in Act V, there are moments when Dekker seems hesitant about damning Bartervile totally. The scene in which Bartervile's client arrives to pay his money and collect his security, but Bartervile prevents him by throwing gold over the document is an anticlimax.[55] It is just not heinous enough, nor is it particularly wily. Yet Dekker knew a great deal about the workings of the financial world, and its corrupt practices. In his prose work, *Lanthorne and Candle-Light* (1609), he gives an elaborate account of goings-on in the shady side of the business world, including how young gentlemen are tricked

[51] *The Whole Treatise of the Cases of Conscience*, in *The Works of William Perkins* (printed by John Legatt, 1613 edn.), sig. L3.

[52] *A Golden Chaine or The Description of Theologie*, in Perkins, *Works* (1603 edn.), 64.

[53] 'Vpon the First Epistle to the Thessalonians', *The Works of the Very Learned and Reverend Father in God Iohn Ievvell* (John Norton, London, 1609), sig. ☛ G3ᵛ–4.

[54] *ITBNAGP*, IV. i. 80–2.   [55] *ITBNAGP*, II. ii. 140–50.

out of fortunes by clever merchants.[56] It is a pity Dekker did not introduce more details like this into the play, and their absence may be attributed to a sudden loss of conviction that young gentlemen being swindled out of their inheritance was such a terrible thing. Dekker seems to go flaccid at this point, unable to sympathize with either party. He solves his dilemma in the last Act, by sending Bartervile to hell, but sending him there in company with a Prodigal, perhaps one of the usurer's own foolish victims. It was not long since Dekker had expressed his view of rich drones and prodigals in one of his most successful pieces of satire, *The Gvls Horne-booke* (1609).

If Dekker's Bartervile appears to be a pale shadow of Shylock, or of Marlowe's Barabas, he is unlike them in one vital respect: he is not a Jew. His avarice is found in the Christian community, not among a handful of aliens suffering under a hereditary curse. As a characterization, Bartervile is weaker, but Dekker's criticism of society is much stronger.

The third devil, Shackle-Soule, is sent to corrupt a monastery. When Shackle-Soule, in his guise of Friar Rush, teaches the monks that charity is a sin, his heresy could be described as a Puritan one:

> PRIOR. How? sin to feed religious votaries!
> SHAC. Rather to nourish idle vagabonds:
>   The Cleargy of other lands, haue with much pietie
>   And thrift destroyde those drones, that lazily
>   Liue eating vp the labours of the bee.
>   A churchman there cares but to feede the soule,
>   He makes that charge his office. Almisdeeds! alas!
>   They through the Lawyers hands are fitt'st to passe.[57]

Some contemporary English Puritans were taking the view that charitable gifts were harmful and encouraged the poor to be lazy. William Perkins quoted St Paul to support his teaching, that it was 'Vniust . . . to feede, or clothe stout and lustie rogues or beggars'.[58] Dekker sees the danger of this attitude as a front for meanness. Of course he was aware of

---

[56] Grosart, iii. 228–37.
[57] *ITBNAGP*, I. iii. 163–70.
[58] Perkins (1603 edn.), p. 64.

the trickery of professional rogues and beggars, which he had warned against in many earlier pamphlets. Normand Berlin has argued that in the plays of this period, including *Westward Ho!* and *Northward Ho!* (which Dekker wrote with Webster) and *The Roaring Girl*, Dekker took a much more lenient view of the tricks of the poor, and a more severe one of the tricks of the rich and well-off. This seems to be true, but I cannot see why Berlin deduces from it that Dekker had been 'corrupted'.[59]

With Court, City, and Church all ruled by the Devil, Naples is on the verge of collapse, and is invaded by the Duke of Calabria. The King's uncle, Octavio, deserts him and goes to fight on the Calabrian side, and many of Alphonso's other subjects turn against him, raising the spectre of civil war. At the nadir of his fortunes, King Alphonso suddenly has a change of heart and asks the forgiveness of heaven. When the denouement is reached in the monastery, Alphonso has been completely reformed; he is reunited with Erminhild, that is, with rightful government, and the blame for all that is past is put on his favourite, the devil Rufman. Alphonso's other favourites, Narcisso, Jovinelli, Brisco, and Spendola, are beheaded, a piece of news Alphonso hears with equanimity.[60] To put the blame for bad rule on the monarch's advisors was an immemorial tradition necessary in order to bring about some kind of satisfactory conclusion within the bounds of existing institutions, and within the conventions of comedy: it was a convention also shared by tragi-comedy. King Alphonso's speedy and total reform is not very believable, but it provides a model of the speedy and total reform that militant Protestants would have liked to behold in King James, who had evidently failed to live up to the great hopes expressed for him in *The Wonderfull Yeare*.[61]

There is good reason to think that Dekker's prologue and epilogue to this play were added at a later stage. The senior devil who appears in them is called Pluto, while the one who appears in the middle of the play is called Lucifer. And in his preface, addressed to the Queen's Men, Dekker writes that

---

[59] Normand Berlin, 'Thomas Dekker: A Partial Reappraisal', *Studies in English Literature*, 6 (1966), 273–5.
[60] *ITBNAGP*, V. iii. 85–6.   [61] Grosart, i. 97–9.

after the play was spurned by Fortune—i.e. the Fortune Theatre—the Queen's Men 'gently raizd it vp (on the same *Columnes,*) the *Frontispice* onely a little more *Garnished*'.[62] If this refers to the prologue, in hell, it must also refer to the epilogue.

One likely reason for the addition of this prologue and epilogue is that they make the play more politically acceptable. The King and his policies have been criticized throughout the play, but in the epilogue we see the devils tormenting Guy Fawkes and Ravaillac, along with Bartervile and a 'Puritane'. This epilogue was surely appended to the play in order to provide a safe and loyal (though rowdy) conclusion.

When Dekker uses the term 'Puritan' he evidently means an extreme non-conformist. At one point in the play Farneze remarks of Bartervile, 'the diuels turn'd puritane I feare, / He hates (me thinkes) to heare his own child sweare.'[63] The oath Bartervile has just broken was, however, no casual imprecation, of the kind that were sometimes cut out of contemporary plays. It was a solemn declaration sworn on a book, presumably a Bible, and amounts to perjury. The 'Puritane' who is brought into hell in the epilogue evidently belongs to some group such as the Brownists. He is dressed wholly in black, refers to his church as a 'Synagogue' and his fellow-believers as 'the brethren and sisters'.[64] They were apparently in exile from England: 'Wee were all smoakt out of our owne Countrey, and sent to *Rotterdam*.'[65] In 1608 a group of English separatists had set up a church in Amsterdam, under the leadership of John Smyth. He was succeeded by Thomas Helwys, who is considered to be the founder of the Baptist Church.[66] Dekker's attitude to these breakaway groups is shown when the 'Puritane' is thrown out of hell in case he brings the place down, as he has brought down the Church above. In *Basilicon Doron* King James had denounced Puritans, i.e. Presbyterians, because he saw them as a threat to hierarchy and monarchy.[67] Dekker, on the other hand, sees some of the more extreme groups as a threat to the Church.

---

[62] Bowers, iii. 119.

[63] *ITBNAGP*, III. iii. 52–3.

[64] *ITBNAGP*, V. iv. 270, 279.

[65] *ITBNAGP*, V. iv. 276–7.

[66] *DNB* entry under Helwys. Not to be confused with Edward Helwys the militant Protestant.

[67] Craigie, xvi. 74.

Along with Bartervile and the Puritan, we see two regicides being toasted merrily by the devils. Significantly, both are anti-Protestant regicides. François Ravaillac, who murdered Henri IV in 1610, was motivated by Catholic extremism. Although Henri IV had joined the Church of Rome in 1593, he still supported a balance of power between Protestant and Catholic Europe. When he was assassinated, he was preparing to lead an international military alliance in which France would side with the Protestant powers against Spain and the Empire. This was prevented by his murder, and the result was a swing in the direction of Rome, since Henri was followed by Marie de Medicis who became regent. From the militant Protestant point of view, Henri's assassination was therefore undesirable. In a later play, *The Noble Spanish Soldier*, Dekker took Henri IV as the basis for a reprobate king, and Ravaillac's appearance in hell here does not mean that Dekker took an uncritical view of the apostate monarch (though many Protestants admired him).[68]

The case of the would-be assassin Guy Fawkes was even clearer. The Gunpowder Plot was a Catholic conspiracy against both Parliament and King, rather than a simple case of regicide. There was nothing in it to tempt a militant Protestant—as there was for instance in the Essex rebellion, and that of Sir Thomas Wyatt. If Dekker had shown his devils tormenting Jacques Clement, the Dominican friar whose assassination of Henri III in 1589 had brought Henri IV—at that time a Protestant—to the throne of France, that would indeed be inconsistent. Clement was a Catholic and a regicide, but he does not appear in Dekker's militant Protestant hell.

The play's epilogue is an affirmation of loyalty, but an affirmation which avoids looking too closely at the basis of that loyalty or its potential limitations.

In *If This Be Not A Good Play*, as in *The Whore of Babylon*, Dekker was struggling to find a form that would provide a vehicle for his religious-political ideas. The result is not totally satisfactory, but it is far from being a failure. It may well have influenced Thomas Scott's famous *Vox Populi*

---

[68] Jones-Davies, i. 143. See also my article, pp. 223–32.

or Newes from Spayne. Scott's work takes the form of a
dialogue between Gondomar, the Spanish ambassador, and
the Spanish Council to whom he reports his success in
guiding King James in a Roman Catholic direction, and
sowing rifts and dissension. One could compare this to
Dekker's Rufman reporting to Lucifer how successfully he
has perverted the King and Court of Naples. At the time of
the Spanish Match, Gondomar's reputation in England was
very much that of a Machiavell or devil.[69] *Vox Populi* is
brought to a close by the arrival of a messenger, who
interrupts the Council to announce the death of 'our most
trusty and able Pensioner *Barnevelt*'.[70] In the epilogue to *If
This Be Not A Good Play* the devils bring Pluto news of the
arrival, that is the death, of several well-known figures: as
well as Ravaillac, they announce the pirate Danztiger and a
sergeant called Cutlar. In Scott's sequel, *The Second Part of
Vox Populi, or, Gondomar Appearing in the Likenes of
Matchiauell in a Spanish Parliament* (1624), the frontispiece
shows a picture of the Spanish Council chamber, with a
horned devil peeping from behind the throne.[71]

B. Troia-Nova Triumphans

Dekker's city pageant, *Troia-Nova Triumphans*, was written
at most a year after *If This Be Not A Good Play*, for the Lord
Mayor's show on 29 October 1612. But it is far more
optimistic than the play.

This new mood of optimism among militant Protestants
was the result of several occurrences. In April 1612 King
James signed a defence treaty with the German Evangelical
Union. At the same time his daughter, Princess Elizabeth,
was betrothed to the young Elector Frederick V of the
Palatinate, a Calvinist with family and political ties linking
him to the Huguenots. The murder of Henri IV and the
consequent change in the balance of power were probably

[69] Charles H. Carter, 'Gondomar: Ambassador to James I', *Historical Journal*,
VII (1964), 190.
[70] *The Workes of the Most Famovs and Reverend Divine Mr. Thomas Scot*
(Printed at Vtrick, 1624), sig. Dᵛ.   [71] Ibid. sig. A.

influential in causing King James to take a more Protestant line on foreign policy.[72] In addition to this, Prince Henry had now reached maturity, and was actively supporting the Palatine alliance; he was even showing interest in a Calvinist bride for himself, the sister of the Elector. These events gave militant Protestants hope that the era of political frustration, which had characterized *The Whore of Babylon* and *If This Be Not A Good Play*, might soon be over.

In the autumn of 1612 the Elector and his uncle the Duc de Bouillon arrived in London to prepare for the marriage, which was then fixed for November. They were present at the Lord Mayor's show, and Dekker refers to them in his induction:

. . . the fruites whereof shoot forth and ripen, are gathered, and taste sweetly, in the mouthes not onely of this *Citty*, but also of our best-to-be-beloued friends, the *Noblest strangers*. Vpon whom, though none but our *Soueraigne King* can bestow *Royall welcomes*; yet shall it be a *Memoriall* of an *Exemplary Loue* and *Duty* (in those who are at the *Cost* of these *Triumphs*) to haue *added* some *Heightning* more to them then was intended at first, of purpose to do honor to their Prince and Countrey.

For to haue bene leaden-winged now, what infamy could be greater? When all the streames of *Nobility* and *Gentry*, run with the *Tide* hither. When all *Eares* lye listning for no newes but of *Feasts* and *Triumphs*: All *Eyes* still open to behold them: And all harts and hands to applaud them.[73]

The feasts and triumphs are the pre-nuptial festivities. The pageant itself is intended to be part of these celebrations, in honour not only of the royal visit and the forthcoming marriage, but of the confessional alliance so welcome to militant Protestants:

. . . obserue what honorable entertainement the Citty affoords to their new *Praetor*, and what ioyfull salutations to her noble *Visitants*.[74]

---

[72] Simon L. Adams, 'Spain or the Netherlands: The Dilemmas of Early Stuart Foreign Policy', in *Before the English Civil War*, ed. Howard Tomlinson (Macmillan: London, 1983), 86. Also Adams, 'Protestant Cause', p. 183.
[73] Bowers, iii. 231–2, lines 28–42.   [74] Ibid. iii. 232, lines 58–60.

When Dekker writes:

Ryot hauing no hand in laying out the *Expences*, and yet no hand in plucking backe what is held decent to be bestowed: A *sumptuous Thriftinesse* in these *Ciuil Ceremonies* managing *All*,[75]

this could be another shaft at the extravagance of the Jacobean Court, such as he made in *If This Be Not A Good Play*. In *The Dead Tearme*, a pamphlet of 1608, Dekker voiced this criticism as explicitly as he could:

Prodigality . . . thou Darling of *Great Brittaine*, thy Princes call thee *Their Treasurer* and thou art so.[76]

The expenditure of the City in honour of a worthy cause is carefully distinguished from the pointless extravagance and display of Whitehall.

The pageant, which is not a long one, consists of five devices, representing Neptune, the Castle of Virtue, the Castle of Envy, the House of Fame, and finally, Justice. There were also some water-shows, but as they included no poetry Dekker does not detail them. He refers a little disdainfully to the amusement of '*Powder* and *Smoake*', the kind of entertainment Rufman provided for the Naples Court and which was favoured by the Philistine monarch.[77] Virtue's speech praises the 'Ciuill, Popular gouernment' of the City, with its 'free election' of the aldermen and mayor: a somewhat idealized image, and a notably republican ideal. The fourth device, the House of Fame, is designed as a compliment to Prince Henry. It represents all the princes and distinguished people who had over the centuries been honorary members of the Merchant Tailors Company, the guild to which the mayor being inaugurated in 1612, Sir John Swinnerton, belonged. 'In other seuerall places sit Kings, Princes, and Noble persons, who haue bene free of the *Marchant-tailors*: A perticular roome being reserued for one that represents the person of *Henry* the now Prince of *Wales*.'[78] Prince Henry had accepted honorary membership of the Merchant Tailors Company, unlike his father, who had turned down the similar

[75] Bowers, iii. 230, lines 10–13.   [76] Grosart, iv. 14.
[77] Bowers, iii. 236, lines 222, 229.   [78] Ibid. iii. 240, lines 342–5.

offer made by the Mercers in 1604. Since Prince Henry, the heir apparent, was now in the Privy Council and regarded as the emerging leader of English militant Protestants, his membership of a guild gave it considerable prestige, and it was also a token that the Prince had more respect for the City and its inhabitants than his father appeared to have. Prince Henry had actually agreed to be at *Troia-Nova Triumphans*, hosting the Elector Palatine, but illness prevented him from attending. In the absence of the Prince, the Elector Frederick went to dine at the Guildhall.

Fame says of Henry:

> A *Sprig* of which *Branch* (*Highest* now but *One*)
> Is *Henry Prince of Wales*, followed by none:
> Who of this *Brotherhood*, last and best steps forth,
> Honouring your Hall.[79]

Troia-Nova Triumphans is a militant Protestant triumph, which celebrates the Palatine match, the inauguration of a Mayor who was a Merchant Tailor, and the emergence of a new religious-political figurehead who was a future king: Prince Henry. Roy Strong has written that the Prince Henry cult, with its revival of Elizabethan mythology, was essentially nostalgic and backward-looking, but there is more to it than that.[80]

It may have been a memory of Dekker's pageant which prompted Webster when in 1624, many years after Prince Henry's death, he placed a figure of Prince Henry in a prominent position in his city pageant, *Monuments of Honour*. The Prince appeared in the 'Character of a Perfect Ruler', and M. C. Bradbrook has interpreted this as an implied criticism of King James and Prince Charles.[81] Webster was himself a Merchant Tailor and so is unlikely to have been absent from *Troia-Nova Triumphans*.

This euphoric pageant has a postscript even more melancholy than does *The Magnificent Entertainment*. Only a few days after the performance, Prince Henry was dead, and militant Protestant hopes were dashed again. The era of

---

[79] Ibid. iii. 241, lines 384–7.
[80] Strong, *Cult of Elizabeth*, p. 187.
[81] Bradbrook, *John Webster*, p. 181.

wishful thinking, and political frustration, now returned with a vengeance. Dekker was not one of the throng of writers who rushed to produce elegies for the Prince, but this may have been due to the pressing concerns of his own life. In the last weeks of the year, he was arrested for debt and spent the next seven years in prison.[82]

But Dekker resumed writing while he was in gaol, and in one of the works he wrote there, *Dekker His Dreame* (1620), envisaged the eschatological confrontation that would precede the end of the world, a war that would be accompanied by famine, pestilence, and disorder:

> Peace fled to Heauen (me thought), And as she went
> Her Roabe fell from her, which Warre finding Rent
> Into a thousand Ragges, dying them in Gall
>
> .   .   .   .
>
> Religion (all this while) a Garment wore,
> Stayned like a Painters Apron, and turn'd Whore
> To seuerall Countries, till from deepe Abysme
> Vp her Two Bastards came (Error and Schisme).[83]

A lesser-known poem he wrote at this time, *The Artillery Garden*, returns to the subject of Prince Henry and the lost hopes of the militant Protestants. The war-like Prince Henry had been the patron of the artillery garden, or yard, the area just outside London where the local militia trained for battle, and he himself often exercised there. The poem begins with the praise of London, whose virtues have been crowned in Dekker's eyes by its recent Protestant alliance:

> Nor wash my braines in purer *Helicon*
> Than in thy Thames: no draught of *Hipocrene*
> Tastes like it, as tis now mix't with the *Rhene*.[84]

---

[82] Leslie Hotson and Mary Edmond have suggested that his debts may have been incurred as a result of *Troia-Nova Triumphans*, since one of his creditors was John Webster, the dramatist's father, a Merchant-Tailor and coachmaker who made the rolling-stock for the city pageants. If this was so, it is strange that Webster the dramatist did not—or could not—intervene with his father on Dekker's behalf. See Mary Edmond, 'In Search of John Webster', TLS, 24 Dec. 1976. 1621–2. Jones-Davies considers this theory unconvincing.

[83] Grosart, iii. 13–14.

[84] *The Artillery Garden*, ed. F. P. Wilson (1616; facsimile, privately printed, Oxford, 1952), sig. Di.ᵛ.

In a letter of February 1613, Sir Henry Wotton refers to the Palatine marriage as 'the conjunction of the Thames and the Rhene, as our ravished spirits begin to call it'.[85]

Dekker's poem glorifies the martial arts, of which Henry had been so fond, and includes a passionate 'Inuectiue against Peace'. To militant Protestants, who had welcomed the treaty with the Evangelical Union, King James's policy of prolonged peace was not an achievement, but a symptom of decadence. *The Artillery Garden* laments that the City's training in the use of arms is despised by the Court:

> War hath forgot her name: our Language yeelds
> No words so full of Horror, as Pitchd Fieldes.
> Peace Spurnes the Drum, all broken and vnbrac'd,
> Cullors wrapt vp, the Soldier is disgracd,
> And like a garment out of fashion Growne,
> Laugh'd at . . .[86]

Only the City remains war-like:

> Against the day of Fight, they learn to Fight,
> And in their braue Artillery more delight,
> Than feasts or triumphes; off are Scarlets layd
> To put on armors. Senators vpbraid
> Our fethered Gulls cold resolution . . .[87]

Earlier, in *If This Be Not A Good Play*, Dekker's Charon had deplored the fact that all the English gallants nowadays died of diseases, and not from wounds of battle.[88] Here, Dekker actually castigates peace:

> Thou graue of Noble action, that interres
> Spirits for bodies
>
> .   .   .   .
>
> The depthles Gulph, wher euery mischeife flotes,
> Earth-quake of Kingdomes, shaking Cities more,
> With Sensuall Feauers, then could Feilds before,
> Of armed men . . .[89]

---

[85] *Letters of Sir Henry Wotton*, ed. Logan Pearsall Smith (2 vols.; OUP, 1907), ii. 12.   [86] *Artillery Garden*, sig. C.

[87] Ibid. sig. C2ᵛ. I have altered the placing of the full stop after 'armors', which is clearly an error in the printed text.

[88] *ITBNAGP*, I. i. 35–8.   [89] *Artillery Garden*, sig. C1ᵛ.

The paradox is matched by another later in the poem, when Dekker extols the cannon as 'Preseruer of the world'.[90] The poet describes how he watched (presumably from his prison window) a group of children playing at soldiers in the street:

> Euery Boy-man in this Infantery,
> Shewing like *Mars* in his Minority,
> These by Diuine instinct perhaps being led,
> To rouze dull peace, who in her sloth seemes dead.[91]

He is overjoyed at this, wondering if it is 'a prognosticating signe' that the next generation will be less effete than the present one, and that God is preparing England for the Armageddon to come. The phrase 'Perhaps being led' is one of our rare glimpses of the limits of Dekker's religious certainty.

The Artillery Garden concludes with a lament for Prince Henry:

> I cannot but with Teares of bloud condole,
> Of one most stately Columne the Sad Fall,
> Which from the Pedestal to'th Capitall
> Stood all for Soldiers: when that fell, the Land,
> Her *Generall* lost, and warre her selfe a *Hand*.
> Had not that sumptuous Frame, bin rak'd & torne
> To earth, your *Sons* would haue bin warriors borne.
> But tis our curse: and therefore though an Vrne,
> Be with *His* Ruines filld, (that did adorne,
> The Armes he wore and Loude) to Memorize
> His worth; Nource you, of *Armes* the exercize.[92]

Such a passage, written three or four years after Prince Henry's death, provides a much stronger indication of Dekker's allegiance than an obituary written at the time.

One contemporary described Prince Henry in a letter as, 'that vigorous young Prince, whose extraordinary great parts and virtues made men hope and believe, that God had reserved and destined him, as a chosen instrument, to be the Standard-bearer of his quarrel in these miserable times, to work the restoration of his church and the destruction of the

[90] *Artillery Garden*, sig. D1ᵛ.
[91] Ibid. sig. C2.
[92] Ibid. sig. D2ᵛ.

Romish idolatry.'[93] But these prospects, like their hopes for Essex, had to be abandoned.

Faced with the death of Prince Henry, militant Protestants transferred their hopes to the Elector Frederick, and the single piece of legislation passed by the Addled Parliament of 1614 was the naturalization of the Elector and his children, in case they should become England's heirs.

[93] Thomas Birch, *Life of Henry, Prince of Wales* (1760), 406.

5

The Virgin Martyr and the War in Germany

The Virgin Martyr, a collaboration between Dekker and the young Massinger, has attracted quite a lot of critical attention, but for the last twenty years the accepted view of it has been that it is a Roman Catholic *tragedia sacra*, something which would be totally inconsistent with the works of Dekker and furthermore a unique anomaly on the Elizabethan or Jacobean stage. While *The Virgin Martyr* is a remarkable play, it is not such a total anomaly, and it is best understood in its proper place in the Dekker canon.

Not all critics have insisted that *The Virgin Martyr* is a Catholic play. The Victorian Henry Hallam suggested that it might have some connection with the Spanish Inquisition.[1] His idea was taken up by A. W. Ward in 1875, and then mouldered.[2] A recent book by Simon Shepherd revives the idea, in passing, but assumes rather casually that the play is entirely the work of Massinger.[3]

The Catholic theory rests on an article by Louise G. Clubb, '*The Virgin Martyr* and the *Tragedia Sacra*', whose conclusions are regarded with approval by Hoy.[4] But many of Clubb's arguments are extremely challengeable and questionable. She compares *The Virgin Martyr* to a number of Italian saints' plays dating from the fifteenth century onwards, some featuring St Dorothea.[5] But all the common elements are present in the play's known sources, and in innumerable

[1] Henry Hallam, *Literary Essays and Characters* (John Murray: London, 1852), 156.

[2] A. W. Ward, *A History of English Dramatic Literature to the Death of Queen Anne* (3 vols.; Macmillan: London, 1875; 2nd edn., rev. 1899), iii. 13.

[3] Simon Shepherd, *Amazons and Warrior Women* (Harvester Press: Brighton, 1981), 193–8. Shepherd has in conversation with me revised his view of the authorship of this play (June 1988).

[4] Louise G. Clubb, '*The Virgin Martyr* and the *Tragedia Sacra*', *Renaissance Drama*, 7 (1964), 103–26. Hoy iii. 181–90. [5] Clubb, p. 106.

other martyrologies; and none of these Italian plays could possibly have been known to the dramatists, since neither of them understood Italian. Clubb asserts that after the Reformation, only Catholics wrote religious drama on post-biblical subjects, and that there were no saints' plays on the Elizabethan stage.[6] But Protestant authors like Buchanan did write sacred dramas, some with a strong political motivation— like his *Baptistes*, which was translated by Milton. And many of the exceptions on the Elizabethan stage involve Dekker and the Foxean tradition. *Sir Thomas Wyatt* and *The Whore of Babylon* both have constituents of a saint's play. *The Shoemakers' Holiday* is based on the story of Sts Crispin and Crispianus. *The Honest Whore* is an obvious Magdalene play, so it is no exaggeration to describe Dekker as an indefatigable Protestant hagiographer.

The *tragedia sacra* in Counter-Reformation Italy is said by Clubb to be written in *verso sciolto*, using strictly neoclassical forms and conventions.[7] But *The Virgin Martyr* ignores the classical unities, has no prologue or chorus, and presents acts of horror and violence on stage in full view of the audience. It is written in a mixture of prose and verse, like most Elizabethan plays.

Clubb says that the *tragedia sacra* often featured devils who are usually pitted against angelic adversaries.[8] But Dekker introduces devils in many other plays, such as *If This Be Not A Good Play* and *The Witch of Edmonton*, neither of which has any connection with Catholic tradition. Devils also appear in Marlowe's *Faustus*, which, with its scene of farce in the Vatican, is hardly a Catholic play. And if *tragedia sacra* sometimes used personified vices and virtues, so did many Elizabethan plays, such as *Faustus*.[9] Even if there were any generic resemblance it would not prove what Clubb is trying to prove: the seventeenth-century English play that seems to correspond most closely to Clubb's specifications for the *tragedia sacra* is *Samson Agonistes*. This is because Milton, like the Italian authors, followed classical models. It would be a little rash to deduce that *Samson Agonistes* must be a Catholic or Catholic-influenced play.

[6] Ibid. 106–7.   [7] Ibid. 108–10.   [8] Ibid. 111.   [9] Ibid.

Clubb lists certain examples of the *tragedia sacra* which told the story of St Dorothea, but they have two drawbacks: firstly, they were in Italian, which neither Dekker nor Massinger could read. No translations were made into English.[10] Secondly, none of them are extant, as she freely admits. The first, by Giambattista della Porta, was written some time before 1591 but never printed; and if, as Clubb says, Porta usually kept to a strict neo-classical form, this would make it very different from *The Virgin Martyr*. The second, by Orazio Persio, is also lost. And a third, by Tristano, was only published in 1642, when Dekker and Massinger were both dead.[11] Since Italian theatre companies did not tour in England, nor English ones in Italy, the practical opportunities for influence seem non-existent.

Clubb suggests that *The Virgin Martyr's* source may have been *XII Virgines et martyres*, by Paolo Emilio Santori, Archbishop of Urbino, a work which was dedicated to the Pope.[12] The subject of the play's sources is actually a very complicated one. The dramatists used as many as four sources, some Catholic, some—like Foxe—Protestant, and others pre-Reformation. But Santori was definitely not one of them, as it was unavailable in England in 1620, and reveals no independent links with the play that cannot be traced to much more accessible sources.[13]

According to Clubb, the early Italian *sacre rappresentazione* often transferred elements of one saint's life to another, as is done in *The Virgin Martyr*, but this practice is typical of all hagiography (and of dramaturgy in general, one could say).[14] Furthermore the stories of St Agnes and St Dorothea were already intermingled in *The Golden Legend*, and so the dramatists were merely continuing a process begun in their source.[15]

Clubb asserts that when *The Virgin Martyr* was written, censorship of Catholic books had been relaxed, because of the

---

[10] Mary A. Scott, *Elizabethan Translations from the Italian* (Vassar Semi-Centennial Series; The Riverside Press: Cambridge, Mass., 1916), contains a list of all known translations.   [11] Clubb, pp. 114–15.   [12] Ibid. 116.
[13] See my D.Phil. thesis, 'The Protestant Plays of Thomas Dekker' (Oxford, 1987), 129–48. Also my article on *The Virgin Martyr* forthcoming in the *Review of English Studies*.   [14] Clubb, p. 117.   [15] See my thesis, pp. 139–40.

negotiations for the Spanish Match.[16] Hoy echoes this, referring to the 'relaxed tolerance of the early 1620s (so different from the shrill hatred and fear of popery in the period following the Gunpowder-plot)'.[17] Relaxed tolerance seems a questionable description of a period which Jenny Wormald characterizes as one of 'war-fever' and when, as Margot Heinemann has pointed out, two London apprentices were lashed, one of them to death, for insulting the Spanish ambassador, Gondomar.[18] If Clubb is thinking of the decree of 2 August 1622 which ordered that 'from hope of favour by foreign Princes' there would now be fewer restrictions on recusants and those who possessed 'Popish books', not only was this decree issued two years after the play, but it referred to ecclesiastical censorship of printed books, which was quite separate from theatrical censorship.[19]

While the decree reflected the King's policy, it certainly did not indicate that the London public had become any friendlier towards Rome. Neither does it seem to have had any effect on the Church's censorship of books, which continued as before. A secret Catholic press was suppressed in Lancashire in 1621, and there were routine seizures by Customs of smuggled Catholic books in 1620, 1623, and 1626.[20] Moreover, the whole picture of theatrical censorship in this period is complicated by the fact that the same people may have been acting as patrons or censors (or both), depending on which theory we believe. There is no documentary evidence of Dekker ever working for a patron, but Massinger had connections with the Herbert family, and the 3rd Earl of Pembroke, Lord Chamberlain in 1620, was a literary patron as well as a supporter of Frederick and Elizabeth's cause.[21] However any such notions must remain speculative.

[16] Clubb, p. 119.   [17] Hoy, iii. 198.

[18] Jenny Wormald, 'James VI and I: Two Kings or One?', *History*, 68, no. 223 (June 1983), 199; Heinemann, p. 151.

[19] *Cal. State Pap. Dom.*, CXXXII, p. 437, entry 84.

[20] Helen C. White, *English Devotional Literature 1600–1640* (University of Wisconsin Studies in Language and Literature, 29; University of Wisconsin Press: Madison, 1931), 133–6.

[21] S. L. Adams, 'Foreign Policy and the Parliaments of 1621 and 1624', in *Faction and Parliament*, ed. Kevin Sharpe (OUP, 1978), 143.

It is probably more helpful to consider that *The Virgin Martyr* was written for the Red Bull, the playhouse outside the City in Clerkenwell which had for years specialized in putting on militant Protestant plays such as Wentworth Smith's *Hector of Germany, or the Palgrave Prime Elector*, written in 1612 at the time of the Palatine marriage. Dekker knew his public, and went for it.

Clubb argues that Massinger's name 'has often been linked with Popery'.[22] This is another complex subject, but the case for Massinger's Catholicism originated with the guesswork of his nineteenth-century editor Giffard, and has been questioned by many modern scholars. The arguments brought for it are variants on the one about Catholic sources, or the presentation of Catholic characters in a favourable light in certain plays. But using Catholic sources does not necessarily mean an author is Catholic: after all, both Foxe and Martin Luther used a lot of Catholic sources. There are various ways of using them. Thomas A. Dunn discusses these arguments, but concludes that Massinger was probably not converted to Catholicism.[23] Donald Lawless calls the theory 'plausible', but A. H. Cruickshank rejects it altogether.[24] The editors of Massinger's collected plays, Philip Edwards and Colin Gibson, say that the theory is 'not very convincing', and they bring no new evidence for it.[25]

While Clubb has asked some of the right questions, seeking to place *The Virgin Martyr* in a European context, and to find some contemporary significance in its choice of subject, her answers are altogether implausible. Even if we regard Massinger as taking the lead in *The Virgin Martyr* (which there is no reason at all to do), the Catholic case is still extremely weak. Hoy for instance writes: 'How, one may ask, did the author of *The Whore of Babylon* become involved in such a sophisticated theatrical project as *The Virgin*

[22] Clubb, p. 117.

[23] Thomas A. Dunn, *Philip Massinger: The Man and the Playwright* (Nelson and Sons Ltd.: Edinburgh, 1957), 49–51.

[24] Donald Lawless, *Philip Massinger and His Associates* (Ball State Monographs, 10; Ball State University: Muncie, Ind., 1967), 9. A. H. Cruickshank, *Philip Massinger* (Basil Blackwell: Oxford, 1920), 3.

[25] Introduction to *The Plays and Poems of Philip Massinger*, ed. Philip Edwards and Colin Gibson (5 vols.; OUP, 1976), vol. I, p. xlv.

Martyr, touched as it is with the wings of the Catholic baroque?'[26] A better question might be, how can we comprehend *The Virgin Martyr* unless we understand the highly developed tradition of Protestant historiography which underlies both this play and *The Whore of Babylon*?[27]

Both Hoy and Clubb avoid mentioning that there is a rival theory, at least equally strong, that several of Massinger's plays show support for the cause of the Protestant Elector Frederick. Not everybody who sympathized with this cause would necessarily have been a militant Protestant: some did so merely because Frederick was King James's son-in-law, and husband to the Princess Elizabeth, who was second in line to the English throne. Plays with such a stance had considerable audience appeal in London in the 1620s, and it is an interpretation which makes Massinger's collaboration with Dekker on *The Virgin Martyr* comprehensible.

The Massinger plays which have been interpreted in this way are *The Bondman* (1623), *The Maid of Honour* (1625), *The Emperour of the East* (1631), and *Believe As You List* (1631), all of which are discussed usefully by Heinemann.[28] Most of the evidence in the case of *The Bondman* was put forward by B. T. Spencer in his edition of the play.[29] Edwards and Gibson are cool towards this theory too, and it is no more open to absolute proof than the other.[30] But in the case of *Believe As You List*, Massinger's prologue drops a broad hint that we are to look for some contemporary parallel with the events of the plot:

> yf you finde what's Roman here,
> *Grecian*, or *Asiaticqe*, drawe to nere
> a late, & sad example, tis confest
> hee's but an English scholler at his best,

[26] Hoy, iii. 197.

[27] Apart from the Catholic interpretation, a further possibility was suggested in 1970 by Peter F. Mullany, 'Religion in Massinger and Dekker's *The Virgin Martyr*', *Komos*, II, no. 3 (Mar. 1970), 89–97. He argues that the play is completely lacking in sincerity, and offers only 'the pretence of serious concerns', being 'designed to entertain'. I draw the same conclusions about Mr Mullany's article.

[28] Heinemann, pp. 213–20.

[29] *The Bondman by Philip Massinger*, ed. B. T. Spencer (Princeton University Press: Princeton, 1932), introduction, pp. 38–43.

[30] Discussed by Edwards and Gibson, i. 302.

> a stranger to Cosmographie, and may erre
> in the cuntries names, the shape, & character
> of the person he presents . . .[31]

The first version of the play was rejected by the censor in January 1630/1, as containing 'dangerous matter', and the most likely explanation of this is that audiences would have seen in the story of a sad king's exile a reference to the Elector Palatine, deposed King of Bohemia.[32]

This can provide the basis for a consistent interpretation of this group of dramas and *The Virgin Martyr*. *The Bondman* was written in 1624 for the Lady Elizabeth's servants, otherwise known as the Queen of Bohemia's Company, the same company who had in 1620 put on *The Virgin Martyr*, a play they were reviving in 1624. The Queen of Bohemia's Company might well have wished to support the Bohemian cause, and it seems that Massinger in the later plays was essentially continuing the practices established earlier in *The Virgin Martyr*.

Massinger seems to have disliked all forms of religious persecution, as is suggested by Dunn, who points out that Massinger never satirizes the Puritans anywhere in his works.[33] This makes it believable that he collaborated on *The Virgin Martyr*, a play which is among other things a protest against persecution of the Protestants. Edwards and Gibson call it 'a most uncharacteristic work' for Massinger to have written.[34] Yet Edwards and Gibson believe that Massinger had collaborated with Fletcher on *Sir John Van Olden Barnavelt* in 1619.[35] This play is a candid depiction of contemporary events which names all its personages, and quite plainly takes the part of the Calvinist Maurice of Nassau against the Arminian Barnavelt who had been executed a few months before. If so then the evidence that Massinger was a Protestant is conclusive.

I would draw the final inference that Massinger was a Protestant, but not so militant a Protestant as Dekker, and

---

[31] Edwards and Gibson, iii. 305.   [32] Ibid. iii. 293, 298.
[33] Dunn, p. 191.   [34] Edwards and Gibson, vol. I, p. xix.
[35] Ibid. vol. I, p. xxi, also ii. 187. The attribution was first put forward by A. H. Bullen, who included it in *A Collection of Old Plays in IV Volumes* (Privately printed, 1882–5), vol. II.

that the apocalyptic framework of *The Virgin Martyr*, which has no parallels elsewhere in Massinger, reveals that Dekker, the senior dramatist, took the lead in its design.

The censor of 1620 certainly took a great interest in *The Virgin Martyr*, when it was licensed on 6 October: 'For new reforming the Virgin-Martyr for the Red Bull, 40s.' When additions were made to the play in 1624, the same difficulty was encountered: 'Received for the adding of a new scene to The Virgin-Martyr, 10s.'[36] G. E. Bentley pointed out that these charges were exceptionally high and must indicate that the censor had found a lot of work to do: the usual charge for a whole play was only 20s.[37]

The only other contemporary plays for which such a high fee was charged were *Keep the Widow Waking* by Dekker, Webster, Ford, and Rowley, and *The Dutchess of Suffolk* by Thomas Drue, both licensed in 1624. The former commented on a murder case *sub judice*, and its authors had to appear in Star Chamber.[38] *The Dutchess of Suffolk*, which took its plot from *Actes and Monuments*, has recently been discussed in detail by Heinemann, and also by Jerzy Limon.[39] Ostensibly portraying events set in the previous century, it makes an analogy between these and the plight of the Elector Palatine and his wife, the Princess Elizabeth, by then fleeing as refugees all over Europe. It even introduced a historical Elector Palatine in a very heroic role.[40] But since King James was, in January 1624 when the play was licensed, pursuing a policy of non-intervention in his son-in-law's cause, parts of it were suppressed.

Drue's play was surely imitating the technique established by earlier militant Protestant plays such as *Sir Thomas Wyatt* and *The Virgin Martyr*, which had drawn on Foxe for their plots or ideas. The assertion that *The Virgin Martyr* draws on

[36] *The Dramatic Records of Sir Henry Herbert*, ed. J. Quincy Adams (Cornell Studies in English, 3; Yale University Press: New Haven, 1917), 29.

[37] G. E. Bentley, *The Jacobean and Caroline Stage* (5 vols.; OUP, 1941–56), iii. 265.

[38] C. J. Sisson, *Lost Plays of Shakespeare's Age* (CUP: Cambridge, 1936), 80–124.

[39] Heinemann, pp. 203–13; Jerzy Limon, *Dangerous Matter: English Drama and Politics 1623–4* (CUP: Cambridge, 1986), 40–61.

[40] Thomas Drue, *The History of the Dutchess of Suffolk* (Imprinted by A. M. for Iasper Emery at the Flowerdeluce in Paules-Church-yard, 1631).

Foxe may appear somewhat surprising, but of the four sources the dramatists used, *Actes and Monuments* is certainly the most significant. Although St Dorothea has a very minor place in Foxe's vast work, the fact that she is there at all clears up the main problem that has dogged this play, the idea that Protestants regarded every saint's legend with absolute disbelief and disapproval. Foxe writes cautiously:

I haue oftentimes before complayned that the stories of Sayntes haue bene poudered and sawsed with diuers vntrue additions and fabulous inventions of men, who either of a superstitious deuotion, or of a subtill practise, haue so mingle mangled their stories and liues, that almost nothing remaineth in them simple and uncorrupt.[41]

It is during his account of the tenth and last persecution of the early Church that Foxe mentions Dorothea. He writes that this persecution was started by Diocletian and Maximinian, and carried on by Maximinus, the latter's son. It included a pogrom of Christians in Cappadocia. *The Virgin Martyr* is set in Caesarea, a city in Cappadocia, in the reign of Dioclesian and Maximinus, a fictional merger. Foxe states his source as Eusebius's *Ecclesiastical History*, which was regarded as reliable by Catholics and Protestants alike. The marginal heading reads, 'Cosmas, Damianus, Dorothea, with other martyrs'. The list runs: 'Erasmus, Bonifacius, Iuliana, Cosmas, Damianus, Basilinus with seuen others, Dorothea, Theophilus, Theodosia, Vitalis, Agricola, Acha, Philemon, Hireneus, Ianuarius, Festus'.[42]

Fourteen lines below Dorothea, Foxe mentions St Agnes, whose martyrdom is usually attributed to the same period of persecution. He tells her story in more detail a few pages later, but his bare account differs from those in Catholic martyrologies because he omits 'divers and sundry straunge miracles by her done' on the grounds that they are dubious.[43]

Foxe relates that Agnes, a Christian maiden of Rome, refused to sacrifice to the pagan gods even when threatened with torture and death. As a form of coercion, Agnes is displayed naked in a street where prostitutes solicit, but a young man who approaches her lustfully gets struck down by

---

[41] Foxe, i. 95.   [42] Ibid. i. 83.   [43] Ibid. i. 94.

fire from heaven. She prays and he is restored from this apparent death—whether real or not, Foxe does not say. Agnes is then executed, intransigent to the last.[44] This provided the outline of the events in Act IV, scene i of the play, and Foxe's ambiguity is carefully preserved. Dorothea herself says, when Sapritius is struck down, 'I can no myracles worke.'[45] Between miracles worked by a saint and miracles worked by heaven on a saint's behalf the path is a tricky one, but it is due to the influence of Foxe that the dramatists attempt to trace it in *The Virgin Martyr*. The way that the dramatists freely amalgamated the stories of Agnes and Dorothea (a combination first noted by Joseph M. Peterson in his study of the play) hints that they did not regard them with superstitious reverence, nor expect the audience to take the play literally.[46] They were aiming to present a type of story, recognizable as such, and open to contemporary and metaphorical interpretation.

In his preface to *Actes and Monuments*, entitled 'The vtilitie of this Story', Foxe says something which illuminates the dramatists' choice of subject in *The Virgin Martyr*, and how they expected their audience to regard it:

A comparison betweene the Martyrs of the Primitiue Church and of the latter Church.

I see no cause why the Martyrs of our tyme deserue any less commendation, then the other in the Primatiue Churche, which assuredly are inferiour vnto them in no poynt of prayse: whether we view the number of them that suffered, or greatnes of theyr tormentes, or theyre constancie in dying, or also consider the fruite that they brought to the amendment of posteritie, and encrease of the Gospell. They did water the truth with theyr bloud, that was newly springing vp: so these by theyr deathes restored it agayne, being sore decayed and fallen downe. They standing in the forewarde of the battell, did receaue the first encounter and violence of theyr enemies, and taught vs by that meanes to ouercome such tyranny: These with like courage agayne like old beaten souldiours

---

[44] Ibid. i. 94–5.   [45] *VM*, IV. i. 178.

[46] Joseph M. Peterson, *The Dorothea Legend*, Ph.D. thesis (University of Heidelberg, 1910), 53. The dramatists also incorporated elements of other saints' stories, which Peterson did not notice, including those of St Agatha and St Paul (see my thesis, pp. 136–8).

did winne the field in the rereward of the battayle. They like famous husbandmen of the world did sow the fields of the Church, that first lay vnmanured and wast: these with fatnes of their bloud did cause it to battell and fructifie. Would to God the fruite might be speedely gathered into the barne, which onely remayneth behinde to come.[47]

The analogy between the martyrs of the early Church and those of the Protestant Reformation was second nature to Elizabethans, who were brought up on Foxe's book. Foxe believed that history would include two great ages of persecution for the Church, each consisting of ten separate persecutions, and that the second age of persecution, which had begun with the precursors of the Reformation, was nearing its end in his own time. Foxe's metaphor, 'the fruite that they brought to the amendment of posteritie' could also supply a less literal interpretation of the miracle of St Dorothea, with which *The Virgin Martyr* concludes.

The whole Foxean tradition of drama depends on thinking by analogy, and this is derived from the nature of Protestant historiography itself. History was destined virtually to repeat itself, and these duplications were the key to understanding the events of the present age.

The fact that Foxe authenticates both Sts Dorothea and Agnes enabled the dramatists to use the material, but to find more details of the stories they went to pre-Reformation or contemporary Catholic books, quarrying them for materials to suit their purpose, not in a spirit of credulity. One of their sources was probably *Flos Sanctorvm*, an English Catholic work, by the brothers William and Edward Kinsman, which was more recent than any of the works suggested by Peterson, Jones-Davies, or other critics; it was also small and inexpensive. The first edition of Kinsman appeared in 1609 and it was reprinted in 1615. Another martyrology which they probably consulted was *The Golden Legend*, in Caxton's English translation, and there may have been one or two more whose influence was slight.[48]

The most important material they gathered from these works was the idea that there was a second motive in the mind of the judge who persecuted and tortured the young virgin saint: she had rejected his marital advances, or those of his

---

[47] Foxe, i. sig. *vi[v].   [48] See my thesis, pp. 132–45.

son. The sexual persecution of a female saint is an ancient and widely used motif, which in this case lent itself to allegorical use by the dramatists. Their Dorothea–Agnes preserves her integrity in preserving her virginity from pagan suitors. We have only to look back at Dekker's use of the image of the persecuted virgins of the Netherlands, in *The Whore of Babylon* and *The Magnificent Entertainment*, to see how naturally this could be used to represent any member of the True Church in distress.

In 1620 the Thirty Years' War had just broken out, but the crisis had been growing for the last ten years. In 1609 an insurrection in Bohemia had forced the Catholic Emperor officially to ratify religious freedom for the Utraquists, Lutherans, and Calvinists there. In 1617 Ferdinand of Styria, a Hapsburg and a Catholic, was elected King of Bohemia and soon after started to infringe the Protestants' rights. In May 1618 the Bohemian nobles rebelled, defenestrated Ferdinand's deputies in Prague, and took control of the country. In August 1619 they chose another King, the Calvinist Elector Palatine, and Frederick was crowned in November 1619. But at the same time Ferdinand was elected the new Holy Roman Emperor, to the disappointment of those who had hoped for a Protestant to win. Ferdinand immediately started a campaign to subdue the rebellion spreading in the Empire, making war between him and Frederick for the Bohemian crown inevitable.

Without British support not only Bohemia but the Palatinate as well would soon fall to Catholic forces, opening up the Rhine for a Spanish campaign into the United Provinces when the Truce of Antwerp expired there in April 1621. Militant Protestants saw this as the resumption of the great Protestant–Catholic war which they had been waging until 1604 against Spain. Even the Archbishop of Canterbury, George Abbott, saw the outbreak of this war in apocalyptic terms, expressing his view in a letter.[49] An alliance of militant Protestant powers would destroy the forces of Babylon at last. Many clergy expressed their support for Frederick's cause by leading public prayers for him as King of Bohemia, and as a result they were disciplined.[50]

---

[49] Quoted in ch. 3 above.   [50] S. L. Adams, 'Protestant Cause', p. 290.

For, despite the alliances he had made in 1612, King James refused to go to war. Gratified though he would have been at his son-in-law's promotion to royal rank by a more conventional procedure, he disapproved of the Bohemians' action in deposing their monarch and put the interest of monarchy before all else. It was a case of not supplying or trusting other princes' rebels. Moreover, he was pursuing an alliance with Spain, which he hoped would combat 'a creeping disposition to make popular states and alliances to the disadvantage of monarchy', to quote the instructions given to the English ambassador who was negotiating the Spanish Match.[51]

So there were several political issues at question here: the choice between interventionism and non-interventionism; between confessional alliance and others which seemed more pragmatic; and the conflict between James's absolutism and 'popular states and alliances', represented by the United Provinces and now also by Frederick, the elected King of Bohemia.

Public interest in the crisis generated, and was generated by, a rapidly increasing spate of pamphlets and newsletters in 1618–20; indeed the crisis stimulated the appearance of the first corantoes, forerunners of the modern newspaper. One of 1619 was entitled *Trovbles in Bohemia and Diuers Other Kingdomes, Procured by the Diuellish Practises of State-meddling Iesvites*.[52] In the same year appeared an official statement from Bohemia, translated by John Harrison, *The Reasons which Compelled the States of Bohemia to Reiect the Archduke Ferdinand &c. & Inforced Them to Elect a New King*. It asserted the legality of Frederick's election, firstly because the Bohemian Crown was electoral and not hereditary, and secondly on the grounds that Ferdinand had used bribery and threat to get elected in 1617, and that he had subsequently

[51] S. L. Adams, 'Foreign Policy', p. 141.

[52] Trans. out of the French (anon., London, 1619). See also *Exemplar Litterarum* (two Latin newsletters; n.p., Sept. and Oct. 1618); *The Last Newes from Bohemia . . . Wherein is Related all the Passages that have Happened since the Elector Palatine of the Rhine was Elected and Crowned King of Bohemia* (anon., n.p., 1620); *Articles of the League Made betweene Fredericke, King of Bohemia . . . and . . . Gabriel, Prince of Hungaria* (anon., n.p., 1620); *The Declaration and Information of the High and Puissant King of Bohemia, against the Vniust Mandates Published in the Name of the Emperour . . .* (anon., n.p., 1620); and *A Plaine Demonstration of the Unlawful Succession of Ferdinand II* (anon., 1620).

violated the terms of his election by refusing to recognize the Protestants' rights: an anti-absolutist argument that would have enraged James. It said that Ferdinand's aim was 'to roote out the true Religion in those partes' and accused him of persecution: he 'no sooner entred the government of the country then he persecuted those of the Religion . . . and exercised such crueltyes vpon them, as might have converted a very barbarous education to a gentleness of nature, by beholding, or but by hearing only of the hatefulnes of the persecution.'[53]

An echo of this last passage may be suspected in Theophilus's speech in the play (a Dekker speech):

> Haue I inuented tortures to teare Christians,
> To see but which, could all that feeles Hels torments
> Haue leaue to stand aloofe heere on earths stage,
> They would be mad till they againe descended,
> Holding the paines most horrid, of such soules,
> May-games to those of mine, has this my hand
> Set downe a Christians execution
> In such dire postures, that the very hangman
> Fell at my foote dead hearing but their figures.[54]

Another, extremely learned, pamphlet which appeared in 1620, *Bohemiae Regnum Electiuum*, provided a legal defence of the Bohemians' traditional right to elect and depose their kings. It takes examples from nine hundred years of Bohemian history.[55]

Militant Protestants feared that the Hapsburg dynasty was aiming at the total eradication of the True Church. The twentieth-century historian C. V. Wedgwood says of Ferdinand, 'He desired the political and economic destruction of all those who had been concerned in the revolt, the extinction of national privileges and the extermination of the Protestants.'[56] When the Jesuit-educated Emperor got control of Bohemia in 1621, he did abolish electoral monarchy, together with the religious freedom of Utraquists, Lutherans,

---

[53] *The Reasons which Compelled the States of Bohemia to Reiect the Archduke Ferdinand &c. & Inforced Them to Elect a New King*, trans. John Harrison (Dort, 1619), 1, 2–4, 5, 13.   [54] *VM*, II. ii. 66–74.

[55] *Bohemiae Regnum Electiuum* (anon., n.p., 1620).

[56] C. V. Wedgwood, *The Thirty Years War* (Jonathan Cape: London, 1938).

and Calvinists. There were large-scale executions and con-
fiscations of property to enforce this.[57]

The Virgin Martyr portrays the persecution of Christians
under the Roman Empire. Both Catholics and Protestants
regarded the Holy Roman Empire of the Hapsburgs as the
successor to the ancient Roman Empire in a revived though
interrupted line. This was no invention of the dramatists' but
an assumption taken for granted by their contemporaries. The
German Emperors had adopted the double-headed eagle of the
later Roman Empire as their symbol and the Roman eagle was
an instantly understood symbol of the H.R. Empire in
sixteenth- and seventeeth-century political pamphlets on the
Continent, both Catholic and Protestant. In a typical
example, from Germany in 1621, an eagle symbolizes
Ferdinand, while a classical Roman column and laurel wreath
represent the Empire.[58]

In the opening scene of *The Virgin Martyr* exactly these
symbols have been used, so that the audience can be quite
sure from the start what the play is about. The Emperor
Dioclesian makes a ceremonial state entrance and the stage
directions specify, 'Antoninus *and* Macrinus *carrying the
Emperors Egles*, Dioclesian *with a guilt laurell on his head.*'[59]
Even the choice of the scene, Caesarea, is a useful one for this
purpose, as the Hapsburg Emperors were quite customarily
referred to as Caesar.[60]

While there was nothing at all esoteric about this idea, it did
have a further connection with apocalyptic theology. Protestants regarded the Holy Roman Empire as a secular arm of the
Church of Rome, and in *The Whore of Babylon*, the second of
the Empress's minion kings represents the Empire. George
Giffard interpreted the sea beast of Rev. 13 as being the Holy
Roman Empire, and the land beast as the papacy.[61] He was

---

[57] Wedgwood, 142–3.

[58] Wolfgang Harms, *Illustrierte Flugblatter aus den Jahrhunderten der Reformation* (Kunstsammlungen der Veste Coburg: Coburg, 1983), nos. 52, 64, 76.

[59] *VM*, I. i. 118–19.

[60] *Exemplar Litterarum* refers to Ferdinand as 'S. Caes. M.tem.' Surius' *De
Probatis Sanctorum Historiis* (7 vols.; Cologne, 1571–8), a possible source for the
play suggested by Koeppel and Jones-Davies, says on its title-page that it is printed at
'Coloniae Agrippinae' and 'Cum priuilegio . . . CAESAREAE Maiestatis'.

[61] Giffard, pp. 246, 255.

probably influenced by Bullinger, who had identified the sea beast as 'the olde, and the newe, Roman Empire'.[62] The fact that the Holy Roman Empire had been ruled since 1438 by the Hapsburg dynasty, who were also Kings of Spain and held the title of 'Catholic monarch', encouraged the Protestant view that Rome was a single beast with many heads. In the play there are two simultaneous Emperors, Dioclesian and Maximinus, and this could provide to a Protestant audience an image of the allied dominions of the Hapsburg dynasty, threatening a Catholic universal monarchy.

Apart from the obvious analogy between the Roman Empires past and present, there is another reason why a play about St Dorothea would have been particularly applicable to the crisis in Germany. The cult of St Dorothea had been centred in the Holy Roman Empire since the Middle Ages, particularly in the areas of the Rhine, Saxony, and Bohemia.[63] This is evident from the way that so many versions of the Dorothea story, including the one in *The Golden Legend*, originate in Germany.[64] Whether the dramatists could have known this, and whether they could have expected even the more learned and travelled members of their audience to be aware of it is a separate point, but one small and specific clue about St Dorothea's association with Bohemia was within their reach, and as so often John Foxe provides the vital link.

English reaction to the events in Bohemia, and the warmth of militant Protestants' interest in it, was greatly influenced by Foxe as well as by Frederick's tie with the British royal family. Most of what people knew about Bohemia would have been drawn from *Actes and Monuments*, in which Foxe gives a prominent place to the history of Bohemia and its native religious reformers.

In Foxe's interpretation, the religious reforms which took place in Bohemia at the beginning of the fifteenth century anticipated the Protestant Reformation. Foxe saw the influence of Wycliff as the decisive force in the Utraquist movement of Jan Hus, and argued that this in turn influenced the Reformation in Germany and England. He chronicles the

---

[62] Bullinger, pp. 367–8.
[63] *Biblioteca Sanctorum* (12 vols.; Istituto Giovanni XXIII, Rome, 1964), iv. 825.
[64] See my thesis, pp. 138, 144.

history of Bohemia in the fifteenth century in great detail, and the series of wars against the papacy and the Emperors in which it struggled for its religious freedom. He gives detailed accounts of the careers of Hus, of Jerome of Prague, and of Zisca, the Bohemian national leader. Most editions also have large pictures of Hus and of Jerome being burnt alive as heretics.[65] All three were included in Foxe's calendar of saints, 'John Hus, martyr' on May 2, 'Zisca, confessor' on February 5, and 'St Hierome of Prague, martyr' on June 1, a high festival: the same distinction granted to Canmer, Latimer, and Ridley.

In mapping out his scheme of history, Foxe often refers to 'the tyme of Iohn Wickliffe, & Iohn Husse', a very significant point when the fifth age, that of reformation, had its beginning. This is why the name of the Bohemian John Hus occurs so frequently throughout the book, even on its first page. In supporting the Bohemian cause, the English could feel that they were continuing an old tradition of religious solidarity.

In his account of the Hussite movement, Foxe translates the original document sent by Archbishop Conradus of Prague to the University of Prague in 1413/14, declaring that Hus was a heretic and that the entire University must publicly disavow his and Wyclif's doctrines. This is followed by the declaration which the University drew up in response: it refused to comply with the Archbishop's terms, defended Hus, and demanded 'that the kingdome of Boheme remain in his former rites, liberties and customes' in matters of religion.[66] This document, the official charter of the Hussite movement, is taken, as Foxe states in the margin, from Johannes Cochlaeus's *Historia Hussitarum* (1549), a Catholic work.

If any readers of Foxe had been interested enough in Bohemia to consult Cochlaeus as well, they would have found that the full title of the document (which Foxe uncooperatively left out) was: 'Consilium pro parte Hus & sibi adhaerentium, datum & exhibitum in congretatione Cleri, in die S. Dorotheae, Anno Domini M.CCCC.XIII'.[67] If the Hussites had declared their religious autonomy on

---

[65] Foxe, i. 588–695; illustrations, pp. 624, 636.

[66] Foxe, i. 589.

[67] Johannes Cochlaeus, *Historia Hussitarum* (Bohemia, 1549), i. 32.

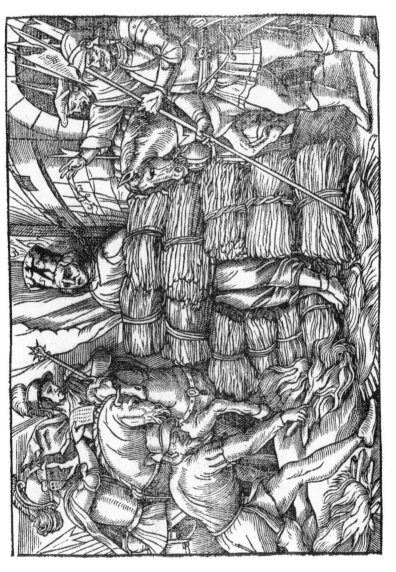

3. The Martyrdom of Jan Hus, from John Foxe's *Actes and Monuments*, i (1583 Edition)

4. The Martyrdom of Bishop Jerome of Prague, from John Foxe's *Actes and Monuments*, i (1583 Edition)

St Dorothea's day, St Dorothea could be taken as a symbol of Bohemian religious independence. Was the dramatists' choice of subject just an inspired chance, a one in three hundred and sixty-five coincidence? Cochlaeus was obviously available in England, since Foxe drew on it, and there were other copies in circulation.[68] This is an intriguing, but elusive, aspect of the play's allegory, which is not easy to prove.

In October 1619 the news that Frederick had accepted the Crown of Bohemia reached England, and Chamberlain reports that James 'did not allow of the Palatines election, but esteemed it rather a faction, which he would in no wise favour nor further, and that his subjects were as deere to him as his children, and therfore wold not embarke them in an unjust and needlesse quarrell'.[69] If he feared that his own subjects might assume this dangerous right to depose their monarchs once he lent it any countenance, his fear was a perfectly logical one. For the militant Protestants, it was one more experience of political frustration.

In January 1620 Frederick's ambassador from Bohemia, Achatius von Dohna, arrived in England to press for aid in defending Bohemia and the Palatinate. At the same time the Spanish ambassador Gondomar arrived on his second embassy to promote the Spanish Match. In February 1620 Andrew Gray, a Scot, arrived from Bohemia and tried to levy volunteers to fight for Frederick's cause.[70] Dohna and his English agent Abraham Williams were hoping for an official campaign financed through a Parliament, but James refused to call a Parliament. So Dohna, with Abbott's support, launched a series of appeals for loans, first in March to the City of London, and then in the summer extended this to the whole of England. The response was disappointing because many supporters of the cause held back, fearing that the private loan would prevent a Parliament being called.[71]

In June 1620 the Spanish forces of Flanders, commanded by Spinola, advanced on the Palatinate, while those of the

[68] See my thesis, p. 158.
[69] *Letters of John Chamberlain*, ed. H. E. McClure (2 vols.; Philadelphia Amen Philosophical Society; Lancaster Press: Philadelphia, 1939), ii. 226.
[70] Ibid. ii. 290, 295, 300.
[71] S. L. Adams, 'Protestant Cause', p. 290.

Emperor Ferdinand marched on Bohemia. Spain's active alliance with Ferdinand could no longer be doubted, but James still refused to drop his *entente* with Spain, hoping to bring about a peaceful solution. In July he permitted a tiny force of two thousand volunteers commanded by Sir Horace Vere to go to the Palatinate, in response to the appeals of Princess Elizabeth and of the Prince of Orange, who feared the capture of the Rhine. Vere succeeded in the very difficult task of occupying the fortresses of Frankenthal and Mannheim, where they were soon surrounded by Spinola's invading force and cut off. The force held out under siege for over two years, receiving no supply from England. James's indifference to them was aggravated by Buckingham's hostility, resulting from a personal grudge the favourite had conceived towards Vere.[72]

Literary involvement in the crisis took many forms. There were sermons, such as Thomas Gataker's *Sparke toward the Kindling of Sorrow for Sion* (1621), and poems, such as Chapman's *Pro Vere, Autumni Lachrymae*, about Vere's doomed enterprise. The latter pleaded with the King not to let Protestant hopes perish 'In a Dutch Cytadell':

> For who can
> Resist God, in the Right of such a Man?
>
> .   .   .   .
>
> But thou hast now a kind and Pious King,
> That will not suffer his immortall Spring
> To die vntimely; if in him it lye,
> To lend him Rescue . . .[73]

Chapman's use of the word 'Dutch' to mean German highlights the lack of a clear distinction between Dutch and Deutsch at this time. The Anglo-German alliance could be seen as an extension of the Anglo-Dutch alliance militant Protestants had been supporting for so long.

John Harrison translated such pamphlets as *A Declaration of the Causes for which Wee Frederick . . . have Accepted the Crowne of Bohemia*, aimed at the English public. And the Elector's agents, Dohna and Williams, are thought to have

---

[72] *DNB*, xx. 329, entry under Villiers.
[73] *The Poems of George Chapman*, ed. P. B. Bartlett (OUP, 1941), 341.

organized a propaganda campaign for his cause in England in the middle of the year, promoting such productions as the anonymous dialogue, *The Popes Complaint to His Minion Cardinals against the Good Successe of the Bohemians and Their Generall Proceedings*, very comparable in its technique to Scott's *Vox Populi*, which appeared in several editions in 1620. Adams believes that the latter was written in 1619 and printed under Dohna's aegis, while Scott's later pamphlet, *Vox Spiritus, or Sir Walter Rawleighs Ghost*, was both written and printed as part of Dohna's campaign.[74] Of course, the term 'propaganda' would not have been used at this time: the Jacobeans would simply have called it 'news'. But a campaign to raise money and volunteers does go a long way to answering the question 'What was the point in stirring up public opinion when people had no votes?' Some of them had money, and most of them had arms and legs.

The Virgin Martyr, which was licensed in October 1620, was probably written in the summer of 1620 and inspired by Frederick's cause. For the stage, as well as the press and the pulpit, to make its contribution would have been quite normal. Perhaps it was a German, or somebody who had visited Germany in the retinue of the Elector and his wife, who suggested to the dramatists this subject which is so intimately connected with the German Empire and with Bohemia in particular. There are many features of *The Virgin Martyr* which make it recognizable as a propagandist play. The violence of its subject-matter is remarkable, and Dekker very rarely presents torture or killing on stage—never without some strong reason. In many ways *The Virgin Martyr* is an extremely emotive and manipulative work, skilfully calculated to arouse pity, fear, and anger in its audience.

Atrocity propaganda, the familiar accompaniment of all modern warfare, had already reached a high level during the Thirty Years' War. Pamphlets circulated in England with titles like *A Relation of the Bloody Execution at Prague* (1621); they were often illustrated with all the details of

---

[74] S. L. Adams, 'Captain Thomas Gainsford, the *Vox Spiritus* and the *Vox Populi*', *Bulletin of the Institute of Historical Research*, XLIX (May 1976), 141–4.

tongues being cut out, bleeding stubs, and so on. In the play the degree of violence is carefully built up: it begins with Theophilus's descriptions of torture, goes on to show him murdering his daughters, then proceeds to a victim who is tortured before her execution. The last victim, Theophilus himself, is tortured to death in full view of the audience. The intention is to arouse pity and terror, not for mere sensation or catharsis, but to galvanize the audience into active support for the Protestant cause in Europe at that very moment. Such a technique makes entering the war seem a moral obligation, less an act of violence than one of opposition to violence. There is also the very good argument that one's own country may be next on the list for such treatment. In Act V, just before his conversion, Theophilus reads out a plan of the atrocities which he is carrying out for the Roman Emperors in Great Britain: hot irons, people buried alive, mutilations, and so on.[75]

To say that *The Virgin Martyr* possesses such an aspect is not to deny that it is a good play. Hagiography and propaganda for a religious-political cause are very closely related activities, and it would be foolish to deny that there can be good hagiographical art.

Central to this propagandist technique is the threat of rape to which Dorothea is subjected. Her refusal of Antoninus's legitimate advances, rich and great though he is, symbolizes the refusal of the True Church to enter into non-confessional alliances (such as the detested Spanish Match for Prince Charles). It is followed by a series of violent assaults, in which she is only protected by a miraculous power. The rape metaphor can seem in some respects rather distasteful. To define fully why it is objectionable to exploit the heroine's virginity and attractiveness by having her threatened with rape as Dorothea is in Act IV would entail analysing the whole tradition and significance of the St Agnes legend—a very interesting subject, but rather major to go into here. It is, of course, in no way peculiar to this play, or to these authors, and in fact Shakespeare uses it in *Pericles*. The playwrights would not have used it without a serious metaphorical

---

[75] *VM*, V. i. 1–45.

purpose in mind: as in the allegorical entertainment given for Leicester in 1586, virginity is a symbol of autonomy.

As long ago as 1606 Dekker had used the same metaphor for the United Provinces:

Those seuenteene Dutch Virgins of *Belgia*, (that had Kingdoms to theyr dowries, and were worthy to be courted by Nations) are now no more Virgins: the Souldier hath deflowered them, and robd them of theyr Mayden honor: Warre hath still vse if their noble bodyes, and discouereth theyr nakedness like prostituted Strumpets. Famine hath dried vp the fresh bloud in theyr cheekes, whilest the Pestilence digd vp theyr Fields, and turned them into Graues.[76]

So automatic was this metaphor in Reformation thinking that the German Lutheran city of Magdeburg which held out so long in the 1540s against the Catholic forces of the Emperor came to regard its name—originally Magataburg—as meaning Virgin-City, and changed the spelling accordingly. It placed over its gate a statue of a young girl holding a virgin's wreath, and the words 'Who will take it?' When the city fell to Tilly's army in 1631 during the Thirty Years' War, the tradition took an ironic twist: Magdeburg was known as the Protestant Lucretia.[77]

In the course of Act IV, a British slave is summoned by Sapritius to rape Dorothea, but he refuses contemptuously.[78] This bold, heroic figure, who proclaims he would do almost anything for liberty, is the dramatists' invention, and he is put there to involve the audience as much as possible. It is an appeal to their national moral pride which, it must be said, stoops to rather an obvious level in comparison with the rest of the play. It is over-direct, and there are some episodes in *Sir John Van Olden Barnavelt* which introduce British characters in a very similar way.[79]

Simon Shepherd has written that *The Virgin Martyr*'s 'consistent attack on ritual and idolatry is in line with any Protestant play'.[80] This is best seen in Dorothea's debate with Christeta and Caliste when they come to convert her to paganism. The idols made of gold, silver, brass, and wood

---

[76] Grosart, *The Seanen Deadly Sinnes* ii. 9.   [77] Wedgwood, pp. 242, 289.
[78] *VM*, IV. i. 126–60.   [79] Bullen, ii. 234.   [80] Shepherd, p. 195.

which Dorothea ridicules would have been easily recognized by a Protestant audience as images in churches, worshipped by the superstitious and ignorant.[81] Dorothea reminds the sisters that the temples of Flora and Venus are run like brothels:

> Yet *Venus* whom you worship was a whore,
> *Flora* the Foundresse of the publike Stewes,
> And has for that her sacrifice . . .[82]

It is unmistakably aimed at the Whore of Babylon.

When Dorothea has triumphed in the debate, she, Christeta, and Caliste refuse to burn incense in front of Jupiter's image; instead, they spurn it and spit on it. In the Protestant mind, incense had become an abhorrent symbol of Roman mystagogy and the sacrificial mass. The playwrights specify that the priest of Jupiter should enter carrying an image and 'Censors', and if the Red Bull production had burned real Catholic incense, that would have aroused some very precise associations in the audience.

The dramatists were not very sympathetic to the idea of relics either. They specify that Dorothea's body should

> Be cast forth with contempt in some high way,
> And be to Vultures and to Dogs a prey.[83]

This does not happen to Dorothea in any of the sources: no Catholic writer would have included something that was such bad news for the relic business. The Elector Frederick, on his arrival in Prague as King in 1619, set about destroying all the relics there, together with the images in churches.[84]

Propaganda has to be careful not to make its picture so gloomy that the fight appears to be over. The play carefully balances fear and hope, a purpose for which the Dorothea story is ideally suited. At the beginning of the last Act, when Dorothea has been executed, Theophilus is found in his study reviewing and planning the continued persecution of the Christians, i.e. the Protestants. When Dorothea's angel visits him, Theophilus is immersed in his horrible plans, his own will intent on them, but the appearance of the miraculous

---

[81] *VM*, III. i. 117–21.   [82] *VM*, III. i. 139–41.
[83] *VM*, IV. iii. 193–4.   [84] Wedgwood, p. 120.

fruit tempts him to taste of it and, as if by a symbolic reversal of original sin, he is overtaken by grace and converted. The forces of heaven and hell, represented by Harpax and Angelo, struggle over him, but Harpax is defeated. This repentance seems to dramatize the Calvinist doctrine of irresistible grace. The source-story had been accepted by Catholics as orthodox, but so had the biblical texts used by Calvin to prove all his teachings. The writers have ingeniously proved a Protestant doctrine out of material accepted by both Catholics and Protestants. The sophisticated archaism of this Dekker scene, with its medieval touches, should not distract us from its theological statement. The conversion of the persecutor by irresistible grace is the fittest possible conclusion for a Protestant propaganda play.

Before he dies, Theophilus releases two shiploads of Christians who escape as refugees.[85] In 1620 there were already Protestant refugees fleeing from areas threatened by the advancing Catholic forces, along the Rhine and in Bohemia. Hope and fear are mingled in the play's conclusion. Dorothea's triumph in spiritual terms is weighed against a renewed consolidation of the Imperial Roman forces. Dioclesian marries his daughter to Maximinus, and with this even closer bond between them, they increase their determination to stamp out Christianity totally:

> The persecution that is here begun,
> Through all the world with violence shall run.[86]

It is the strongest possible argument for intervention.

In late November 1620, a month after *The Virgin Martyr* was licensed for its first performance, news reached London that the unaided Frederick had been defeated by the Catholics in the Battle of the White Mountain outside Prague, and had fled Bohemia together with his wife. Public anger and disappointment were severe, and in December of 1620 the famous proclamation against 'lavish speech' was issued, indicating that presumptuous criticisms of royal policies had reached royal ears.[87]

[85] *VM*, V. ii. 68–81.
[86] *VM*, V. ii. 241–2.
[87] *Cal. State Pap. Dom.*, CXVIII, p. 202.

But Frederick's cause was not abandoned for many years, and *The Virgin Martyr* remained, for political or artistic reasons (or both), extremely successful for some time after this. When it was printed in 1622 it immediately ran into a second impression, and the title-page says that it has been 'DIVERS times publickely Acted with great Applause, By the seruants of his Maiesties Reuels'.[88] So a second company had taken it up.

In July 1624 an additional scene for it was licensed, though never printed. This indicates that *The Virgin Martyr* was revived in the summer of 1624, when Middleton's *Game at Chess* was put on by the King's Men. We have no way of knowing what was in the additional scene, or even whether it was by Dekker, but it probably responded in some way to the changing political situation, for by the summer of 1624, it began to seem that England would enter the European war after all. Buckingham was now determined to declare war on Spain, but Parliament refused to finance his plans, since these were all 'either militarily, politically or financially absurd'.[89] Parliament wished for a diversionary attack on Flanders, carried out jointly by Britain and the Dutch United Provinces in order to force Spinola to withdraw from the Palatinate. In essence, this was a revival of the Anglo-Dutch alliance that Dekker had always supported (and which he in a sense embodied).

Two years later, in 1626, *The Virgin Martyr* was performed again, this time in Protestant Germany. The touring company of John Green and Robert Browne travelled to Dresden in 1626 and there between May and December put on a dozen plays, including one called 'The Martyr Dorothea'. This has long been identified with *The Virgin Martyr*, not unreasonably since no other English play about St Dorothea has ever been written.[90] Not only would the story have been familiar to a German audience, but its propaganda aspect would have been

[88] Bowers, iii. 365.

[89] S. L. Adams, 'Foreign Policy', p. 139. Roger Lockyer, *Buckingham: The Life and Political Career of George Villiers, First Duke of Buckingham* (Longman Group Ltd: London, 1981), 190 is incorrect in stating that the 1624 Parliament wanted an attack on Spain.

[90] Alfred Harbage, *Annals of English Drama 975–1700*, rev. by S. Schoenbaum (Methuen: London, 1964), 206–7.

timely and suitable. By 1626 England had entered the war, but it was a desperately low point for the Protestant cause. Since the loss of Bohemia and the Palatinate, the Protestant Christian IV of Denmark had been defeated by Tilly and Wallenstein, and large parts of northern Germany were being overrun and laid waste. Dresden in Saxony was a Protestant city whose inhabitants hated the Imperial forces, and celebrated Protestant victories with a public holiday; but the Elector of Saxony had consistently supported the Emperor in the belief that this maintained the constitution.[91] A performance of *The Virgin Martyr* might well have expressed an English hope that Saxony would translate its sympathy for the Protestant cause into action.

Another play performed by Green's company in Dresden at this time could also have had a propaganda purpose. Entitled 'The King of Denmark and the King of Sweden', it is usually identified with the lost play *Gustavus King of Swethland* which was attributed to Dekker when it was entered on the Stationers' Register on 29 June 1660.[92] Martin Butler, assuming a date of 1632, relates the title to Gustavus Adolphus and suggests that it was 'presumably a play on Gustavus's recent Continental victories against the Catholics'.[93] However, Gustavus Adolphus did not land in Germany until June 1630, and did not win any victories until late the following year. So unless we abandon the link with Green's tour, we must assume that this play concerned the earlier King Gustavus of Sweden, Gustavus Vasa, who also happens to be a Protestant hero. In the previous century, he had brought the Reformation to Sweden, and had been elected King, winning Sweden's freedom from Danish domination. Gustavus's struggle with Christian II of Denmark provides a subject that fits the records of Green's company, and which could have provided an excellent historical analogy on which to base a propaganda play for Frederick's cause in Bohemia. There is no doubt that plays which supported the

[91] Wedgwood, p. 302.   [92] Jones-Davies, ii. 413.

[93] Martin Butler, *Theatre and Crisis 1632–1642* (CUP: Cambridge, 1984), 235. The date of 1632, or pre-1632, has been given in various reference books simply because that was the year that Dekker died. Pre-1626 would be a more accurate date. Dekker seems to have stopped writing plays around that time.

Elector's cause continued to be written and performed in England well into the 1630s: Butler, who notes that the Caroline theatre did not express 'monolithically and un-critically the point of view of the King',[94] shows that there was an upsurge of this theatrical lobbying in 1635–7 when Frederick's son visited the English Court.

The Virgin Martyr was reprinted in 1631, 1651, and 1661, and it was given two theatrical revivals at the Drury Lane Theatre in 1661 and 1668.[95] In 1715 an adaptation by Benjamin Griffin was performed at Richmond and so *The Virgin Martyr* remained popular for a century, during which time its Protestant motive was probably well understood. In 1715, at the accession of King George I, Griffin's production of *The Virgin Martyr* might have been a suitable way of celebrating the arrival of a German, thoroughly Protestant King, who was the grandson of Frederick and Elizabeth of Bohemia. George I's mother, Sophia, had been Frederick's daughter, and it is possible that a surviving reputation in 1715 still associated this play with the Bohemian cause.

To categorize *The Virgin Martyr* as a propagandist play is in a sense misleading, since the terms 'propaganda' and 'hagiography' suppose that politics and religion are separate spheres, a notion that the dramatists did not share. Even to class *The Virgin Martyr* as a tragedy (as does its 1622 title-page) is misleading, since it is concerned with the triumph, not the fall of its subject. Perhaps we should call it a *tragoedia apocalyptica*. Nevertheless, the term propaganda is useful since it reminds us that the play is an event in a continuum of other events, active as cause, not only as effect, and in this case the dramatists were deliberately trying to maximize that effect.

While the propaganda aspect of the play would have been its most observable feature to its original audience, a modern reader may find *The Virgin Martyr* more interesting as an example of how militant Protestants of the Jacobean era engaged in a process of self-mythologizing. This is true of all their best plays, including *The Whore of Babylon*, and *The*

---

[94] Martin Butler, 'Entertaining the Palatine Prince: Plays on Foreign Affairs 1635–1637', *English Literary Renaissance*, 13, no. 1 (Winter 1983), 323.
[95] The performance is recorded by Samuel Pepys: see Hoy, iii. 193.

Virgin Martyr is among the most artistically successful of the Foxean dramas. It provides us with an insight, not only into their political frustration, but into how they viewed themselves and the world through their own historiographical myths. Dorothea, like any Foxean heroine, defies secular authority, and her clash with absolutism betrays the tensions inherent in militant Protestant beliefs.

6

Match Me In London and the Spanish Match

Match Me In London was probably written in or around 1621, soon after *The Virgin Martyr*.[1] One clue to this date is to be found in the play's title. *Match Me In London* is an odd name for a play set in Spain. One meaning is suggested by the play's last lines:

> KING. Come *Tormiella*, well were that City blest,
> That with but, Two such women should excell,
> But there's so few good, th'ast no Paralell.[2]

It could be Tormiella's example of fidelity that London is being invited to match, i.e. to emulate. But there are two other meanings that an audience could have noticed much earlier. One is 'Marry me in London rather than in Spain.' The word 'match', particularly in a play concerned with Spain and with enforced marriages, would immediately have suggested the Spanish Match, the great issue of the times.

A third possible meaning might have occurred to the audience when the King of Spain first enters in Act I. Like King Alphonso in *If This Be Not A Good Play*, the King of Spain in *Match Me In London* is being used as a vehicle for criticizing King James. In certain scenes he is a personal caricature, and the title can be taken to mean, 'Find a King like this in London.'

Although the play was described as 'An Old Play' when it was relicensed for the Cockpit in August 1623 by Herbert, one thing proves that it cannot have been written before 1619.[3] It is scattered with references to Admirals. Tormiella's father Malevento is made a Vice-Admiral by the King of

---

[1] Hoy, iii. 148. Allison's *Bibliographical Catalogue*, p. 30 also gives 1620–3, though Jones-Davies, ii. 392 suggests a date as early as 1611–13.
[2] *MML*, V. v. 86–8.   [3] J. Q. Adams, p. 25.

Spain, as a reward for condoning the King's seizure of her:

> KING. *Andrada Maleuento* we make you
> Vice-Admirall of our Nauy.
> CORDO. Oh spitefull Comedy, he's not a Courtier of halfe
> an houres standing, and he's made a Vice already.[4]

This makes him the second Admiral in the play, since Valasco, the King's son-in-law, is also an Admiral and is frequently referred to as such.[5] This peculiar bandying of the title of Admiral in a play which includes neither ships, ports, nor battles, was a joke at the expense of the royal favourite, Buckingham, who had been made Lord Admiral of England in January 1619. This was the only time the office of Admiral changed hands in King James's reign.

Buckingham's appointment as Admiral epitomized all that was worst in royal favouritism. The previous Admiral, the aged Lord Nottingham, had commanded the fleet at the time of the Armada victory, and taken a leading part in the Cadiz expedition; by contrast, Buckingham was only twenty-six and his nautical experience consisted of a Channel crossing.[6] The King gave him a present of a diamond brooch in the shape of an anchor, which he thought was suitable for an Admiral's attire.[7] John Chamberlain noted the appointment in a letter dated 6 February 1618/19, and in July of the same year he reports that 'oure younge Lord Admirall' was taken by the King to inspect some ships at Chatham, 'and that was all he could do'.[8]

It was not until the siege of La Rochelle in 1626 that Buckingham got a chance to prove his spectacular incompetence as a commander (an incompetence that was ultimately the cause of his assassination by Felton), but public dismay over his appointment did not quickly die down. In *The Bondman* (1623), Massinger makes what are usually taken to

---

[4] *MML*, IV. i. 18–21.

[5] *MML*, III. i. 38, 55; III. ii. 63–4; IV. iii. 3–6, 54; IV. iv. 61–2.

[6] D. H. Willson, p. 397. Roger Lockyer, 50, 90, 183, etc., attempts to defend Buckingham in this and other respects. *DNB*, xx. 327, entry under Villiers.

[7] John Nichols (ed.), *Progresses of James I* (4 vols.; Society of Antiquaries, 1828), iv. 834.

[8] Chamberlain, ii. 210, 254.

be criticisms of Buckingham, by making references to a
Carthaginian Admiral who does not appear:

> LEOSTHENES.   Who commands
>   The *Carthagenian* Fleet?
> TIMAGORAS.   Gisco's their Admirall,
>   And tis our happinesse: a rawe young fellow,
>   One neuer traind in Armes, but rather fashiond
>   To tilt with Ladyes lips, then cracke a Launce,
>   Rauish a Feather from a Mistrisse Fanne
>   And weare it as a Fauour; a steele Helmet
>   Made horrid with a glorious Plume, will cracke
>   His womans necke.[9]

A different sort of attack on Buckingham can be seen in *The
Maid of Honour* (1621), where the cowardly Fulgentio,
favourite of King Robert, behaves in a dishonourable way to
the heroine.[10] In *Match Me In London* more of the blame falls
on the King for making the appointment than on the
unsuitable recipient. Dekker's lines are fairly coarse squibs,
designed to raise a laugh from the audience, and Malevento's
title 'Vice-Admirall' is obviously a pun: a scurrilous ballad of
the early 1620s (written before May 1623 as it refers to
Buckingham as a Marquis and not a Duke) listed most of the
Villiers family in scathing or indecent terms, and alludes to
Buckingham himself as 'Great George, our brave *viceroy*'.[11]

But the laughter expressed a political hostility, since, until
late 1623, Buckingham was supporting the Spanish Match,
and was enlisted in what contemporaries such as Thomas
Scott called the 'Spanish faction'.[12] Because of Buckingham's
power over the King, his extensive clan rapidly rose to
dominate the Court, and D. H. Willson goes as far as to say,
'Buckingham's ascendancy brought favouritism, corruption
and debauchery, while his system of plunder poisoned the
atmosphere . . . at Westminster.'[13]

---

[9] Edwards and Gibson, i. 130 (I. i. 48–55), quoting Spencer, p. 173.

[10] Discussed by Heinemann, p. 217.

[11] Frederick W. Fairholt (ed.), *Poems and Songs Relating to George Villiers, Duke
of Buckingham* (Percy Society Reprints, vol. XXIX, 1850), no. i.

[12] Thomas Scott, *The Second Part of Vox Populi, or, Gondomar Appearing in the
Likenes of Matchiauell in a Spanish Parliament* (Goricom, 1624), sig. C.

[13] D. H. Willson, p. 389.

The bawd in the play describes the power of a royal favourite:

> Would you not stoope to take it, and thrust your hand
> Deepe as a King's in Treasure, to haue Lords
> Feare you, t'haue life or death fly from your words.[14]

When the King is told that Tormiella has a husband, he says, 'if he storme, giue him a Court-Loafe; stop his mouth with a Monopoly,' and later Iago tempts Cordolente with 'Sweet notes of place and office'.[15] Monopolies given to courtiers as rewards or favours were a mounting grievance in the later years of King James's reign. The Parliament which met early in 1621 attacked monopolies, particularly those so lavishly granted to Buckingham and his family. The monopolist Sir Giles Mompesson was impeached, and the monopolies held by Buckingham's two brothers were declared to be 'illegal and oppressive'.[16] Actually, Dekker had attacked monopolies as long ago as 1606 in *The Seuen Deadly Sins*.[17]

The play gives a picture of a degenerate, nepotistic Court and a resentful public, and by comparing the English Court and King to those of Spain, delivers the ultimate insult.

When *Match Me In London* was relicensed by Herbert on 21 August 1623, he wrote that it had been 'formerly allowed by Sir George Bucke'.[18] But John Chamberlain reports in a letter of 30 March 1622: 'Poor Sir George Bucke master of the Revells is in his old age faln starke madd, and his place executed by Sir John Ashley [*sic*] that had the reversion.'[19] Bucke's derangement, or oversights connected with it, may help explain how (while Catholic books were being seized by censors in Lancashire) a play which included a hostile skit of the King himself could be put on in London more than once. Perhaps Bucke was having one of his convenient periods of

---

[14] *MML*, II. ii. 38–40.
[15] *MML*, I. iv. 139–40, IV. i. 45.
[16] Farmer, p. 35. *DNB*, xx. 329, entry under Villiers.
[17] Grosart, ii. 74.
[18] J. Q. Adams, p. 25.
[19] Chamberlain, ii. 430. The date given in the *DNB*, vii. 171, of 30 Mar. 1620, is an error obviously arrived at by adjusting Chamberlain's old-style date '1621' back a year instead of forward.

dementia, or perhaps, as Heinemann has suggested, some of those who performed the office may have had sympathies with the dramatists, or connections with the Protestant cause.[20]

In *Match Me In London* the King of Spain is both the villain and the clown. He can be described as a political sketch or caricature, far more hostile and personal than anything in *If This Be Not A Good Play*. The King of Spain is a tyrant, a lecher, and a buffoon: he is also suspicious, timorous, vain, and jumpy in a way that is totally undignified throughout. One of his courtiers refers to him almost pityingly by saying:

> Wretched state of Kings, that standing hye,
> Their faults are markes shot at by euery eye,

and this closely echoes *Basilicon Doron*: 'A King is as one set on a skaffold, whose smallest actions and gestures al the people gazingly do behold.'[21]

When he first appears, the King of Spain is in the middle of describing a ghost. He tells Valasco, Martines, and Alphonso how on seeing it he called for help, and was found 'dead with feare!'[22] This causes some embarrassment, as Valasco does not believe in the ghost, and when Martines refuses to corroborate the King's statement, the King becomes furious and sends him away, accusing him of being a spy. The rest of his hearers decide to humour the King:

> VAL.   Sooth him vp, y'are fooles,
> If the Lyon say the Asses eares are hornes
> The Asse if he be wise will sweare it, la Sir
> These tell me they all saw it.
> OMN.   Yes my Lord.[23]

It is an extraordinary comic opening, and it is not really part of any plot. Later, in Act V, no sooner has the King been told that his wife is dead than he thinks he sees her ghost, too, and reacts with alarm.[24] In fact, she is still alive.

King James was a great believer in ghosts, always fascinated

---

[20] Heinemann, p. 166.
[21] *MML*, V. i. 46–7; Craigie, xvi. 162.   [22] *MML*, I. iv. 14.
[23] *MML*, I. iv. 20–3.   [24] *MML*, V. i. 38–9.

by the macabre and the supernatural. Shakespeare must have
known this when he wrote *Macbeth* in the hope of attracting
royal favour. Sir John Harrington relates how he was once
embarrassed by King James describing to him a premonition
seen in Scotland before his mother's death, in the form of a
bloody head dancing in the air.[25] It is this kind of embarrassment that the play is reproducing, and it is a type of
embarrassment that subtly undermines the conventions of
kingship.

In the strange scene where the King of Spain tricks one of
his courtiers into appearing to attack him, he displays an
absurd mixture of fearfulness and vanity. This incident has
absolutely no function in the plot, nor has the report of the
ghost: both are a cruel burlesque of King James. The King of
Spain first instructs Martines to meet him in half an hour's
time in the privy gallery with 'two naked Poniards'.[26]
Martines trots off to get the poniards, although the King gives
no reason for wanting them. In the next scene, Martines meets
the King in the gallery holding the poniards, and the King's
astonished escort cries out 'Treason!' Instead of explaining
what has happened, the King encourages the misunderstanding
so that he can give a display of courage:

> KING.   Stay, none touch him
> On your liues; on Kings shoulders stand
> The heads of the Colossie of the Goddes
> (Aboue the reach of Traitors) were the beds
> Of twenty thousand Snakes layd in this bosome,
> There's thunder in our lookes to breake them all,
> Leaue vs.
> OMN.   You are too venturous.[27]

His entourage exclaims in admiration, and the King's only
motive is to stage a petty display of regal fearlessness. The
references to Jove and to the godlike nature of kings would
have been immediately recognizable as James, who had once
told the Parliament of 1605 that monarchs were furnished
with 'some sparkles of divinity'.[28]

---

[25] D. H. Willson, p. 288.   [26] *MML*, IV. iv. 105.
[27] *MML*, IV. v. 7–13.   [28] D. H. Willson, p. 226.

The irony is increased when Martines has left, and the King of Spain asks his followers if the assassin did not look terrible, reminding them to guard him closely:

> KING. Are all weapon'd?
> OMN.   All, all.[29]

He is so suspicious he even thinks that his wife is setting spies on him.[30]

King James's personal timidity was well known, and many of its signs were comical, from his heavy armed guard to his frequent assertions that God was protecting him. The heavy guard has been doubted by some historians, but whether or not it is true, Dekker is referring to a belief about the King held by Weldon and other contemporaries.[31] James had quoted in *Basilicon Doron* the proverbial view that 'Suspicion is the Tirantes sicknes, as the fruits of an euil Conscience.'[32] As a theme, cowardice may also be related to foreign policy. Militant Protestants could have regarded James's refusal to go to war to defend the Palatinate as a sign of cowardice.

The unregal impression made by the King of Spain is increased by his bad temper. He constantly accuses people of lying, while at other times he tries to get them to tell lies.[33] When he is told that Tormiella has gone mad, he first accuses Malevento of lying, and then hits Gazetto in front of Valasco, Malevento, and Alphonso.[34] In 1618 when Prince Charles at Court behaved with playful disrespect towards Buckingham (at that time an earl), James immediately and publicly cuffed the heir to the throne. There were other similar occasions.[35]

Added to all this, the King of Spain displays an egregious preoccupation with his own majesty. This is evinced by his constant references to himself as a lion (which was James's dicton), an eagle, or thundering Jove. In one speech to Tormiella he jumbles all these majestic images into four lines.[36]

---

[29] *MML*, IV. v. 29–30.
[30] *MML*, I. iv. 19–21.
[31] D. H. Willson, p. 380–1; Wormald, p. 189.
[32] Craigie, xvi. 158.
[33] *MML*, I. iv. 75–85.
[34] *MML*, V. i. 1–6.
[35] D. H. Willson, pp. 242, 395, 407.
[36] *MML*, III. iii. 67–71.

King James was notorious for this kind of vanity. Not only did he write books about monarchy, but he often took occasion to hold forth about the kingly function and dignity in a way that was indeed comical. It was also a dangerous form of overkill. Willson writes that 'no adulation was too gross, no praise too strained or fulsome' for James.[37] His was the kind of vanity and egotism that suggested a fundamental insecurity, and this is well captured in Dekker's caricature.

On stage it must have been very funny, though it is attached to a plot which is not ideally suited to it, concerning the King of Spain's pursuit of Tormiella. The caricature is least recognizable when it is involved in this plot. Probably Dekker had to take the precaution of placing his skit in a context which could be used to argue that it was not really like James, and this gives it a disadvantage when compared to the parody of Horace/Jonson in *Satiromastix*.

But the satire is not altogether lightweight. In the first scene in which the King of Spain appears, after Valasco has reflected, aside, that it is wise to humour the lion whatever he says, the King, who does not hear him, goes on to tell Valasco a tale, in somewhat pedagogic style, about a lion, a fox, and an ass:

> KING. Father Ile tell you a Tale, vpon a time
> The Lyon, Foxe and silly Asse did jarre,
> Grew friends and what they got, agreed to share:
> A prey was tane, the bold Asse did diuide it
> Into three equall parts, the Lyon spy'd it,
> And scorning two such sharers, moody grew,
> And pawing the Asse, shooke him as I shake you.
> VAL. Not too hard good my Lord, alas I am craz'd.
> KING. And in rage tore him peace meale, the Asse thus dead,
> The prey was by the Foxe distributed
> Into three parts agen; of which the Lyon
> Had two for his share, and the Foxe but one:
> The Lyon (smiling) of the Foxe would know
> Where he had this wit, he the dead Asse did show.[38]

---

[37] D. H. Willson, pp. 226, 243, 168.
[38] *MML*, I. iv. 27–40.

It is derived from Aesop's fable of the Lion and Other Beasts. In Aesop's story the Lion goes hunting with three other animals, but when the prey is caught the Lion insists on having all four portions to himself.[39]

The King of Spain proceeds to expound his tale as a political allegory, but gives an exposition that is clearly wrong.

> VAL. An excellent Tale.
> KING.   Thou art that Asse.
> VAL.   I!
> KING.   Thou:
> You, and the Foxe my Brother cut my Kingdome,
> Into what steakes you list, I haue no more,
> Then what you list to giue.
> You two broach Warre or Peace; you plot, contriue,
> You flea off the Lyons skinne, you sell him aliue,
> But hauing torne the Asse first limbe from limbe
> His death shall tell the Foxe Ile so serue him.[40]

This does not correspond to the story he has just told. The lion starts by agreeing with the other animals that they will share the prey they take, but when it is divided he kills the ass and seizes an extra share. The cowed fox accepts this injustice out of necessity. The King's interpretation is quite nonsensical: he claims it is the other animals who are encroaching on the rights of the lion, when clearly it is the royal lion who is the tyrant, and is usurping the rights of the other beasts. The King of Spain accuses the fox and the ass of trying to flay the lion, but this is the opposite of what happened: it was the lion who was blatantly attacking the fox and the ass.

The fable is about tyranny, and points to King James as being a tyrant. By wrongly expounding his own story, the King of Spain reveals himself as both a tyrant and a fool. The royal lion is an absolute monarch, ruling lawlessly without respect for the rights of others. Whether the subject, or the law courts, or Parliaments actually had such rights in Great Britain, and if so how they originated, was a matter of

---

[39] Aesop's *Fables*, trans. A. Caldecott (Macmillan and Co.: London, 1887), 38–9.
[40] *MML*, I. iv. 41–8.

dispute; but this fable suggests that Dekker thought that they had, and that King James was violating them. The King of Spain's accusation that he is being sold alive might describe the sensations of militant Protestants who discovered that their religion was to be put at risk in exchange for the Infanta's dowry.

Valasco's reply to the King's accusation is that a man would have to be a real ass to oppose the interests of his own son-in-law, or turn against his own posterity, and this is surely a dig at King James's abandonment of Frederick.[41]

In using a beast-fable to criticize tyranny, Dekker is continuing a militant Protestant tradition established in the previous generation.[42] Sidney used a similar kind of fable for the same purpose in the Third Eclogues of *The Arcadia*. There the song of Philisides tells how the world was once populated only by beasts, who ruled peacefully through their own senate. But tiring of this the beasts ask Jove to give them a king. Jove warns them of the consequences, but they insist, and so he gives them man. All the beasts contribute something to man's creation. When instated as king, man proves to be a pitiless tyrant.[43]

This fable, which combines elements of Aesop's *Frogs Desiring A King* with other stories, is an allegory that contrasts the benefits of aristocratic rule with the tyranny of absolute monarchy. Languet, the shepherd to whom Philisides attributes the story, was the name of Sidney's tutor in political affairs. The poem has been interpreted as a protest against the Alençon marriage, which Sidney opposed openly in his *Letter to Queen Elizabeth*.[44]

A similar interpretation has been put on the Second Eclogue of Spenser's *Shepheardes Calender*, which he dedicated to Sidney in 1579. In the argument which prefaces the February Eclogue, Spenser writes: 'This Aeglogue is rather morall and generall, then bent to any secrete or particular

---

[41] *MML*, I. iv. 49–55.
[42] Animal fables were also useful to uphold absolutism at times: see Anthony G. Petti, 'Beasts and Politics in Elizabethan Literature', *Essays and Studies*, 16 (1963), 68–90.
[43] Sir Philip Sidney, *The Countess of Pembroke's Arcadia (The Old Arcadia)*, ed. Jean Robertson (OUP, 1973), 254–9.   [44] Ibid. 465.

purpose.'[45] Such a disclaimer only implants curiosity to know what secret or particular meaning anyone could suspect in it. The story concerns an old oak tree that had once been King of the field, and a young briar that springs up beside it. The briar scorns the oak, and boasts of its own red and white flowers, 'Colours meete to clothe a mayden Queene', surely a reference to the Tudor rose and Queen Elizabeth.[46] Eventually the ambitious bramble persuades the farmer to cut down the venerable oak; and when winter comes the briar, lacking the shelter of the oak, dies.

The briar or bramble symbolizes the Tudor dynasty, and the oak tree 'an auncient tree, / Sacred with many a mysteree', represents the English nobility, many of whose families had held high rank long before the Tudors.[47] When the overweening monarchy weakens the aristocracy in order to impose absolutism, it eventually courts its own downfall. The opposition to the Alençon marriage was led by the Earl of Leicester, and so the issue could have been seen as a constitutional choice between despotism or a mixed government with a powerful nobility.

Dekker is reviving this literary tradition because the same issues of religion and despotism had recurred after a generation. Nor was there yet any solution to this problem. The Spanish Match brought up all the same questions that had been raised by the Alençon marriage, questions Dekker had touched on in *The Whore of Babylon*. And the marriage of Queen Mary to Philip of Spain, which had provoked Sir Thomas Wyatt's rising, had raised the same problems in a slightly different way. What were the limits of the monarch's power?

All three of these fables, by Sidney, Spenser, and Dekker, offer some form of primigenial myth: they appeal to an earlier contract or state of society in order to condemn tyranny, and this was the usual method of argument among those who opposed absolutism at this time, whether they opposed it in favour of aristocracy, republicanism, or any other system.

In *Match Me In London* there is a second beast-fable, quoted by Cordolente when he spurns the King's offers of

---

[45] Smith and Selincourt, p. 423.   [46] Ibid. 425.   [47] Ibid. 426.

place and office. It is Aesop's fable of how the Wolf saw the shepherds eating a lamb in the fold, and reflected that those who make laws do not themselves keep them:

> You oft call Parliaments, and there enact
> Lawes good and wholesome . . .
>
> . . . .
>
> Great men make Lawes, that whosoe're drawes blood
> Shall dye, but if they murder flockes 'tis good.[48]

It was James's theory that the king is above the law; Dekker interprets this as a criminal despotism.

Cordolente's reference to Parliaments is one of the few references of its kind in Dekker's plays. In *If This Be Not A Good Play* Octavio uses the metaphor of a Parliament to describe how the king makes laws:

> This is that booke of statutes, were enacted
> In the high Parliament of thy roiall thoughts
> Where wisedome was the speaker.[49]

It is an extraordinarily paradoxical image. The laws have been dictated by Alphonso, yet his thoughts are compared to a Parliament as if Parliaments are the true source of legality. This suggests some crucial uncertainty about what the real source of legality is. Is the King's mind a Parliament in itself, or do Parliaments have sovereign power?

Cordolente's speech is also a little ambiguous. He says that the King enacts laws in Parliament, rather than Parliaments themselves enacting laws. Yet it suggests that the King cannot enact laws without a Parliament, or not at any rate 'Lawes good and wholesome'. Laws which lack the consent of a Parliament are presumably not good but tyrannical. Cordolente does not say whether the 'Great men' who make laws are kings, members of one of the houses of Parliament, or advisors of the King (such as Buckingham). He is less concerned with who exactly makes the law, than with the problem that some great men act as though they are above it. It may be that because there was in 1620–1 no Leicester, Essex, or Prince Henry to lead the militant Protestant cause,

---

[48] *MML*, IV. i. 56–7, 67–8.   [49] *ITBNAGP*, II. i. 3–5.

Dekker's thoughts are turning more to Parliaments as a remedy against tyranny.

Speaking of the King of Spain's plan to force Tormiella to marry him, Gazetto says to her.

> Because I know he'll force the tye a knot,
> The Church must see and sigh at.[50]

Without its metaphorical dimension, *Match Me In London* becomes the rather strange story of a King who wants to marry a shop-girl. One clue to the presence of this metaphorical dimension is the use of a dumb show at the climax of the play, when the King of Spain tries to force Tormiella to marry him, but is prevented by thunder and lightning. Dekker had used dumb shows in a similar way in *Satiromastix* and *The Whore of Babylon*. The analogy between tyranny and violation, which Dekker had recently used in *The Virgin Martyr*, was ubiquitous in Jacobean drama. For us, this kind of metaphor may (like the apocalyptic allegories) pose certain problems, and it has to be seen as an attempt on the part of the drama to deal with subjects that could not be discussed in too direct and overt a fashion. However, Dekker was certainly not merely taking over themes from other, younger, dramatists (as G. R. Price and Hoy have claimed, comparing this plot to several of Fletcher's[51]). Dekker had been one of the first to make use of the tragi-comic motif of the heroine persecuted by a lustful tyrant, in *Satiromastix*, which had appeared in 1601, seven years before Fletcher started to write plays. If the lustful tyrant was a stock figure on the Jacobean stage, then Dekker had bought first-issue stock; maybe Fletcher was imitating him.

The likenesses between *Match Me In London* and *Satiromastix* are quite extensive. Most readers of *Satiromastix* are so absorbed by the Horace–Tucca plot that they barely notice the verse-plot concerning Celestine, Sir Walter Terrill, and King William Rufus, who tries to seduce Celestine on her wedding-night. But this plot has distinct parallels with the story of Tormiella, Cordolente, and the King of Spain in *Match Me In London*. Both plays combine a potentially tragic plot with some contemporary satire; in *Satiromastix* it is Ben

---

[50] *MML*, V. ii. 63–4.   [51] Price, p. 79; Hoy, iii. 148.

Jonson who is satirized, and in *Match Me In London* it is the King. *Match Me In London*'s attempt to merge the tyrant and the clown into a single figure is not, artistically, a formula for success, but it remains extremely interesting.

The plot of *Match Me In London* makes an analogy between private and public tyranny. First we see the tyranny of father over daughter, then the tyranny of monarch over subject. Malevento tries to force his daughter, Tormiella, to marry Gazetto, and makes a promise on her behalf. But she does not consent to this and refuses to be dictated to:

> From that my Fathers promise to *Gazetto*
> That he should haue me: contract is there none,
> For my heart loath'd it.[52]

She elopes with Cordolente, and remains devoted to him, despite the assaults of the King, who has her carried off to Court to be his mistress, and tries to constrain her to go through a marriage ceremony with him in church. Despite all his threats and violence she remains steady in her own will, and her rebellion is finally sanctioned and upheld by divine intervention. This is a bold plot, and it suggests a further meaning for the title *Match Me In London*. It might be inviting London to emulate not only Tormiella's constancy but her heroic insubordination.

Tormiella would rather murder the King of Spain than marry him, and she says so from the start:

> Let goe your hold, keepe off, what violent hands
> Soeuer force mee, ne're shall touch woman more,
> Ile kill ten Monarches ere Ile bee ones whore.[53]

For this, the bawd calls her a 'puritan foole'.[54] Later, encouraged by Gazetto, Tormiella takes a vow to murder the King in bed if he forces her to marry him.[55] She is not one to swear lightly, and she has the weapon, a knife, with her. Only a miracle averts it.

One problem we face with the Elizabethan use of the rape metaphor for tyranny or conquest is that it was not very consistent with their prevailing attitudes to rape itself. The

---

[52] *MML*, I. ii. 8–10.
[54] *MML*, II. ii. 60.
[53] *MML*, II. ii. 57–9.
[55] *MML*, V. ii. 68–9.

inhabitants of a captured city were not usually branded apostates or traitors, nor were they encouraged to commit suicide as a form of expiation. In *Satiromastix* Dekker's earlier heroine, Celestine, starts by questioning the 'rape of Lucrece' morality:

> CEL. I may be constant still, and yet not true.
> TER. As how?
> CEL.   As thus, by violence detain'd,
>   They may be constant still, that are constrain'd.[56]

This is one of the few intelligent things said on the subject of rape by any Elizabethan writer. But, under the influence of her father, Celestine yields to more conventional standards. She takes what she believes is poison, to avoid being violated by King William, and to prove that she is 'a constant wife'.[57]

The weakness of this 'rape of Lucrece' morality is that it is not about rape: it fails to distinguish between participation and victimization. This is all the more unsatisfactory in *Satiromastix*, because Celestine's bridegroom, Terrill, has partly connived at the King's designs on her, and he rather than she is guilty if the assault takes place. So we listen with a sense of discomfort when the climax comes and Terrill denounces King William over the motionless body of Celestine:

> I blush not King,
> To call thee Tyrant: death hath set my face,
> And made my bloud bolde . . .[58]

In returning to this kind of plot in *Match Me In London*, Dekker's aim is more consciously metaphorical. There is no irony when Cordolente denounces the King of Spain as a tyrant: he is recognized as one by everyone in the play. The bigamous marriage that he tries to force on Tormiella is an act of tyranny, just as to militant Protestants the Spanish Match, an alliance forced on England without its consent, was a violation.

In *Satiromastix* it is clear that the heroine never undergoes physical violation, but in *Match Me In London* it is

---

[56] *Sat.*, III. ii. 57–9; Bowers, i. 347.
[57] *Sat.*, V. ii. 89, 90; Bowers, i. 376.
[58] *Sat.*, V. ii. 63–5.

considerably less clear. For a considerable part of the plot, Tormiella is imprisoned at Court by the King, where everybody, including the Queen, thinks she is the King's mistress. Gazetto tells Cordolente that Tormiella has been 'taken away by the King to his priuate bed-chamber', and Cordolente believes Tormiella is guilty of infidelity.[59] According to English common law at this time, to abduct a *mulier honesta* from her husband or father constituted a crime, often referred to as rape, and was enough to involve the woman in loss of reputation, and to entitle her husband or father to financial compensation.[60] But what of rape in the modern sense (which is what the rape metaphor entails)? On the grounds of physique, we might argue that it would be very difficult for the King to fail under these circumstances, in the long run; but on the grounds of psychology, we might argue that he would not remain interested in marrying Tormiella if he had already raped her. Dekker does seem to maximize the uncertainty, for instance by giving Tormiella so little to say when she is taken to Court in Act II, and nothing at all thereafter until Act III, scene iii. Her protestation of innocence to the Queen then has to be read in the light of Celestine's view that those who are constrained are not inconstant. Is her constancy moral or corporeal?

It would be very unusual by Jacobean literary standards for a husband to take a wife back, as Cordolente does at the end of the play, if she had been constrained in such a manner. This ethical blind spot is at the very centre of Jacobean tragicomedy: time and time again tragi-comedy hinges on the inability to condemn a tyrant or exonerate a raped woman. If this is the case, then no wonder the metaphor is deeply flawed. Furthermore, if a dramatist wishes to avoid tragedy he is supposed to avoid irreversible injury to any character, particularly a heroine. But generalizations do not help us to decide what happens in one particular play. The majority of

---

[59] *MML*, IV. i. 81.

[60] Michael Dalton, *The Covntry Iustice* (1618), 225–6, 248, considers rape under the section 'Burglarie', but restricts the crime of elopement to cases when the girl was, like Tormiella, under sixteen. T. E., *The Lavves Resolvtions of Womens Rights* (1632), 378 gives the proper meaning of rape as the abduction of a virgin '*volente vel nolente*' from her parents or guardians.

the audience would have wished to believe that Tormiella is not physically raped, and that is certainly the happiest ending, though not the most rigorous from a moral or philosophical point of view. The play's conclusion condemns the tyrant, by divine intervention, for the act he is attempting, regardless of whether he has succeeded, and this compromise may be the only way for the play to transcend its own metaphor and avoid becoming tragedy.

M. C. Bradbrook suggested that the plot of *Match Me In London* 'is closely related to the plot of Middleton's *Women Beware Women* with a happy end instead of a tragic one'.[61] There does appear to be a relationship between *Match Me In London* and *Women Beware Women*, but of a much less direct and simple kind. Both of them belong to a group of Jacobean plays which debate the moral issue of a woman's right to choose her own husband without paternal dictatorship. *Othello* and *Cymbeline* can be placed in this group (though it is doubtful whether either intended any larger-scale political metaphor). In all these plays, the heroine marries in defiance of her father's wishes: both Bianca and Tormiella actually elope, and the difficulties which beset the ensuing marriages are meant to be seen in relation to this beginning. *Women Beware Women* ends, like *Othello*, in tragedy, and this tragedy can be seen as the outcome of ethical choices made at the start of the play: the self-determination of Bianca, and the romantic idealism of Leantio, are by no means held up for approval if we are to judge from the speed with which corruption and disaster follow.[62] *Match Me In London* is the only one of these plays in which the heroine's right to choose for herself is fully endorsed from a moral standpoint. In Dekker one can detect the kind of views defined by William and Malleville Haller as 'Puritan romanticism'.[63]

Middleton is quite aware of the political aspect of marriage theology, and allows Leantio himself to remind us of it:

[61] Bradbrook, *Growth and Structure*, p. 247.

[62] T. S. Eliot asserted that Middleton has some special insight into female psychology (*Selected Essays* (Faber and Faber: London, 1927; rpt. 1972), 163, 166), but one is baffled at his presumption in making such a claim. Being a great poet does not necessarily make you a good critic.

[63] William Haller and Malleville Haller, 'The Puritan Art of Love', *Huntingdon Library Quarterly*, V, no. 2 (1942), 235–72.

> As fitting is a government in love
> As in a kingdom; where 'tis all mere lust
> 'Tis like an insurrection in the people,
> That raised in self-will wars against all reason.[64]

It is an ironic speech, since Leantio himself is one of the rebels, and gets his retribution when Bianca is unfaithful to him. Then he expresses remorse for the sin of their elopement, and the argument he uses—that it is rough justice to steal what was stolen in the first place—reveals the Common Law attitude: that women are property, and marital fidelity is a law of ownership. According to this view, Leantio and Cordolente are guilty of 'rape' whether or not the woman concerned agreed to elope. 'Here stands the poor thief now that stole the treasure.'[65] Such a view is really built into the argument of Middleton's play.

In *Match Me In London* Dekker gives this very argument to the corrupt King, and it could be an intentional echo of Middleton:

> Thou art his whore, he plai'd the theefe and rob'd
> Another of thee, and to spoyle the spoyler,
> Is Kingly iustice.[66]

But the foolish old king is reproved in the end, by divine justice itself. There seems to be nothing in Middleton's vocabulary between government and insurrection, or between arranged marriage and wicked lust; in Dekker's vocabulary there is a legitimate self-determination which objects to both private and public tyranny.

In January 1620 King James had issued an instruction to preachers to 'inveigh vehemently against the insolencie of our women, and theyr wearing of brode brimmed hats, pointed dublets, theyre haire cut short or shorne, and some of them stilettoes or poniards'.[67] In *Match Me In London* the heroine is indeed armed with a stiletto or poniard, and for a very good reason. From first to last in the play she has to stand up to threat, assault, and harassment. In one scene Tormiella,

---

[64] Thomas Middleton, *Women Beware Women*, ed. J. R. Mulryne (The Revels Plays; Methuen: London, 1975), 29; *WBW*, I. iii. 43–6.

[65] Mulryne, p. 95; *WBW*, III. iii. 88–9.

[66] *MML*, III. iii. 80–2.   [67] Chamberlain, ii. 286–7.

running from the threats of the King, is insulted menacingly by another man, the disguised Gazetto, in the street. It is interesting to note that Ben Jonson was, as usual, in disagreement with Dekker on this issue. His masque of 1621, *News From the New World*, included some satire on the behaviour of London women, particularly their carrying of weapons, and this was assiduously designed to support the attitudes of the King.[68] Moll Frith, the heroine of Dekker and Middleton's *Roaring Girl*, had warmly asserted her right to bear weapons as long as men did.

In *Match Me In London*, Malevento, Gazetto, Pacheco, the bawd, and Cordolente all at one time or another express anti-feminist moral prejudices, harping on the theme of the guilty Eve:

GAZ. She followes the steps of her old grandam, all euils take their names from her, the ills of *Eue*, thy wife for the hoope ring thou marriedst her withall, hath sworne to send thee a Deathes head.[69]

The irony is that when Gazetto expounds his fictive etymology, he is actually lying to Cordolente. It is not Tormiella, but Gazetto himself who has sworn to murder Cordolente, on the instruction of the King. He is trying to poison Cordolente's mind against Tormiella, and his misogynist views are deceitful, founded in spite. Despite the doubts of her own morally faithless husband, Tormiella's own fidelity confutes all these prejudices. Dekker is using the same grammar of irony here that Middleton uses to discredit the views of Livia and Bianca in *Women Beware Women*, but he is using it to defend the principle of self-determination that Middleton attacks. Malevento calls Tormiella a 'Strumpet . . . a disobedient Child', but this is refuted when we see her courage and constancy.[70] Later on, Malevento's own corruption by the King discredits his claim to exercise authority. He accepts honours in exchange for the seizure of his own daughter. The domestic tyrant grovels to the royal tyrant, and by this logical alliance each reimplicates the other.

In *If This Be Not A Good Play* Dekker avoided taking sides

---

[68] Percy and Simpson, vii. 521–2.

[69] *MML*, V. ii. 96–9; also I. i. 80–1, I. ii. 79–80, I. iii. 14, I. iv. 129–30, II. ii. 69–70, II. iv. 104–6, etc.   [70] *MML*, II. i. 61.

between the Court and the City, but he cannot avoid doing so in *Match Me In London*. The confrontation between the apprentice Bilbo and a Court fop makes this division particularly clear.[71] It is also apparent in the tense scene when the courtiers arrive and escort Tormiella away from her husband's shop.

There are good and bad characters in both City and Court, and Dekker makes subtle parallels between the corruption in both. For instance, when Malevento finds Cordolente's shop in Seville, they pretend to be reconciled but Malevento expresses his lingering resentment in an aside.[72] Likewise, the King's brother Don John pretends to make up his past quarrel with Valasco, and a minute later tries to poison him.[73] Yet although there are dubious characters in the City, they are drawn to the Court as the play goes on because it is the centre and magnet of corruption. The worth of Tormiella and, to a lesser extent, her doubting husband, is shown by their rejection of ambition and faithfulness to their citizen roots. Cordolente is a small tradesman, no magnate or capitalist, but Dekker's leaning reflects a sense that militant Protestantism seemed more securely established in the City at this time than in the Court of King James.

It is typical of tragi-comedy that the happy (or at least non-tragic) ending is arrived at by means of a number of small rebellions against corrupt authority. In *Match Me In London* such rebellions are rife. Both Valasco and Gazetto defy the King's orders to commit murder, and so the lives of Cordolente, the Queen, and Don John, the somewhat ineffective and innocuous traitor, are all saved. Similarly, in *The Winter's Tale*, both Camillo and Paulina disobey the orders of an unjust King, and a happy ending reached by such a means is discreetly anti-absolutist.

But more than individual defiance is needed to resolve the problems in *Match Me In London*. We see in dumb show how the King takes Tormiella to church to marry him. Cordolente rushes in and tries to kill her, but does not do it, and later says that the hand of heaven held him back.[74] He is thrust out of the church and the ceremony begins again. It seems that

---

[71] *MML*, IV. ii.
[72] *MML*, II. iv. 39–40.
[73] *MML*, III. i. 55–206.
[74] *MML*, V. iv. 10–11.

Tormiella will have to carry out her vow to kill the King—a terrible and violent last resort. But just when the King is putting the ring on Tormiella's finger—a symbolic rape— thunder and lightning intervene, the same signs of divine power which the King has boasted in previous scenes that he can wield. The false Jove is reproved by the real one, preventing the union which Cordolente calls 'sacrilegious'.[75] It is a wordless enactment of what had been said in the beast-fable: that James's claims to divine right were, like his current policies, tyrannical in militant Protestant eyes.

After this, the conclusion is summary in the extreme, even more so than usual with tragi-comedy. The tyrant reforms, a few judgements and penalties are awarded to lesser persons, and Tormiella is restored to Cordolente. After the dumb show, there is really nothing more of importance to be said.

Although we do not know the exact date of the first performance of *Match Me In London*, we do know that it was relicensed by Herbert on 21 August 1623, for the Princess Elizabeth's company. This second performance therefore took place while Prince Charles and Buckingham were actually in Madrid trying to finalize the Spanish Match. They had left on their hare-brained and diplomatically embarrassing visit in February of that year, and returned in October, now determined to abandon the match. The London public was overjoyed and celebrated openly, lighting bonfires and singing ballads. Although it took some time before Buckingham persuaded King James to break off the negotiations, some might have felt that there had indeed been divine intervention.

The following year, Middleton's *Game at Chess* was performed by the King's Men, and once more they chose August for its production. August 1619 had been the date when the King's Men had put on Fletcher and Massinger's *Sir John Van Olden Barnavelt*.[76] And we know that the revival of *The Virgin Martyr* in 1624 took place at the same season, since Herbert licensed the additional scene in July of that year. This encourages the speculation that the practice of putting on plays of a highly topical or audacious nature in mid-summer when the King and Court were away from

[75] *MML*, V. iv. 5.   [76] Bentley, iii. 415–17.

London had been going on for some time, and was not invented for *A Game at Chess* as certain editors and critics believe.[77] (Of course the summer was a pleasant time to put on a play of any kind in a roofless theatre.) Doubtless the King's Men were emboldened to put on a play which presented so many contemporary figures by the example Dekker's plays had set at the Cockpit and the Red Bull.

Match Me In London had a discernible influence on *A Game at Chess*, just as Middleton's *Women Beware Women* seems to have influenced Dekker. In fact, *A Game at Chess* seems to have been influenced by several Dekker plays, including *The Whore of Babylon*. In the induction to *A Game at Chess*, Ignatius Loyola wakens Error, representing Roman Catholicism, who tells him what he needs to know about the game in progress.[78] It would be a puzzling choice of speaker, as Error's statements turn out to be quite reliable, but it is surely intended as a parody of the opening of Dekker's *Whore of Babylon*, in which the Protestant Titania awakens the allegorical figure of Truth. Middleton evidently expected his audience to be quite familiar with Dekker's play, and to understand from this joke that his play was related to the apocalyptic dramas, but in a somewhat lighter vein.

The technique of dumb show is something else that Middleton appears to be borrowing from Dekker. In *A Game at Chess* the White Pawn is saved from a bogus marriage to a Jesuit on the Black (Spanish) side, and this plot culminates in a dumb show.

A Game at Chess was written after Buckingham, with Charles in tow, had turned against the Spanish Match, and this enabled Middleton to portray them in the role of heroes, though somewhat stupid ones. Gondomar alone is the play's villain. Even the White King (James) is shown as a kindly, if weak, figure. The play does less to oppose than to apologize for the actions of the Stuart government in pursuing the Spanish Match, and it also provides propaganda for the foreign policies of Buckingham, who was locked in conflict with Parliament at this time over how to conduct the war.

[77] Thomas Middleton, *A Game at Chess*, ed. J. W. Harper (New Mermaid Series; Ernest Benn Ltd: London, 1966), p. xii. Also Bradbrook, *Growth and Structure*, p. 154; Heinemann, p. 166.   [78] Harper, p. 7.

King James had agreed to an invasion of the Palatinate, but Parliament opposed it as impractical and wanted to get its grievances redressed before financing anything at all, so the King prorogued Parliament on 28 May 1624.[79]

Dover Wilson suggested that Buckingham might have been Middleton's patron.[80] But the whole question of direct patronage of the stage at this time is full of uncertainties. One thing that would have pleased Buckingham is that in *A Game at Chess*, Middleton makes a scapegoat out of the recently impeached Lord Treasurer, Lionel Cranfield, Earl of Middlesex. Cranfield is to be identified with the White King's Pawn, who in Act III is unmasked and found to be Black. He is also portrayed as acting as an informer to the Black side, a propagandist fiction comparable to Dekker's portrayal of Lopez at the Babylonian Court.[81] Yet Cranfield, who was one of the few able ministers James had in his Council, had only done what Buckingham had done: supported the Spanish Match. When Buckingham turned against Spain, Cranfield remained consistent in his views and loyal to the King. So Buckingham engineered his downfall by getting him impeached in Parliament for peculations which were modest in comparison with the major industry of bribery and monopoly run by the Villiers clan. Middleton is upholding a political and ethical inconsistency here, in order to present Buckingham as a hero, and to gain popular approval of his Privy Council bullying.

There are many unanswered questions about *A Game at Chess*, one of them being, what is the White side in a chess match doing if it takes most of the game to realize that the Black side is its enemy and not to be trusted? Middleton presents an incredible story of how the Black side (Spain) used wiles and deception on the innocent White side (England), but whether or not Gondomar had ever given

---

[79] G. D. M. Howat, *Stuart and Cromwellian Foreign Policy* (Adam and Charles Black: London, 1974), 32–7.

[80] Dover Wilson, Review of R. C. Bald's edition of *A Game of [sic] Chesse*, *The Library*, 4th series, no. 11 (1930), 105–16. Dover Wilson writes that the play was involved in 'the game of foreign policy that Charles and Buckingham were in 1624 playing against the Spanish ambassador' (p. 111), but the real tension seems to have existed between Buckingham and the Commons.   [81] Harper, p. 88.

James any undertaking that Spain would not invade the Palatinate, James and Buckingham had continued to pursue the alliance with Spain for three years after the invasion took place.[82] As for the conversion of the future monarch, the Spanish had never concealed this was their aim even when a Spanish marriage had been discussed for Prince Henry nineteen years before.

Heinemann asks the very good question, of why the official reaction to *A Game at Chess* was, by Jacobean standards, so lenient.[83] The answer is probably because the play was so supportive of the policies of Buckingham and Prince Charles. The Spanish ambassador protested about *A Game at Chess*, and the King's Men were questioned about it by the Council, but this was probably only a gesture of diplomatic propriety.

The leniency of such treatment is best seen by comparing it with another contemporary example. In the autumn of 1624, Dekker, Webster, Rowley, and Ford became involved in a Star Chamber case concerning their play *Keep the Widow Waking*. Though the case was one of libel and seems to have had no bearings on public affairs, it dragged on for two years. C. J. Sisson's research on the trial shows that Dekker had to present a written defence in Star Chamber as late as 1626.[84] The questioning of the King's Men had lasted only one day.

While Dekker was appearing in Star Chamber because of what was called a 'libellous and scandalous enterlude and play', he must have felt rather uncomfortable about the far more serious risks he had taken, particularly over *Match Me In London* and, by that time, *The Sun's Darling* too. This may have something to do with the fact that after 1626 he seems to have given up writing for the stage, confining himself to city pageants and works in prose.

---

[82] Ibid. 89; D. H. Willson, p. 415; Charles H. Carter, 'Gondomar: Ambassador to James I', *Historical Journal*, VII (1964), 205–8, asserts that Gondomar found honesty the best policy to pursue with James. Wormald asserts that their relationship was one of 'mutual respect between two subtle and wily politicians' (p. 189), but this is hard to reconcile with James's persistence in the Spanish alliance after 1620.

[83] Heinemann, p. 2.   [84] Sisson, pp. 80–124.

7

The Sun's Darling:
An Apocalyptic Masque

'THE Sun's Darling, in the nature of a masque by Decker and Forde for the Lady Elizabeth's Servants', was licensed by Herbert on 3 March 1623/4.[1] The text we have now, printed in 1656, is an adaptation made for a Court revival in 1638 or early 1639 by an anonymous reviser. This reviser added a considerable amount to Act V, and may also have inserted two of the eight songs.

A general consensus on style has deemed that Ford was mainly responsible for the first and fourth Acts, and Dekker for Acts II, III, and V of the original text.[2] This would have been a reasonable division of labour. But Hoy also usefully points out that Acts II–V all incorporate material from Dekker's prose work *The Ravens Almanacke* (1609), which contains descriptions of the four seasons.[3] There are other more fundamental links between the religious-political ideas in *The Sun's Darling* and Dekker's previous work, which suggest that he took a leading role in its conception and design. The Ford scholar Ronald Huebert dismisses it as being totally unlike Ford's work, and calls it 'a regular court masque', which it surely is not.[4]

Herbert's description reveals some uncertainty about the genre of *The Sun's Darling*. Although it contains songs and dances, most of the dialogue is spoken. The 1656 title-page calls it 'A Moral Masque', and it certainly has elements of a morality play. But it could also be called a militant Protestant, or an apocalyptic, masque.

---

[1] J. Q. Adams, p. 27; Jones-Davies, ii. 404.
[2] Jones-Davies, ii. 406.
[3] Hoy, iv. 11.
[4] Ronald Huebert, *John Ford: Baroque English Dramatist* (McGill-Queen's University Press: Montreal, 1977), 127.

The following authorship divisions can be deduced:

Dedication	1656. Non-authorial. Signed by actors.
Commendatory verse	1656. John Tatham.
Prefatory poem on the seasons	1656. Its interpretation of the masque is consistent with the description 'A Moral Masque'.
I. i. 1–85	1624. Principally Ford; though the opening song sounds to me like Dekker, others including Jones-Davies have attributed it to Ford.
I. i. 86–165	A problematical passage. Two details suggest that it is an interpolation of 1638: Folly calls Time '1538', i.e. very old, and as Ford's editor of 1811, Henry Weber, noticed, this would have been apt in 1638 making Time a century old. But Weber also pointed out that the date could easily have been changed.[5] Secondly, Folly here meets Raybright, but later in II. i. 100 they meet again as if for the first time. Yet some of the speeches sound like Dekker, although Time's denunciation of Folly might be more suitable at the end of the masque. I conclude that this passage contains material that was taken out of the original Act V in 1638, in order to make room for the additions there. It has probably been altered, and Folly's meeting with Raybright must have been added, but it does contain material by Dekker. This hypothesis also explains why Folly appears simply to melt out of the existing text at V. i. 77.
I. i. 165–212	1624. Ford.
II. i. 1–47	1624. Dekker.
II. i. 48–59 Nightingale song	Another vexed question. A slightly different version of this song is attributed to Lyly in a posthumous volume of 1632, but W. W. Greg has shown good evidence that it is not by Lyly.[6] Either it is a popular song that was

---

[5] W. J. Lawrence, 'The Problem of Lyly's Songs', TLS, 20 Dec. 1923, 894.

[6] W. W. Greg, 'The Authorship of the Songs in Lyly's Plays', *Modern Language Review*, I (1905), 43; see also Lawrence above.

	inserted by the 1638 reviser, or is by Dekker and later got misattributed to Lyly when both poets were dead. It sounds to me less like Dekker than the song at the start of Act I, and it is not really good enough to fight over.
II. i. 60–323	1624. Dekker.
III.	1624. Dekker.
IV. i. 1–158.	1624. Ford.
IV. i. 159–69 Folly's song	This sounds like Dekker, and is an ironic version of the kind of carefree drinking-songs found in *The Shoemakers' Holiday*.
IV. i. 170–227	1624. Ford, though Dekker may have helped with the comic prose, as Jones-Davies thinks.
IV. i. 228–90	1624. Dekker.
IV. i. 291–9	1638 reviser.
V. i. 1–67	1638 reviser.
V. i. 68–77	Folly's last speech sounds like a fragment of the original 1624 text, by Dekker.
V. i. 78–118	1638 reviser (except perhaps for 108–13).
V. i. 119–302	1624. Dekker.
V. i. 303–end	1624. Ford.

This is a complicated picture, but the original plan of the masque is quite clear despite the later alteration. Raybright travels through the four seasons of the year and is welcomed lavishly by each of them, but he deserts them all to pursue his follies. The revisions to *The Sun's Darling* make it possibly more interesting as a text. Little has been left out, and Hoy is probably right in speculating that Act V originally contained a description of Winter to match the other three seasons, taken from *The Ravens Almanacke*.[7] The interpolations added after Dekker's death can provide us with the basis for some very revealing comparisons.

It was W. J. Lawrence who first suggested that the purpose of the revision in Act V was to introduce references to the events of late 1638 or early 1639, the time just before the First Bishops' War. He also showed from external evidence that the revisions were probably made for a revival of *The Sun's Darling* at Court during the Christmas festivities of 1638/9, and this must be the Court performance mentioned on the

---

[7] Hoy, iv. 12.

title-page.[8] When Raybright arrives in Winter's domains, its inhabitants regard him as an armed invader, and Winter reproves them sternly for being rebels against Raybright's sacred authority:

> What, such murmurings does your gall bring forth,
> Will you prov't true, no good coms from the North.[9]

In late 1638 Scotland was up in arms to resist the new Liturgy imposed on it by King Charles. The Glasgow assembly of November 1638 rejected not only the Prayer Book but episcopacy as well; there had been riots and tens of thousands were signing the Covenant. Charles was determined to put the Scots down by force, and was attempting rather unsuccessfully to raise an army.

In the masque, this incongruous episode ends as abruptly as it begins, and is forgotten by the conclusion. However, the political significance of *The Sun's Darling* is not confined to a few isolated allusions. Though the 1638 reviser seems to have been unaware of it, militant Protestant ideas were fundamental to the conception of the original masque. Considering the choice of protagonist, Raybright, son of the god Phoebus, Bowers suggests: 'Usually the Sun would be the king, and Raybright, as his son, would be the prince. It is tempting to speculate that *The Sun's Darling* was written for performance at Whitehall in 1623 some time after Prince Charles's return from Spain on 5 October, that it was intended basically as a compliment to James I and his son Prince Charles, and that it was subsequently produced at the Cockpit.'[10]

It is true that many internal details suggest Raybright is meant to denote Prince Charles, though 'comment', 'reproof', or 'gentle mockery' might be more appropriate terms than 'compliment' here. The true compliments of the piece are offered not to Prince Charles but to his sister the Princess Elizabeth, Electress Palatine and Queen of Bohemia. And there is no evidence that the work was written for Whitehall.

Hoy has objected to Bowers's suggestion, saying that 'As a welcome home to Prince Charles, *The Sun's Darling* could only be a devastatingly satirical greeting, and it is not to be imagined that anything of the sort was ever intended by the

[8] Lawrence, p. 894.   [9] *SD*, V. i. 14–15.   [10] Bowers, iv. 12.

authors,' since neither would have been 'either naive enough or daring enough'. He adds 'The kind of masque that was in fact written to celebrate the Prince's safe return from Spain can be seen in Jonson's *Neptune's Triumph*.'[11] Dekker was not naïve, though he was, as we have seen, daring. There is no reason to assume that only one kind of text—Jonson's cancelled masque—can be related to a particular context. Even if Dekker and Ford had been writing for the Court, things would not be as simple, or as monolithic, as that. Hoy is correct that the work is most unflattering to Prince Charles, and this is one of the interesting things about it.

The Sun's Darling was written for the Lady Elizabeth's Servants, otherwise known as The Queen of Bohemia's Company, who had revived *Match Me In London* at the Cockpit. It is understandable that the author of *The Virgin Martyr* should have wished to write for the company under the official protection of the Bohemian Queen.

In the last Act of *The Sun's Darling*, Raybright arrives at the Court of Winter, and (after the interpolation) the aged King receives him humbly and apologetically:

> Illustrious sir! I am not ignorant
> How much expression my true zeale will want
> To entertain you fitlie, yet my love,
> And hartie dutie, shall be farr above
> My outward welcome.[12]

Raybright commiserates with Winter over the Sun's neglect of his realm:

> So royall, so aboundant in earth's blessings,
> Should not partake the comfort of those beames,
> With which the *Sun* beyond extent doth cheere
> The other seasons.[13]

Receiving little of the sun's rays is winter's lot by definition, but there could also be a further meaning. Raybright goes on to pay a high tribute to Winter's consort, who is called

---

[11] Hoy, iv. 2.
[12] *SD*, V. i. 125–9.
[13] *SD*, V. i. 144–7.

Bounty, and he offers to serve her, which awakens the jealousy of Lady Humor:

> *Winters* sweet bride,
> All Conquering *Bounty*, queen of harts, life's glory,
> Natures perfection; whom all love, all serve.[14]

Since his loss of the kingdom of Bohemia in 1620, the Elector Frederick had also been known by the melancholy name of the Winter King, because he had reigned for only one winter, and because he was now bereft of everything. Another title his opponents gave him in derision was 'The King of Hearts'—the lowest king in the pack of cards. These names were taken up and skilfully reclaimed by his supporters, who turned the latter into a complimentary title for his wife: Elizabeth became known as the Queen of Hearts.[15] So the Court of Winter in the masque would have been immediately recognizable as a poetic allusion to the Winter King and Queen, Frederick and Elizabeth. No portraiture is intended (Winter is old and decrepit, as suits the allegory) but the political meaning is clear.

Raybright also calls Bounty 'Sole daughter to the royall throne of peace'.[16] Elizabeth was James's sole daughter, and at his accession, King James had added to his titles that of '*Rex pacificus*'.[17] This must have been rather galling to those of his subjects who preferred a policy of war, and when Raybright says that the Sun's rays do not warm Winter's realm, there is a suggestion that James had not done all he could for his son-in-law.

Raybright finds Winter in a dejected state, his fortune in 'extreame', and Bounty's smile is said to warm 'misery' and 'desolation'.[18] Since the loss of Bohemia and the Palatinate, Frederick and Elizabeth had been in exile with a handful of followers, and in 1624 they were living at the Hague in great poverty (by royal standards). King James had withdrawn the last English troops from the Palatinate in 1623, and in August 1623 the Protestant forces fighting on Frederick's behalf under Christian of Brunswick had been defeated at Stadtlohn.

---

[14] *SD*, V. i. 154–6.   [15] Wedgwood, pp. 113, 129.
[16] *SD*, V. i. 162.   [17] D. H. Willson, p. 272; Farmer, p. 65.
[18] *SD*, V. i. 157, 171–2.

The fortunes of Frederick and Elizabeth were indeed miserable, unless England came belatedly to their aid.

A masque by its nature intimates rather than states, and any precise interpretation will sound rather bald. But it seems clear that the entire story, with its zodiacal journey through the four seasons, was designed to culminate at the Court of the Winter King and Queen. Like *The Virgin Martyr*, *The Sun's Darling* is pleading the Bohemian cause, and the climax of the action comes when Raybright, who has previously been in the toils of Humor, promises to serve Winter's Queen:

> Yet where you are, the glories of your smiles
> Would warm the barren grounds, arm hartless misery,
> And cherish desolation. Deed I honor you,
> And as all others ought to do, I serve you.[19]

The titles 'Winter King' and 'Queen' definitely refer to Bohemia and not only to the Palatinate. Frederick's right to the Palatinate was hereditary and not controversial: even King James recognized it. But his right to Bohemia was a different matter: even to refer to Frederick and Elizabeth as King and Queen of Bohemia was tendentious, an expression of militant Protestant solidarity which upheld the subjects' right to depose their monarch and exercise Protestant religious freedom. This was the reason James had forbidden the clergy to offer public prayers for Frederick and Elizabeth as a King and Queen.

The Sun's Darling is a very complex creation. Around the framework of the zodiacal journey are interwoven elements of the traditional morality interlude, apocalyptic ideas, and contemporary politics. The two latter ingredients are certainly more prominent in the sections written by Dekker, Acts II, III, and V. The blend of poetry and comedy in these sections is peculiarly Dekkerian, and there is nothing at all like it in Ford's plays. The plot is reminiscent of the spoof morality play in *Sir Thomas More*, in which Witt deserts Lady Wisdom and runs after Lady Vanitie.

Raybright, the son (or, in some places grandson) of

---

[19] *SD*, V. i. 170–3.

Phoebus, is far from being a hero. He is a pleasure-seeker, weak, indolent, and foolish; he is quick to fall under whatever bad influences he meets. Hoy describes him as a 'prodigal' and the action can be seen as a sort of Rake's Progress.[20] It is easy to lose patience with Raybright: he is really rather silly, and this intimates what Dekker (surely not alone) thought of the behaviour of the heir to the English throne. When Charles and Buckingham turned against the Spanish Match in 1623, there was public euphoria, but by early 1624, when *The Sun's Darling* was written, negotiations for a French Match had already begun.

In Act I, Raybright appears as an aimless dreamer, reluctant to undertake any action. When the Priest of the Sun tells him,

> You have had choice
> Of beauties to enrich your marriage-bed,[21]

he replies,

> I care for no long travels with lost labor.[22]

The Priest goes on,

> Have you been sent out into strange lands,
> Seen Courts of forreign Kings, by them been grac'd,
> To bring home such neglect?[23]

This mockery of Charles and Buckingham's foolhardy trip to Madrid prepares the audience for something related to that theme, before the action proper begins. This sort of introduction is possible because the time-scheme of a masque is more flexible than that of a play.

Starting out on his progress, Raybright first arrives at the Court of Spring, who falls in love with him. She woos him to stay with her, and he promises to do so. But soon the Lady Humor arrives on the scene, heralded by Folly, and Raybright is enticed by the sensuous description that Folly provides of her: 'Creature! of a skin soft as Pomatum, sleek as Jellie, white as blanch'd Almonds'.[24] Humor and Spring contend for Raybright's love. Spring offers him youth, health, and

---

[20] Hoy, iv. 11.   [21] *SD*, I. i. 50–1.
[22] *SD*, I. i. 56.   [23] *SD*, I. i. 67–9.
[24] *SD*, II. i. 96–7.

delight, adding the pleasures of the mind and the spirit to those of the senses. She tempts him with poetry:

> Is't come to who gives most?
> The self same Bay tree into which was turnd
> *Peneian Daphne*, I have still kept green;
> That tree shall now be thine: about it sit,
> All the old poets with fresh Lawrel Crownd,
> Singing in verse the praise of chastity.[25]

The Lady Humor, on the other hand, offers Raybright lust, excitement, and a large dowry, far greater than any wealth Spring can muster:

> SPRING. Bought! art thou sold then?
> RAYBRIGHT. Yes, with her gifts, she buyes me with her graces
> .   .   .   .
> RAYBRIGHT. What dowrie can you bring me?
> SPRING.   Dowrie! ha!
>   Is't come to this?[26]

This is a distinct allusion to the Spanish Match. One of the strongest incentives to the match from King James's point of view was the Infanta's enormous dowry, a sum he hoped would render him independent of Parliaments for the rest of his reign.

Folly describes the Lady Humor to Raybright as an Empress, and she herself asks to be given the title.[27] Otherwise she is called a courtesan:

> SPRING. Oh! thou inticing strumpet, how durst thou
>   Throw thy voluptuous spells about a Temple
>   That's consecrate to me.[28]

Humor is clearly no ordinary courtesan. In the masque's allegory she represents the Whore of Babylon—the only one with whom Charles's name was ever linked. The action of the masque at this point is very reminiscent of the dualism of *The Whore of Babylon*. Raybright stands between two contending female figures, the true and worthy Spring, and the false, corrupting Empress of Babylon: the true religion and the

---

[25] *SD*, II. i. 239–44.   [26] *SD*, II. i. 216–17, 222–3.
[27] *SD*, II. i. 91, 263.   [28] *SD*, II. i. 211–13.

false. When Humor first sees Raybright, she says to Folly that he is 'A bedfellow for a Fairie'. Dekker is echoing Spenser as well as his own play here to hint at the apocalyptic allegory.[29] The Temple that is consecrated to Spring is both Raybright himself—that is, Charles—and the English Church.

Humor is the successor of Foxe's Pornapolis and Spenser's Duessa as well as of Dekker's Empress. Like Duessa and Pornapolis she uses magic and illusion to lure Raybright to follow her:

> I'le raise by art, out of base earth, a pallace;
> Whither thy selfe . . .
> Shall call together the most glorious spirits
> Of all the Kings that have been in the world;
> And they shall come onely to feast with thee.[30]

The Lady Humor has three attendants, sinister, unfunny clowns, one French, one Spanish, and one Italian. Again this is reminiscent of *The Whore of Babylon*, in which the Empress has three minion kings. It is notable that by this time, 1624, Dekker no longer makes the Empire one of Babylon's minions. With the Thirty Years' War well under way, militant Protestants were able to hope that the Empire would soon be free of Roman domination. The apocalyptic element in *The Sun's Darling* is very much more subdued than it is in *The Whore of Babylon*, and masquerades as comedy, but it is still there providing the basic structure.

Raybright foolishly allows himself to be seduced by Humor, and forsakes Spring, who dies of grief. Almost at once he feels remorseful and melancholy, and shows his temper by getting angry with Folly and driving away Humor's three parasites. Then he pointlessly reproaches her, but is soon won back, and continues his journey with Humor and Folly. It is classic stupidity: 'I will not leav my *Follie* for a world.'[31]

The figure of Spring possibly carries some further allusion to Vere and his campaign on the Rhine—it is the same pun used by Chapman—but in a general sense Spring represents

---

[29] *SD*, II. i. 127.
[30] *SD*, II. i. 290–4. I have omitted half a line here that is generally regarded as corrupt. See Bowers, iv. 69 and Hoy, iv. 27.   [31] *SD*, III. i. 99.

the season of hope for militant Protestants, and of lost opportunity. In the following episode, in which Raybright visits Summer, the apocalyptic structure is again visible. Summer has the Sun for her lover, but when Raybright approaches accompanied by Humor, the Sun is clouded and disappears. This special effect (whose difficulty of production on the public stage has been much discussed) has an apocalyptic significance. Raybright is told that it is the presence of the Lady Humor that has caused the Sun to fade away:

> SUMMER. Leav off, the *Sun* is angry, and has drawn
> A clowd before his face.
> DELIGHT.   He is vex'd to see
> That proud star shine near you, at whose rising
> The *Spring* fell sick and dy'd.[32]

The Sun is dimmed by the Lady Humor because it recognizes in her its adversary, the Whore of Babylon. Just as the name 'Titania' implies a hidden identification with the Woman Clothed With the Sun, the True Church, the same symbolic dualism is half-concealed here. Prince Charles's betrothal to the Infanta is represented as a desertion of the True Church, and so the forces of Babylon cast their shadow over the Sun. When Raybright and Lady Humor depart from the realm of Summer, the Sun is able to return.[33]

Act IV, written mainly by Ford, follows a similar pattern. Raybright arrives at the Court of Pomona, Queen of Autumn, and she makes a bid for his love. Once again, the attractions of the Lady Humor prove stronger than those of Raybright's hostess. It is interesting that while the female figures have been retained in this dualistic symbolism, it is no longer a virgin–whore dichotomy, as it was in *The Whore of Babylon*. True, Humor is a whore, and the attractions of the seasons are less sensuous, more cultivated, than hers:

> POMONA. Nor hath his masculine graces in our brest
> Kindled a wanton fire, our bounty gives him
> A welcome free, but chaste and honorable.[34]

But of the four seasons, only Spring is said to be a maiden. Pomona is the wife of Autumn, and Bounty is Winter's

---

[32] *SD*, III. iv. 37–40.   [33] *SD*, III. iv. 106–8.   [34] *SD*, IV. i. 92–4.

Queen. Protestant theology did not equate chastity with virginity, and although it was appropriate to make Titania a virgin, since Queen Elizabeth had been single, this could be seen as having Catholic overtones. In Catholic theology, the Woman Clothed With the Sun was interpreted as the Virgin Mary, but in Protestant exegesis she was the True Church, the Bride of Christ. In *The Sun's Darling* Spring is a virgin, but is nevertheless the mother of Summer. The allegory is a very flexible one, and the apocalyptic elements are blended with nature-mythology. They are least prominent in this Act, where Ford's work predominates.

In Act v, Raybright finally arrives at the Court of Winter, and here the masque grows a little more optimistic. Raybright appears to admire Bounty more extravagantly than any of the other four seasons, and his prolonged praise of her makes the Lady Humor feel jealous. Raybright's Folly seems to have disappeared, finding the climate of Winter's realm too chilly for him, or he may have been driven out in this Act in the original text.[35] At any rate, he has gone. Raybright promises to serve the Winter Queen, and Winter offers to act as his guide and mentor: 'I can direct and point you out a path.'[36] Militant Protestants would have liked to see Charles taking the Calvinist Elector Frederick as his guide and model, instead of philandering with the Catholic powers. The possibility that Prince Charles, under the aegis of Buckingham, was now prepared to fight for the Protestant cause, had made him for the first time the darling of the London public.

But Lady Humor is still tempting Raybright, disparaging Winter, and telling Raybright that they can return to the Spring. Raybright goes on wavering right until the end. He just seems to be yielding to Humor's persuasion to desert Winter, when he is interrupted by the reappearance of the Sun:

> To the *Spring*
> I am resolv'd—Oh! what strange light appears;
> The *Sun* is up sure.[37]

---

[35] *SD*, V. i. 71–7.   [36] *SD*, V. i. 295.   [37] *SD*, V. i. 300–2.

After all we have seen of Raybright's previous fickleness, his protestations of faith to Bounty do not carry much weight. We are bound to hear them sceptically.

The climax of the masque's action is the meeting of Raybright and Bounty: Prince Charles and his sister, the heir to the throne and militant Protestantism. The Queen of Bohemia was a charismatic figure in English eyes, and many regarded her rather than her husband as the chief leader of the Protestant cause. She was energetic, active, and determined.[38] There was talk of Queen Elizabeth being revived in her, just as Prince Henry was supposed to be revived in Frederick. She was in fact more deeply committed to Calvinism and to confessional politics than her namesake had been.

To celebrate this meeting, and the symbolic union of Raybright with Winter, a feast and a masque are presented. But the meeting is one which in actual terms never happened: Frederick and Elizabeth were forbidden by King James to return to England at this time, for fear of the Protestant enthusiasm which might be stirred up by their presence. There was even some apprehension that their popularity might provoke an uprising which would overturn the succession in their favour. They were forced to stay on the Continent, and so the joyful union between Raybright and Bounty in *The Sun's Darling* can suggest two things: either a celebration of Prince Charles's recent reverse in policy, or a criticism of him and King James for not going far enough.

The conclusion of the masque is not really very optimistic, although the Sun rises and prevents Raybright from yielding once more to his weak and easily deluded nature. The Sun pronounces a moral, and commands Raybright to observe a strict obedience to his laws in future. If, heeding the apocalyptic elements, we take the Sun to be symbolic of the True Church, of Protestantism, then Raybright, the heir to the throne, is reminded of the existence of a higher authority, as happened to the King in *Match Me In London*. The terrestrial monarch should remember that he is only a humble subject of the divine King, and should fashion his policies

---

[38] Wedgwood, p. 149.

accordingly. The driving out of Folly at this point would have made a more emphatic ending.

Such a reading of *The Sun's Darling* makes it appear extremely sceptical. Prince Charles was for once the darling of the public, but the masque suggests that his true mettle as a Protestant monarch remains to be proved. He is the offspring of the Sun—that is, the heir to the leadership of the English Church—but he does not seem a very promising leader, much less so in fact than his sister or Frederick.

However, the form of the entertainment itself may point in a direction which is more optimistic than the details of its action. Dekker did not often write masques: in fact, this is the only one that he or Ford ever wrote, extant or non-extant.[39] It was also extremely unusual for a masque to be performed in a public theatre, and this has encouraged Bowers's speculation that it must have been written for an earlier performance at Court.[40] But the earliest record of *The Sun's Darling* is its note of licensing for the Cockpit Theatre in March 1624, and there is no evidence of an earlier production at Court, or of any Court production before the 1638 revival.

There is no need to doubt these records. The paradox is the point. By writing a masque, a courtly entertainment, for a public theatre in Drury Lane, the dramatists were transcending social divisions. It was an expression of the new mood of unity and reconciliation that prevailed now that the detested Spanish Match had been abandoned, and England was seriously contemplating a war against the Catholic powers. In August 1623, only a few months before, the Lady Elizabeth's Servants had been acting *Match Me In London* at the Cockpit Theatre—a play which lampooned King James himself and gave the impression of a country bitterly divided. For the same theatre to put on *The Sun's Darling* was a gesture that showed that the way to reconciliation was, at least temporarily, open.

It also had a further significance. By using the masque

---

[39] Huebert, p. 126, points out that most of Ford's plays contain some sort of masque-episode.

[40] Bowers, iv. 12; Hoy, iv. 3. Masque-like entertainments were sometimes performed for aristocratic patrons outside the Court, but there is no evidence to suggest that was the case here either.

form, the form used to entertain kings and rulers, militant Protestants could assert their sense of their own legitimacy. They were refusing to see themselves as outsiders or subversives, the role in which they had been cast during the years of opposition to the Spanish Match. They were asserting that their principles, the principles to which the Elizabethan Church was for the most part committed, had primacy. A masque symbolized the orderly and harmonious working of the state, and by writing a militant Protestant masque, Dekker could imply that it was the Catholic faction, rather than themselves, who were the real threat to the state.

The Sun's Darling not only offers the public audience a masque, but also a masque-within-a-masque, for at the Court of Winter a masque of the Elements and Humours is presented in honour of Raybright and Bounty. The music is sung by Harmony, and the masque celebrates the new, if somewhat precarious, social harmony that could be hoped for if Prince Charles committed himself to the militant Protestant cause. There are in fact four dances in *The Sun's Darling*, since Spring entertains Raybright with a morris, Summer offers a haymakers' dance, and Autumn a Bacchanalian. The dance of the four elements and four humours, or complexions, continues this pattern of fours which gives the plan symmetry, but the masque at Winter's Court is by far the most stately. Conceit says that the dancers will 'entertain Time in a courtly measure' and tells Harmony to place them in order, using the significant term 'rank them in a mask'.[41] There is a distinct emphasis on social orderliness in this entertainment, which belies the idea that militant Protestants are outsiders or constitute a disruptive force. Yet the kind of ranking and order they observe is a paradoxical one, for as Conceit also says:

> here amongest em none
> Observes a difference; Earth and Ayre alike
> Are sprightly active; Fire and Water seek
> No glory of preheminence.[42]

Hoy describes Winter's masque as a 'transcendence of difference', which is true but deeply paradoxical and problematical.[43] Without distinction of any sort it is difficult to have rank and order. Perhaps it is only some distinctions which are to be left behind, but there is a tension within Winter's masque, just as there is a tension in *The Sun's Darling* itself between its courtliness of form, and the highly critical, even scornful, light in which it presents Raybright.

Before the dance of the Elements and Humours is performed, Conceit (or poetic invention) enters to describe and explain it, and he is accompanied by Detraction, a disputatious pedant who finds fault with everything in it: 'Impossible and improper; first to personate insensible Creatures, and next to compound quite opposite humours; fie, fie, fie, it's abominable.'[44] Conceit attempts to defend his creation, but Detraction ridicules Conceit's claims to be a scholar, and insists that 'pettie penmen' cannot write masques.[45] When the elements appear, Detraction insists that they are all low, vulgar people: aldermen's sons, young brothers, and one of them 'a great lover of news', that is to say, somebody who takes more interest than he should in matters of state above his reach.[46]

This is the funniest part of the masque, and there is good reason to believe that in the carping critic Detraction, Dekker was satirizing Ben Jonson. In *Satiromastix* Crispinus accuses Horace/Jonson,

> Of bitter *Satirisme*, of *Arrogance*,
> Of *Selfe-loue*, of *Detraction* . . .[47]

Jonson can be naturally associated with the humours, since he wrote a series of comedies on that theme, and he had expressed his opinion of the prevailing fashion for news (among the sub-courtly orders) in his masque of 1621, *News From the New World*. He made this point with even more violent satire in *The Staple of News*, two years after *The Sun's Darling*. In *Neptune's Triumph*, written to celebrate Prince Charles's return from Spain, he placed greater emphasis than

---

[43] Hoy, iv. 13.   [44] *SD*, V. i. 222–4.   [45] *SD*, V. i. 199, 234.
[46] *SD*, V. i. 252–3.   [47] *Sat.*, V. ii. 220–1.

ever on social divisions and uncrossable barriers. It opens with a curious anti-masque, the cook's masque, in which a host of presumptuous persons, 'Such as do relish nothing but *di stato*', emerge from a stew-pot and dance.[48] The figure of the cook is thought to be an attack on Inigo Jones, but the satire is aimed at all those whom Jonson considered socially, politically, or artistically vulgar (most of the population of the British Isles).[49] The result is in revoltingly bad taste, and *Neptune's Triumph* was, in its original form, cancelled— perhaps because it was not felt to strike quite the right note at a time when Buckingham was making a bid to become a popular leader.

By introducing Detraction, Dekker anticipates Jonson's probable reaction to *The Sun's Darling* itself: a masque to be put on in Drury Lane, a strange and presumptuous creation. The comedy suggests that Dekker was well aware of the paradoxes involved in a morality-masque for the public theatre. Detraction's cry of 'impossible and improper' could easily have been applied to *The Sun's Darling* so Dekker pre-empted it with this satirical interlude.

Jonson, though he did not remain Catholic, had no sympathy for militant Protestantism, and (without setting up any simple antithesis between Jonson and Dekker) it is interesting to reflect that Jonson's *Alchemist* has been thought to possess a basically anti-apocalyptic structure; much of its comedy derives from 'satire of apocalyptic expectations' according to Gerard H. Cox.[50] In his early comedy, *Every Man Out of His Humour*, Jonson ridicules Foxe, when the farmer Sordido has what he thinks is a religious experience, and the ignorant rustics comment that he should be put into *Actes and Monuments* as he is certainly a martyr.[51] In *Satiromastix* we are told that Horace regards his fellow writers as 'Heritickes and Infidels'.[52] Jonson's Court entertainments had upheld the royal authority throughout the years of the Spanish Match, and so Dekker had no reason to

---

[48] *Jonson: The Complete Masques*, ed. S. Orgel (Yale University Press: New Haven, 1969), 416.   [49] Gordon, p. 85.

[50] Gerard H. Cox, 'Apocalyptic Projection and the Comic Plot of *The Alchemist*', *English Literary Renaissance*, 13 (1983), 75.

[51] Percy and Simpson, iii. 520–1.   [52] *Sat.*, IV. i. 90; Bowers, i. 356.

warm to him over the years; in Dekker's mind, popery is linked with arbitrary government.

The revised state of *The Sun's Darling* was spotted long before the precise allusions which date the original and the additions. This raises the question, how can a reader immediately detect the difference between these two sections of the text? Part of the answer lies in incongruity of mood and characters. Winter is made into two different people, first a sergeant-major hectoring his subordinates, then a gentle, courteous but decrepit figure of allegory. Weber observed that Winter's description of Raybright as a fierce conqueror also sounds rather inappropriate.[53] Raybright sets off in the mood of an idle pleasure-seeker and suddenly announces that if he meets any resistance, he will use military force. The break between the original and the 1638 addition actually comes near the end of Act IV. Raybright's couplet,

> Com let's go taste old *Winter*'s fresh delights,
> And swell with pleasures our big appetites,[54]

rounded off the original scene, and led into the next episode. Raybright has been told by Folly and Humor that Winter's realm is a place of gluttony and self-indulgence. But some very incompatible ideas follow. Almost at once there is a reference to 'four provinces we sway', which would have been premature in 1624, when Charles was not yet King. These four are joined in 'one conjugal ring', a somewhat irregular quadruple marriage, and similar absurdities follow. Winter complains that his subjects do not feel the 'heat . . . of obedience', but it is love or enthusiasm that are reputed to be warm, not obedience. And Winter's comparison of the approaching Prince's nature to 'two Suns' is unnatural and odd, particularly in the context of this masque about the Sun's offspring.[55]

There is an even more fundamental difference than this between the original and the 1638 revision, a difference in the fabric of the poetry which makes the change-over immediately audible before we notice points such as those above. The

[53] Quoted by Lawrence, p. 894.
[54] *SD*, IV. i. 289–90.
[55] *SD*, IV. i. 292, V. i. 20, 25.

interpolated passage is different in the way that it uses words. Take:

> Whose laws are so impartial, they must
> Be counted heavenly, cause th'are truly just.[56]

To scan this, it is necessary to stretch out 'impartial' into four syllables; yet in the next line 'because they are', which naturally has four syllables, is squeezed and clipped into two syllables to make it fit. This kind of thing is visible throughout.

> A most fair pretence,
> To found rebellion upon conscience;[57]

The couplet sounds heavy-handed because it rhymes 'pretence' with 'conscience'. The natural emphasis of 'pretence' falls on the final syllable, but 'conscience' is stressed on the first syllable (e.g. Thus conscience doth make cowards of us all). So either we force the pronunciation to bring out the rhyme, or we pronounce the word 'conscience' naturally and then the line sounds too short. It is as if the words themselves are uncomfortable about having to call anybody's genuine conscience a 'pretence' (i.e. arrogant or upstart). We get the feeling that the writer is bullying the language.

Rhymes in the interpolated passage frequently fall on a final, weak syllable:

> Can you conceive that he,
> Whose every thought's an act of pietie.[58]

The same happens with 'see / destinie', 'me / augurie', 'he / destinie', 'eie / majestie', and 'be / dignitie'. This is inept, not only because it harps on the same sounds as rhymes, but because it goes against the grain of the language. It produces an insistent, strident effect which becomes harsher at each repetition: 'pi-et-*ie*', 'dig-nit-*ie*'.

A comparably insistent effect is created by the use of 'Shall' at the beginning of two consecutive lines:

> Shall all attend our pastimes night and day,
> Shall both be subject to our glorious state.[59]

[56] *SD*, V. i. 27–8.   [57] *SD*, V. i. 52–3.
[58] *SD*, V. i. 60–1.   [59] *SD*, IV. i. 294–5.

The second line merely repeats the first, rubbing it in, as it were. And in,

> Your Princes entrie into this his land,

the repeated sound 'this, his' forces the voice to stress the second word in order to separate it, and so emphasizes its meaning.[60] The effect is aggravated by the structure of Winter's sentences, which tend to be too long and pursue their meaning doggedly through clause after clause.[61] Because the stresses are made so prominent, any irregularity tends to stand out, and the abnormally long line,

> From heaven's sublime height, into the depth of hell,

gives the effect of a pompous peroration, quite alien to an Elizabethan verse-dialogue.[62]

The reviser is coercing the language in order to uphold coercion. The very way he writes forces us to perceive it as such: it is dictatorial poetry both in sense and in sound. If we compare this to the section that follows immediately afterwards, in which we return to the 1624 text, we find that there are no more forced rhymes, and Dekker's use of the language is elastic and idiomatic.

> Never till now
> Did admiration beget in me truly
> The rare match'd twins at once, pittie and pleasure.[63]

It is a strange conceit, and the lines could hardly be more irregular. But 'pittie, and pleasure' stand out in a sensitive way, because the stresses are allowed to fall in the natural place, on the first syllable.

> For you he is no souldier dares not fight,
> No Scholar he, that dares not plead your merites,
> Or study your best Sweetness.[64]

The inversion of the word-order here is easy and unforced.

> Natures perfection; whom all love, all serve.[65]

[60] *SD*, V. i. 22.   [61] *SD*, V. i. 60–7.
[62] *SD*, V. i. 42.   [63] *SD*, V. i. 141–3.
[64] *SD*, V. i. 165–7.   [65] *SD*, V. i. 156.

The long, equal syllables at the end of the line—spondees—are difficult to achieve in English and convey strong feeling. The warmth and power of this tribute to the Queen of Bohemia owe a lot to the way it makes use of the idiomatic properties of the words, instead of imposing conformity on them. There is a sensitive tension between the demands of verse, and the shape of words, which creates expressive variety. The poet governs, but he is not a tyrant.

The result of the 1638 revision is that in *The Sun's Darling* as it now stands, two opposed policies have been yoked together. Perhaps the reviser thought they were compatible because Elizabeth of Bohemia was Charles Stuart's sister, and any Stuart cause was good; or more likely, he did not understand the original masque. The result is gravely inconsistent, because in electing Frederick to the throne of Bohemia its nobles had deposed Ferdinand, their previous King, and asserted their right to the same kind of religious freedom which Charles in 1638–9 was denying the Scots. One can compare Charles I's plan to invade Scotland at the time of the two Bishops' Wars, to the imperial invasion of Bohemia in 1620 when Ferdinand ousted the Winter King. So the principles represented by Bounty are the clean opposite of those introduced by the reviser. It is interesting to note that in 1638 the Scottish commander, Alexander Leslie, was a veteran of the Thirty Years' War and, like many of his troops, had served in the army of Gustavus Adolphus.[66] He fought first for Elizabeth of Bohemia and then against her brother Charles I. In both wars, he was fighting for the Protestant cause.

When the Clown says, 'They say this Prince too would bring new laws upon us, new rights into the Temples of our gods, and that's abominable, wee'l all bee hang'd first—'[67] he could be speaking for the Bohemian Sub-Utraquists and Protestants who organized the Defenestration of Prague and started the Thirty Years' War. Many of them were hanged when Frederick was defeated and Ferdinand reasserted his rule with an iron hand in 1621. The lines the reviser gives to Winter, 'A most fair pretence . . .' would be equally appro-

---

[66] G. Davies, p. 89.   [67] *SD*, V. i. 49–51.

priate for the imperial side in the same conflict. So *The Sun's Darling* is a militant Protestant masque with incongruous Caroline additions.

A great deal of space has been devoted here to the revisions of *The Sun's Darling*, partly because a recent book by Jerzy Limon totally rejects the possibility of revision in 1638. While giving welcome attention to a neglected work, Limon overlooks W. J. Lawrence's detailed and (in my view) conclusive arguments linking the Winter interpolation with the First Bishops' War. Not surprisingly, he comes to the conclusion that *The Sun's Darling* 'fails in artistic unity'.[68]

Limon prefers to interpret the Winter passage as a reference to Buckingham's projects for a war to regain the Palatinate in 1624. But this is not satisfactory, because Mansfeld's expedition to the Palatinate (the expedition whose feasibility was so rightly doubted by the war-party in Parliament) had the aim of expelling the Spanish occupying force, not of suppressing rebellious subjects.

As the Clown's speech quoted above indicates, Winter's subjects in the revised section of text fear that Raybright is going to invade them and force a new religion on them. Winter accuses his subjects of preferring their own religion to that of the royal invader. No such rebellion had been broached by the people of the Calvinist Palatinate. They had remained faithful to their Elector, but had been invaded by a Catholic army led by Tilly, four years before. The expedition planned in 1624 aimed to free the Protestant subjects from occupation, and the invader would anticipate welcome since he was coming to liberate the Calvinists, and not to impose an unpopular creed on them. Limon makes no distinction between 'conquest' and 'liberation', but this distinction was very clear in the minds of the authors of the masque.[69]

The 1638 reviser placed great emphasis on the cold, northerly clime where the rebellion is taking place:

> Will you prov't true, no good coms from the North;
> Bold sawcie mortals, dare you then aspire
> With snow and ice to quench the sphere of fire:

---

[68] Limon, pp. 89–90.   [69] Ibid. 93, 95.

Are your hearts frozen like your clime

. . . .

Hee to the frozen northern clime shall bring
A warmth so temperate, as shall force the *Spring*
Usurp my privilege . . .[70]

The Palatinate is not to the North of England, as Scotland is.
Even if we take these references in an entirely metaphorical
sense as allusions to the domains of the Winter King,
i.e. Bohemia and the Palatinate, that would be equally inapt.
There was no rebellion in Bohemia in 1624: like the
Palatinate, it had been subdued by Catholic forces, four years
previously.

Winter's subjects hear reports that the invader is approaching with 'whole troops and trains of Courtiers'.[71] In 1638
Charles I had to rely on 'Courtiers', that is, untrained
gentlemen-volunteers to fight for him. He had no professional
army in England. Strafford offered him the Irish army, but
Hamilton refused to ship it over.[72] This is one reason why the
Scots won both the Bishops' Wars. By contrast, in 1624,
Mansfeld had a highly experienced and professional force at
his command, which was why King James was prepared to
hire him.[73] The Winter interpolation shows an entrenched
animosity between Courtier and Clown, i.e. commoner, but
this was not the case in 1624, when there was strong support
among all classes for a war on Frederick and Elizabeth's
behalf. When Mansfeld came to London in 1624 he was
cheered in the streets, since the general populace did not make
the same kind of distinctions as were being made in
Parliament between one Protestant strategy and another.

In short, all the evidence supports W. J. Lawrence's theory.
I would agree with Limon in one respect, for he detects
allusions to the Bohemian King and Queen in the original
part of Act v.[74] It would be pleasant to have, as he thinks, an
original 1624 text of this masque, but unfortunately that is not
the case.

The Sun's Darling was neither the first nor the last
apocalyptic masque. David Norbrook has recently shed light

[70] *SD*, V. i. 16–19, 94–6.   [71] *SD*, V. i. 2–8.
[72] Farmer, p. 105.   [73] Wedgwood, pp. 186–7.
[74] Limon, pp. 94–5.

on an earlier one which was devised for the Palatine marriage celebrations, but cancelled at the last minute. The text of the masque is lost but there is a descriptive summary in a French pamphlet which enables us to say that it was a militant Protestant work.[75] Such a masque would have been a suitable way for militant Protestants to celebrate their ascendancy and legitimacy at the time of this hopeful alliance, the same sense of ascendancy and legitimacy they felt when the Spanish alliance collapsed and was succeeded by plans for war in 1624. Norbrook speculates that the cancellation may have had a political motive, since James would not have welcomed such a blatant statement of confessional politics. Other apocalyptic entertainments were staged on the continent to cement Protestant alliances. In 1632 Frederick and Elizabeth, together with the King of Sweden, acted in a Protestant masque themselves.[76]

Some comparison could also be made to *Comus*, though with caution. No equation should be attempted between Dekker's views and those of Milton, nor can the term 'militant Protestant' be applied to the government Milton eventually served—Cromwell's war against the Dutch, which put commercial interests above religious solidarity, is enough to indicate that. However, avoiding all such hasty comparisons, it is still true that a work such as *Comus* has a discernible ancestry in the apocalyptic literature of the previous generation, and its performance in 1634 at Ludlow Castle was not a totally unprecedented event.

While *The Sun's Darling* was not the only apocalyptic masque to be written in England, it seems to be—as far as is known—the only one ever to get itself performed at Court. The damaged state of its text can even be seen as a symptom of the strain this incurred: as a battle injury rather than an accident. The tensions involved in putting on a militant Protestant masque at all were increased by circumstances and textual violence ensued. This 1638 performance seems to have

---

[75] David Norbrook, 'The Masque of Truth: Court Entertainments and International Protestant Politics in the Early Stuart Period', forthcoming. I am grateful to the author for allowing me to see this at present unpublished article.

[76] Ibid. 30–2.

been a very strange one, fraught with ironies. The King and Queen doubtless recognized the reviser's very broad allusions to Charles and to the events of the moment: they are so heavy-handed they could not be missed. But it is very unlikely that either they or the actors suspected the less flattering reflections in the original text. The Spanish Match was by then long forgotten, and doubtless *The Sun's Darling* was by 1638 regarded simply as what its title-page calls it, a moral masque. The Court performance was given by children— the King and Queen's Young Company, or Beeston's Boys— which could have increased its air of innocence, and the boys themselves are not very likely to have scrutinized the text for political meanings or references to events before their own birth. Before that argument is carried too far, however, we should reflect that *Comus* was also performed by children.

Not long after *The Sun's Darling*, Dekker and Ford collaborated on *The Fairy Knight*, which was licensed by Herbert on 11 June 1624. Several suggestions have been put forward about this lost play.[77] In the light of *The Sun's Darling*, it seems most probable that *The Fairy Knight* was a dramatization of some part of Spenser's *Faerie Queene*, or connected with the Oberon cult of Prince Henry. There are two extant late works of Dekker in which we may detect an allegorical element, based on the familiar antithesis between female figures representing the True and the False. One is *Penny-Wise Pound Foolish* (1631), the tale of an erring husband who twice falls into the hands of artful courtesans, but is redeemed from prison and forgiven by his faithful wife.[78] Here we may discern the skeletal outline of the story of the Red Cross Knight, though in this version the Duessa figure is literally double, since there are two seductresses, one English and one Venetian.

The other work is a play, *The Noble Spanish Soldier*, a somewhat sketchy work written in the mid-1620s.[79] Here the

---

[77] Jones-Davies, ii. 407 gives the reasons for rejecting them.

[78] Pendry, pp. 111–44. The story was registered as Dekker's.

[79] It has been dated earlier by many scholars, including Bowers, but it can be dated from its use of the last volume of Jacques-Auguste de Thou's history as its source: see my article 'The Noble Spanish Soldier'. De Thou's great history was condemned by the Vatican, hence perhaps Dekker's interest in it. See Hugh Trevor-Roper, *Renaissance Essays* (Secker and Warburg: London, 1985), 126.

heroine, Onaelia, has been betrothed to the King of Spain but he abandons her and marries a Florentine princess called Paulina, who plots to have Onaelia's son murdered. The child is taken into hiding and saved, eventually becoming King, like the offspring of the Woman Clothed with the Sun, who was snatched away from the dragon and preserved in the wilderness. Details reveal that the plot was originally set in France.[80] It is distantly derived from one about Henri IV, who renounced Protestantism and married Marie de Medicis; the wicked Queen has Jesuits for her advisors, and the hero (if he is a hero), Balthazar, grapples with the problems of both apostasy and regicide.

Early in the play we see Onaelia tending an altar-like table on which stand a crucifix and a stabbed portrait of the renegade King. To stab a portrait of the monarch was regarded as a treasonable act, and in *The Whore of Babylon* the Spanish King suborns a conjuror to stick pins into a picture of Titania, then bury it.[81] This was based on the conspiracy of Hacket against Queen Elizabeth in 1591.[82] But while in the earlier play it was Titania who was the victim, in the late one it is the corresponding figure in the allegory who does the stabbing.

Balthazar, the rugged soldier of the title, having chided the King uselessly for his crimes, goes to Onaelia and asks her if she would like him to murder the King. She is tempted, but shrinks from the crime, whereupon he announces that he was only testing her: 'I would not drinke that infernall draught of a Kings blood, to goe reeling to damnation, for the weight of the world in Diamonds.'[83] So far, we are on safe ground, but in the next Act, Balthazar, forcing his way roughly into the King's presence, casually hacks down one of the guards and leaves him for dead. When threatened with banishment, he replies, 'For a Groomes death?'[84] This ignoble episode discredits all he has said about regicide, and all his claim to be regarded as a hero. A minute later, we are told that the man is

---

[80] See my article, referred to in ch. 4 n. 24, p. 225.

[81] *WB*, II. ii. 165–75.

[82] Fredson Bowers, 'The Stabbing of a Portrait in Elizabethan Tragedy', *Modern Language Notes*, 47 (June 1932), 381.

[83] *NSS*, II. ii. 67–9; Bowers, iv. 259.   [84] *NSS*, III. iii. 58; Bowers, iv. 269.

not dead (Dekker for once being kind and gentle), but the point has been made, as Balthazar spoke in the belief that he was. The gaping gulf between his valuation of a guilty king and an innocent groom casts doubt on all his judgements. It must be intentional since there is no other reason for including such an incident at all.

Earlier in the play, Onaelia has a dialogue with a poet, whom she tries to persuade to write an attack on the King. In a society without legitimate opposition this is a treasonable act analogous to her stabbing of the portrait. He refuses, and she scornfully replies:

> This basenesse followes your profession:
> You are like common Beadles, apt to lash
> Almost to death poore wretches not worth striking,
> But fawne with slavish flattery on damn'd vices,
> So great men act them: you clap hands at those,
> Where the true Poet indeed doth scorne to guild
> A gawdy Tombe with glory of his Verse,
> Which coffins stinking Carrion: no, his lines
> Are free as his Invention: no base feare
> Can shake his penne to Temporize even with Kings,
> The blacker are their crimes, he lowder sings.[85]

Dekker's own works, if we know how to read them, exemplify Onaelia's ideal.

The Sun's Darling is a peculiar work, and its posthumous history tempts us to indulge in the dubious practice of trying to project Dekker's ideas into the future, and ask what he would have thought about the First Bishops' War, or the Civil War, or Charles I's execution, or Cromwell's campaign in Ireland, and so on. Such questions are bound to be fallacious, as is any attempt to categorize the militant Protestants of Dekker's generation with political terminology such as 'right' and 'left', 'authority' and 'revolution': even to call them 'anti-absolutist' raises the question of whether the militant Protestants were not, in their way, just as absolute as King James. They opposed absolute power with powerful moral absolutes. In Frederick the Great's Prussia, Protestant-ism and absolute power proved in no way incompatible, but

[85] *NSS*, III. ii. 49–59; Bowers, iv. 263–4.

of course hereditary succession could not guarantee such a convenient situation forever. Martin Butler, in trying to define the stance of English militant Protestants in the 1630s, refers to their 'conservative opposition' (in an age when opposition was illegal) and 'radical nostalgia'.[86] It may be better to avoid such terms altogether.

One widespread attitude is represented by Jerzy Limon, who has written that 'The more a literary work is "engaged" in contemporary politics and the more the persuasive function becomes a goal in itself, the more confined its meaning becomes to one particular time and society,' adding that this is typical of 'literature which is created in countries with totalitarian regimes, and under severe censorship'.[87] In that case, why does Limon choose to write a book on such a subject? One suspects that he finds in the political frustration of Dekker's generation an apocalyptic revelation of more recent times and events. The present book may not persuade anybody to like Dekker, but if more people could at least remember who he is (instead of confusing him with Middleton or Deloney), that would at least be a step in the right direction.

At any rate, when we look at Dekker's work in the aggregate and survey his career over a span of a quarter of a century, we are forced to the conclusion that Dekker not only possessed a coherent group of principles but applied them consistently to a remarkably varied range of subjects and genres. Ultimately, the attitude we take to his religious-political principles is likely to govern our reaction to his work, and the amount of importance we attach to it.

---

[86] Butler, 'Entertaining the Palatine Prince', p. 338.
[87] Limon, p. 132.

BIBLIOGRAPHY

A. WORKS OF DEKKER

BOWERS, FREDSON (ed.), *The Dramatic Works of Thomas Dekker* (4 vols.; CUP: Cambridge, 1953–61).
GROSART, Revd ALEXANDER B. (ed.), *The Non-Dramatic Works of Thomas Dekker* (5 vols.; The Huth Library: Aylesbury, 1884–5; rpt. Russell and Russell, Inc.: New York, 1963).

PENDRY, E. D. (ed.), *The Wonderful Year . . . and Selected Prose Works of Thomas Dekker* (Stratford-upon-Avon Library, 4; Edward Arnold Ltd.: London, 1967).
RHYS, ERNEST (ed.), *Dekker: Best Plays* (The Mermaid Series; T. Fisher Unwin: London, 1887; rpt. Ernest Benn: London, 1949).
SHEPHERD, R. (ed.), *Dramatic Works of Thomas Dekker* (4 vols.; John Pearson: London, 1871–3).
WILSON, F. P. (ed.), *The Plague Pamphlets of Thomas Dekker* (Clarendon Press: Oxford, 1925).

DAVIES, PAUL C. (ed.), *The Shoemaker's [sic] Holiday by Thomas Dekker* (Oliver & Boyd: Edinburgh, 1968).
MCKERROW, R. B. (ed.), *The Gull's Horn-Book by Thomas Dekker* (The King's Library, ed. Prof. Gollanz; De La More Press: London, 1904).
RIELY, MARIANNE GATESON (ed.), *The Whore of Babylon by Thomas Dekker* (Renaissance Drama: A Collection of Critical Editions, ed. Stephen Orgel; Garland Publishing Inc.: NY, 1980).
RIMBAULT, E. F. (ed.), *A Knight's Conjuring, Done in Earnest: Discouered in Jest* (Percy Society Reprints, vol. V, 1842).
SMALLWOOD, ROBERT, and WELLS, STANLEY (eds.), *The Shoemaker's [sic] Holiday by Thomas Dekker* (The Revels Plays; Manchester University Press: Manchester, 1979).
WILSON, F. P. (ed.), *Foure Birds of Noahs Arke: viz. The Doue, the Eagle, the Pellican and the Phoenix* (Basil Blackwell: Oxford, 1924).
—— *The Artillery Garden* (Fascimile, privately printed, Oxford, 1952).

B. PRIMARY SOURCES

ABBOTT, ROBERT, *Antichristi Demonstratio* (1608).

AESOP, *Fables*, trans. A. Caldecott and illus. R. Caldecott (Macmillan and Co.: London, 1887).

Articles of the League Made betweene Fredericke, King of Bohemia . . . and . . . Gabriel, Prince of Hungaria (anon., n.p., 1620).

Babylon is Fallen (anon., 1594; 2nd edn. 1597). Reprinted 1610, 1619, etc. as *A Prophecy that hath Lyen Hid above these 2000 Years.*

BACON, FRANCIS, *A Declaration of the Practices and Treasons Attempted and Committed by Robert, Late Earle of Essex, and His Complices . . . Together with the Very Confessions* (1601).

BALE, JOHN, *The Ymage of Both Chvrches after the Moste Wonderful and Heauenly Reuelacion of Sainct John the Evangelist* (1550).

—— *King Johan*, ed. J. H. P. Pafford (Malone Society Reprints; OUP: Oxford, 1931).

BIRCH, THOMAS, *Life of Henry, Prince of Wales* (1760).

Bohemiae Regnum Electiuum [sic]; or a Relation of the Proceedings of the States of Bohemia, from the First Foundation of that Province by Free Election of Princes and Kings unto Ferdinand, the 18th King of the House of Austria (anon., n.p., 1620).

BROUGHTON, HUGH, *A Concent of Scripture* (1588; rpt. 1590).

BUCHANAN, GEORGE, *The Powers of the Crown in Scotland* ('*De Iure Regni Apud Scotos*'), trans. with intro. and notes by C. F. Arrowood (University of Texas Press: Austin, 1949).

BULLEN, A. H. (ed.), *A Collection of Old Plays in IV volumes* (Privately printed by Wyman and Sons, 1st Series, 1882–5).

BULLINGER, HEINRICH, *A Hundred Sermons vpon the Apocalips of Jesu Christe* (1561).

CALVIN, JEAN, *Commentaries on the New Testament*, trans. T. H. L. Parker, Ross Mackenzie, *et al.*, ed. D. W. Torrance and T. F. Torrance (12 vols.; Oliver & Boyd: Edinburgh, 1959–65).

—— *Commentary on Seneca's 'De Clementia'*, ed. and trans. F. A. Battles and A. M. Hugo (Renaissance Texts Series, 3; Renaissance Society of America: Leiden, 1969).

CHAMBERLAIN, JOHN, *Letters of John Chamberlain*, ed. H. E. McClure (2 vols.; Philadelphia Amen Philosophical Society; Lancaster Press: Philadelphia, 1939).

CHAPMAN, GEORGE, *The Poems of George Chapman*, ed. Phyllis Brooks Bartlett (OUP: Oxford, 1941).

—— *The Tragedies of George Chapman*, ed. Thomas Marc Parrott (Routledge and Sons: London, 1910).

CHILIANUS, EQUES MELLERSTATINUS, *Comedia gloriose parthenices et martiris Dorothee agoniam passionemque depingens* (Per Baccalarium Wolfgangum Monacensem, Leipzig, 1507).

COCHLAEUS, JOHANNES, *Historia Hussitarum* (Bohemia, 1549).

DANIEL, SAMUEL, *Complete Works in Verse and Prose*, ed. A. B. Grosart (4 vols.; privately printed, 1885).

The Declaration and Information of the High and Puissant King of Bohemia, against the Vniust Mandates Published in the Name of the Emperour . . . (anon., n.p., 1620).

DELONEY, THOMAS, *The Gentle Craft, Part One*, in *The Novels of Thomas Deloney*, ed. Merrit E. Lawlis (Indiana University Press: Bloomington, 1961).

DEVEREUX, ROBERT, 2nd Earl of Essex, *An Apologie of the Earle of Essex* . . . *Penned by himself in Anno 1598* (Imprinted at London, by Richard Bradocke, 1603).

DRAYTON, MICHAEL, *The Works of Michael Drayton*, ed. J. William Hebel (5 vols.; The Shakespeare Head Press; Basil Blackwell: Oxford, 1961).

DRUE, THOMAS, *The History of the Dutchess of Suffolk* (Imprinted by A. M. for Iasper Emery at the Flowerdeluce in Paules-Church-yard, 1631).

E., T., *The Lavves Resolvtions of Womens Rights: or, The Lavves Provision for Woemen* (Printed by the assignes of Iohn More Esq., 1632). Also known as *The Woman's Lawyer*.

EUSEBIUS, ST, *Works of St. Eusebius*, ed. M. Hopperus (2 vols.; Basle, 1559).

Exemplar Litterarum (newsletters; n.p., Sept. and Oct. 1618).

FAIRHOLT, FREDERICK W. (ed.), *Poems and Songs Relating to George Villiers, Duke of Buckingham* (Percy Society Reprints, vol. XXIX, 1850).

FOXE, JOHN, *Actes and Monuments of Matters Most Special and Memorable, Happenyng in the Church, with an Vniuersall history of the same* . . . (1563), 4th edn., newly revised and recognized, partly augmented (2 vols.; 1583).

—— *Christvs Triumphans: Comoedia Apocalyptica* (Basel, 1556; rpt. Nuremberg, 1590).

—— *Le Triomphe de Jesus Christ: comedie apocalyptique*, trans. J. F. [Jean Bienvenu] (Geneva, 1562).

—— *Two Latin Comedies by John Foxe the Martyrologist*, trans. and ed. John Hazell Smith (Cornell University Press: Ithaca, 1973).

GATAKER, THOMAS, *A Sparke toward the Kindling of Sorrow for Sion* (1621).

GENTILLET, INNOCENT, *A Discourse Vpon the Meanes of Wel Governing and Maintaining in Good Peace, A Kingdome or Other Principalitie . . . Against Nicholas Machiavel the Florentine*, trans. Simon Patericke (1602; rpt. 1608).

GENTLEMAN, TOBIAS, *England's Way to Win Wealth* (1614).

GIBSON, JOHN, *The Sacred Shield of Al Trve Christian Sovldiers* (1599).

GIFFARD [or GIFFORD], GEORGE (1548–1600), *Sermons Vpon the Whole Booke of the Revelation* (1596; rpt. 1599).

GUEST, Lady CHARLOTTE (trans.), *The Mabinogion* (Everyman's Library, 97; J. M. Dent & Sons: London, 1906; rpt. 1924).

HELLWIS [or HELLWYS], EDWARD, *A Marvell Deciphered, Being an Exposition of the 12th Chapter of the Revelation* (1589).

HERBERT, Sir HENRY, *The Dramatic Records of Sir Henry Herbert*, ed. Joseph Quincy Adams (Cornell Studies in English, 3; Yale University Press: New Haven, 1917).

HOLINSHED, RAPHAEL, *Chronicles of England, Scotland and Ireland*, augmented edn. (4 vols.; 1587).

JACOBUS DE VORAGINE, *Legenda Sanctorum Aurea (Historia Lombardica)* (Ulm, 1469). English trans. by W. Caxton, *The Golden Legend* (1483, rpt. 1503, 1527).

JAMES VI and I, *The Basilicon Doron of King James VI*, ed. J. Craigie (Scottish Text Society, 3rd series, vols. 16, 18; Edinburgh, 1944–50).

—— *A Fruitefull Meditation . . . of the 7, 8, 9 and 10 Verses of the 20 Chapter of the Reuelation* (Edinburgh, 1588; 2nd edn. printed for John Harrison, London, 1603).

—— *The Trve Lawe of Free Monarchies, or The Reciprock and Mutuall Dutie betwixt a Free King, and His Naturall Subiects* (Edinburgh, 1598; 2nd edn. London, 1603).

—— *The Workes of the Most High and Mighty Prince, James* (1616).

JEWELL, JOHN, *The Works of the Very Learned and Reverend Father in God Iohn Ievvell* (John Norton, London, 1609).

JONSON, BENJAMIN, *Complete Works*, ed. C. H. Herford Percy and Evelyn Simpson (11 vols.; OUP: Oxford, 1941).

—— *Jonson: The Complete Masques*, ed. S. Orgel (Yale University Press: New Haven, 1969).

KEYMOR [or KEYMER], JOHN, *John Keymor's Observation Made upon the Dutch Fishing about the Year 1601* (Printed 1664), Facsimile, ed. M. P. Lloyd Pritchard (NY, 1967).

KIRCHMEYER, THOMAS [NAOGEORGIUS], *Tragoedia noua Pammachius* (Wittenberg, 1538).

KYFFIN, MAURICE, *The Blessedness of Britain or a Celebration of the Queenes Holyday* (1587).

The Last Newes from Bohemia ... *Wherein is Related all the Passages that have Happened since the Elector Palatine of the Rhine was Elected and Crowned King of Bohemia* (anon., n.p., 1620).

A Letter Written Out of England to an English Gentleman Remaining at Padua, Containing a True Report of a Strange Conspiracie, Contriued between Edward Squire, Lately Executed for the Same Treason as Actor, and Richard Wallpoole a Iesuite, as Deuiser and Suborner against the Person of the Queenes Maiestie (anon., printed by Christopher Barker, 1599).

MACHIAVELLI, NICCOLO, *The Literary Works of Niccolo Machiavelli*, trans. and ed. J. R. Hale (OUP: Oxford, 1961).

—— *The Prince*, trans. with introd. by W. K. Marriott (Everyman's Library, 280, gen. ed. Ernest Rhys; J. M. Dent and Sons: London, 1908; rpt. 1944).

MARLOWE, CHRISTOPHER, *Doctor Faustus*, ed. Keith Walker (Oliver & Boyd: Edinburgh, 1973).

MASSINGER, PHILIP, *The Bondman by Philip Massinger*, ed. Benjamin Townley Spencer (Princeton University Press: Princeton, 1932).

—— *The Plays and Poems of Philip Massinger*, ed. Philip Edwards and Colin Gibson (5 vols.; OUP: Oxford, 1976).

MIDDLETON, THOMAS, *A Game at Chess*, ed. J. W. Harper (New Mermaid Series; Ernest Benn Ltd.: London, 1966).

—— *Women Beware Women*, ed. J. R. Mulryne (The Revels Plays; Methuen and Co.: London, 1975).

MORNAY, PHILIPPE DU PLESSIS, *Le Mystere d'iniqvité* (Saumur, 1611).

—— *The Mystery of Iniquity*, Englished by Samson Lennard (1612).

MUN, THOMAS, *A Discovrse of Trade, from England vnto the East-Indies* (1621).

—— *England's Treasure by Forraign Trade* (1664).

—— *The Petition and Remonstrance of the Governor and Company of Merchants of London Trading to the East Indies* (1628).

NEGRI, FRANCESCO, *A Certayne Tragedie Wrytten Fyrst in Italian by F. N. B. Entituled, Freewil, and Translated into English by Henry Cheeke* (1589).

PARSONS, ROBERT, SJ [under pseud. R. DOLEMAN], *A Conference abovt the Next Succession to the Crowne of Ingland* [sic] (1594).

PERKINS, WILLIAM, *The Works of William Perkins* (Printed by John Legatt, 1613).

PHENICE, THRASIBULE [THEODORE DE BEZA], *Comedie dv Pape malade et tirant a la fin* (Orleans, 1575).

PHILIP, W. (trans.), *Newes from Bohemia; an Apologie Made by the States of the Kingdome of Bohemia, Shewing the Reasons Why Those of the Reformed Religion were Moved to Take Armes* (1619).

A Plaine Demonstration of the Unlawful Succession of Ferdinand II (anon., 1620).

The Popes Complaint to His Minion Cardinals against the Good Successe of the Bohemians and Their Generall Proceedings (anon., n.p., n.d. (*c.*1620)).

PRICKETT, ROBERT, *Honors Fame in Trivmph Riding, or, the Life and Death of the Late Honorable Earle of Essex* (1604).

—— *Time's Anotomie* [sic] (1606).

PROCTOR, JOHN, *The Historie of Wyates Rebellion* (1554; rpt. 1555).

R., I. [ROBERT KAYLL?], *The Trades Increase* (1615).

The Rates of Marchandizes, as They are Set Downe in the Booke of Rates for the Custome of Poundage (n.p., n.d.). Also known as *Salisbury's Book of Rates*, issued 1608.

The Reasons which Compelled the States of Bohemia to Reiect the Archduke Ferdinand &c. & Inforced Them to Elect a New King, trans. John Harrison (Dort, 1619).

A Relation of the Bloody Execution at Prague (anon., 1621).

SANCTORIUS [or SANTORI/IO], PAULUS AEMILIUS, *XII Virgines et martyres* (Rome, 1597).

SCOTT, THOMAS, *Robert Earle of Essex His Ghost, Sent from Elizian: To the Nobility Gentry and Commvnaltie of England. Virtutum Comes Invidia. Printed in Paradise* (1624).

—— *The Second Part of Vox Populi, or, Gondomar Appearing in the Likenes of Matchiauell in a Spanish Parliament* (Goricom, 1624).

—— *Vox Populi* (1620).

—— *The Workes of the Most Famovs and Reverend Divine Mr. Thomas Scot Batchelor in Diuinitie Sometimes Preacher in Norwich* (Vtrick, 1624).

SENECA, LUCIUS ANNAEUS, *Moral Essays*, with a trans. by J. W. Basore, Loeb Classical Library (3 vols., William Heinemann: London, 1928).

SHAKESPEARE, WILLIAM, *The Merchant of Venice by William Shakespeare*, ed. John Russell Brown, The Arden Shakespeare (Methuen: London, 1955; rpt. 1984).

—— and FLETCHER, JOHN, *King Henry VIII*, ed. J. C. Maxwell, The New Cambridge Shakespeare (CUP: Cambridge, 1969).

SIDNEY, Sir PHILIP, *Miscellaneous Prose of Sir Philip Sidney*, ed. Katherine Duncan-Jones and J. Van Dorsten (Clarendon Press: Oxford, 1973).

—— *The Countess of Pembroke's Arcadia (The Old Arcadia)*, ed. Jean Robertson (OUP: Oxford, 1973).

SMITH, HENRY, *Ten Sermons Preached by Henry Smith* (1596).

SMITH, WENTWORTH, *The Hector of Germany, or, the Palgrave Prime Elector* (1615; written 1612).

SPENSER, EDMUND, *The Poetical Works of Edmund Spenser*, ed. J. C. Smith and E. de Selincourt (OUP, 1912; rpt. 1937).

The Statutes at Large from Magna Charta to George III, ed. O. Ruffhead, new edn. rev. by C. Runnington (14 vols.; 1786–1800).

STOWE, JOHN, *Annales of England . . . until 1601*, augmented edn. (1601).

SUETONIUS TRANQUILLUS, GAIUS, *The Twelve Caesars*, trans. Robert Graves, The Belle Sauvage Library (Cassell & Co.: London, 1962).

SURIUS, LAURENTIUS, *De Probatis Sanctorum Historiis* (7 vols.; Cologne, 1571–8).

TENNYSON, ALFRED, *The Works of Alfred Tennyson, Poet Laureate* (Kegan Paul, Trench and Co.: London, 1883).

Trovbles in Bohemia and Diuers Other Kingdomes, Procured by the Diuellish Practises of State-meddling Iesvites, trans. out of French (anon., 1619).

VILLEGAS, ALFONSO, *Flos Sanctorvm. The Lives of Saints. Written in Spanish by the Learned and Reuerend Father Alfonso Villegas Diuine, of S. Dominicks Order. Translated out of Italian into English and conferred with the Spanish, by W. & E. K. B.* [i.e. William and Edward Kinsman] (2 vols.; Douai, 1609).

WEBSTER, JOHN, *Three Plays of John Webster*, ed. D. C. Gunby, The Penguin English Library (Penguin Books: Harmondsworth, 1972; rpt. 1980).

WOTTON, HENRY, *Letters of Sir Henry Wotton*, ed. Logan Pearsall Smith (2 vols.; OUP: Oxford, 1907).

C. SECONDARY SOURCES

ADAMS, H. M., *A Catalogue of Books Printed on the Continent of Europe 1501–1600 in Cambridge Libraries* (2 vols.; CUP: Cambridge, 1967).

ADAMS, SIMON L., 'Captain Thomas Gainsford, the *Vox Spiritus* and the *Vox Populi*', *Bulletin of the Institute of Historical Research*, XLIX (May 1976), 141–4.

—— 'Eliza Enthroned? The Court and its Politics', in *The Reign of Elizabeth I*, ed. Christopher Haigh (Macmillan: London, 1984).

ADAMS, SIMON L., 'Foreign Policy and the Parliaments of 1621 and 1624', in *Faction and Parliament: Essays in Early Stuart History*, ed. Kevin Sharpe (OUP: Oxford, 1978).

—— 'The Protestant Cause: Religious Alliance with the European Calvinist Communities as a Political Issue in England, 1585–1630', D.Phil. thesis (Oxford, 1972).

—— 'The Queen Embattled: Elizabeth I and the Conduct of Foreign Policy', in *Queen Elizabeth I: Most Politick Princess*, ed. Simon L. Adams (A History Today Production, series editor Juliet Gardiner, 1984).

—— 'Spain or the Netherlands: The Dilemmas of Early Stuart Foreign Policy', in *Before the English Civil War*, ed. Howard Tomlinson (Macmillan: London, 1983).

ADLER, DORIS RAY, *Thomas Dekker: A Reference Guide* (G. K. Hall and Co.: Boston, 1983).

ALLISON, A. F., *Thomas Dekker: A Bibliographical Catalogue of the Early Editions* (Pall Mall Bibliographies; Dawsons of Pall Mall: Folkestone, 1972).

—— and ROGERS, D. M., *A Catalogue of Catholic Books in English Printed Abroad or Secretly in England 1558–1640* (The Arundel Press: Bognor Regis, 1956).

ANDREWS, MICHAEL CAMERON, '*The Virgin Martyr* and Sidney's *Arcadia*', *American Notes and Queries*, XIV, no. 7 (March 1976), 107.

ARDOLINO, FRANK R., ' "In Saint Iagoes Park": Iago as Catholic Machiavell in Dekker's *Whore of Babylon*', *Names*, 30 (1982), 1–4.

BAUCKHAM, RICHARD, *Tudor Apocalypse* (The Courtenay Library of Reformation Classics, 8; The Sutton Courtenay Press: Oxford, 1978).

BENTLEY, G. E., *The Jacobean and Caroline Stage* (5 vols.; OUP: London, 1941–56).

BERGERON, DAVID M., *English Civic Pageantry, 1558–1642* (Edward Arnold Ltd.: London, 1971).

—— 'Harrison, Jonson and Dekker: The *Magnificent Entertainment for King James*', Note in *Journal of the Warburg and Courtauld Institutes*, 31 (1968), 445–8.

—— 'Prince Henry and English Civic Pageantry', *Tennessee Studies in Literature*, 13 (1968), 109–16.

—— 'Thomas Dekker's Lord Mayor's Shows', *English Studies* (Amsterdam), 51 (1971), 2–15.

BERLIN, NORMAND, 'Thomas Dekker: A Partial Reappraisal', *Studies in English Literature*, 6 (1966), 273–5.

BEVINGTON, DAVID M., *Tudor Drama and Politics: A Critical*

Approach to Topical Meaning (Harvard University Press: Cambridge, Mass., 1968).

BIRCH, T., *The Court and Times of James I* (2 vols.; Henry Colburn: London, 1848).

BLACK, J. B., *The Reign of Elizabeth, 1558–1603* (OUP: London, 1959).

BLOW, SUZANNE K., *Rhetoric in the Plays of Thomas Dekker* (Jacobean Drama Studies, III; Dr James Hogg Institute, University of Salzburg, Austria, 1972).

BOAS, FREDERICK S., *University Drama in the Tudor Age* (OUP: London, 1914).

BOWERS, FREDSON, 'Essex's Rebellion and Dekker's *Old Fortunatus*', *Review of English Studies*, NS 3 (1952), 365–6.

—— 'The Stabbing of a Portrait in Elizabethan Tragedy', *Modern Language Notes*, 47 (June 1932), 378–85.

BRADBROOK, MURIEL C., *The Growth and Structure of Elizabethan Comedy* (Chatto and Windus: London, 1955).

—— *John Webster, Citizen and Dramatist* (Weidenfeld and Nicolson: London, 1980).

BURELBACH, FREDERICK M., 'War and Peace in *The Shoemakers' Holiday*', *Tennessee Studies in Literature*, 13 (1968), 99–107.

BUSH, DOUGLAS (ed.), *The Oxford History of English Literature*, rev. edn. (OUP: Oxford, 1962).

BUTLER, MARTIN, 'Entertaining the Palatine Prince: Plays on Foreign Affairs 1635–1637', *English Literary Renaissance*, 13, no. 1 (Winter 1983), 319–44.

—— *Theatre and Crisis 1632–1642* (CUP: Cambridge, 1984).

CAPLAN, JOEL H., 'Virtue's Holiday: Thomas Dekker and Simon Eyre', *Renaissance Drama*, NS 2 (1969), 103–22.

CHAMBERS, E. K., *The Elizabethan Stage* (4 vols.; OUP: London, 1923; rpt. with corrections, 1951).

CHAPMAN, HESTER W., *Lady Jane Grey* (Jonathan Cape: London, 1962; rpt. Cedric Chivers Ltd.: London, 1972).

CHEYNEY, EDWARD P., *A History of England from the Defeat of the Armada to the Death of Elizabeth* (2 vols.; Longmans, Green & Co.: London, 1926).

CLUBB, LOUISE G., '*The Virgin Martyr* and the *Tragedia Sacra*', *Renaissance Drama*, 7 (1964), 103–26.

COLLINSON, PATRICK, 'The Elizabethan Church and the New Religion', in *The Reign of Elizabeth I*, ed. C. Haigh (Macmillan: London, 1984).

—— *The Elizabethan Puritan Movement* (Jonathan Cape: London, 1967).

COLLINSON, PATRICK, *Godly People: Essays on English Protestantism and Puritanism* (The Hambledon Press: London, 1983).
—— 'The Jacobean Religious Settlement: The Hampton Court Conference', in *Before the English Civil War*, ed. H. Tomlinson (Macmillan: London, 1983).

COOPER, ELIZABETH, *The Life and Letters of Lady Arabella [sic] Stuart* (2 vols.; Hurst and Blackett: London, 1866).

COX, GERARD H., 'Apocalyptic Projection and the Comic Plot of *The Alchemist*', *English Literary Renaissance*, 13 (1983), 70–87.

CRUICKSHANK, A. H., *Philip Massinger* (Basil Blackwell: Oxford, 1920).

CUNNINGHAM, WILLIAM, DD, *Alien Immigrants to England* (Social England Series, ed. K. D. Cotes; Swan Sonnenschein & Co.: London, 1897).

DAVIES, GODFREY, *The Early Stuarts*, Vol. ix of *The Oxford History of England*, gen. ed. Sir George Clark (OUP: London, 1937; rpt. 1967).

DOBSON, DANIEL B., 'Allusions to the Gunpowder Plot in Dekker's *Whore of Babylon*', *N & Q* VI (1959), 257.

DUNN, T. A., *Philip Massinger: The Man and the Playwright* (Nelson and Sons Ltd.: Edinburgh, 1957).

DURANT, DAVID M., *Arbella Stuart: A Rival to the Queen* (Weidenfeld and Nicolson: London, 1978).

DUST, PHILIP, 'A Source for John Donne's Seventeenth Meditation in Rowley, Dekker and Ford's *The Witch of Edmonton*', *N & Q* CCXXIX (June 1984), 231–2.

ECCLES, MARK, 'Thomas Dekker (or rather Heywood) and Eliot's "Rhapsody on a Windy Night" ', *N & Q* CCXXVI (June 1981), 435.

EDMOND, MARY, 'In Search of John Webster', TLS, 24 Dec. 1976, 1621–2.

EDMUNDSON, GEORGE, *Anglo-Dutch Rivalry 1600–1653; The Ford Lectures 1910* (Clarendon Press: London, 1911).

ELIOT, T. S., *Elizabethan Essays* (Faber and Faber: London, 1934).
—— 'Plague Pamphlets', TLS, 5 Aug. 1926, 522.
—— *Selected Essays* (Faber and Faber: London, 1927).

ELLIS-FERMOR, UNA, *The Jacobean Drama: An Interpretation* (Methuen and Co.: London, 1936).

FARMER, D. L., *Britain and the Stuarts* (G. Bell and Sons Ltd.: London, 1971).

FEUER, LEWIS S. (ed.), *Marx and Engels: Basic Writings on Politics and Philosophy* (Fontana Classics of History and Thought; Anchor Books: NY, 1959; rpt. Fontana Books: Glasgow, 1976).

FIRTH, KATHERINE ROBBINS, *The Apocalyptic Tradition in Refor-*

mation Britain 1530–1645 (Oxford History Monographs; OUP: Oxford, 1979).

FISHER, J., PROCKTER, A., and TAYLOR, R., *A–Z of Elizabethan London* (Harry Margary, Lympne Castle, Kent. In association with the Guildhall Library, 1979).

FLEAY, FREDERICK GARD, *A Biographical Chronicle of the English Drama 1559–1642* (2 vols.; Reeves and Turner: London, 1891).

FLETCHER, ANTONY, *Tudor Rebellions* (Seminar Studies in History, 3; Longmans: London, 1968).

FOAKES, R. A., and RICKERT, R. T., *Henslowe's Diary* (CUP: Cambridge, 1961).

FREEMAN, A., 'The Date of Dekker's *If This Be Not A Good Play*', *Philological Quarterly*, XLIV (1965), 122–4.

GARDINER, SAMUEL R., *A History of England from the Accession of James I to the Outbreak of the Civil War, 1603–1642* (10 vols.; Longmans: London, 1883; 3rd edn. 1889).

GASPER, JULIA, '*The Noble Spanish Soldier, The Wonder of A Kingdom*, and *The Parliament of Bees*: The Belated Solution to a Long-standing Dekker Problem', *The Durham University Journal*, LXXIX, no. 2 (June 1987), 223–32.

—— 'The Protestant Plays of Thomas Dekker', D.Phil. thesis (Oxford, 1987).

GOLDBERG, JONATHAN, *James I and the Politics of Literature* (Johns Hopkins University Press: Baltimore, 1983).

GORDON, DAVID JAMES, *The Renaissance Imagination, Essays and Lectures*, ed. Stephen Orgel (University of California Press: Berkeley, 1975).

GREEN, MARY ANN EVERETT (ed.), *Calendar of State Papers, Domestic, Reigns of Elizabeth I and James I* (104 vols.; 2nd series; Longmans, Brown, Green, Longmans and Roberts: London, 1858).

GREER, GERMAINE, *The Female Eunuch* (MacGibbon and Kee: London, 1970; rpt. Paladin Books, Granada Publishing: London, 1979).

GREG, W. W., 'The Authorship of the Songs in Lyly's Plays', *Modern Language Review*, I (1905), 43–52.

—— *A Bibliography of the English Printed Drama to the Restoration* (2 vols.; The Bibliographical Society, 1939–51).

—— *Henslowe's Diary* (2 vols.; A. H. Bullen: London, 1904–8).

HAIGH, CHRISTOPHER (ed.), *The Reign of Elizabeth I* (Problems in Focus Series; Macmillan and Co.: London, 1985).

HALLAM, HENRY, *Literary Essays and Characters* (John Murray: London, 1852).

HALLER, WILLIAM, and HALLER, MALLEVILLE, 'The Puritan Art

of Love', *Huntingdon Library Quarterly*, V, no. 2 (1942), 235–72.

HARBAGE, ALFRED B., *Annals of English Drama 975–1700*, rev. by Samuel Schoenbaum (Methuen and Co.: London, 1964).

—— 'The Mystery of Perkin Warbeck', in *Studies in English Renaissance Drama*, ed. J. W. Bennet *et al.* (Peter Owen: London, 1959).

HARDER, KELSIE B., 'The Names of Thomas Dekker's Devils', *Names*, 3 (1955), 210–18.

HARMS, WOLFGANG, *Illustrierte Flugblatter aus den Jahrhunderten der Reformation* (Kunstsammlungen der Veste Coburg: Coburg, 1983).

HARRISON, G. B., *The Life and Death of Robert Devereux, Earl of Essex* (Cassell and Co.: London, 1937).

HARVEY, PAUL (ed.), *The Oxford Companion to English Literature* (OUP: Oxford, 1967).

HEINEMANN, MARGOT C., *Puritanism and Theatre: Thomas Middleton and Opposition Drama under the Early Stuarts* (Past and Present publications; CUP: Cambridge, 1980).

HILL, CHRISTOPHER, *Puritanism and Revolution* (Martin Secker and Warburg: London, 1958).

—— *Society and Puritanism in Pre-Revolutionary England* (Martin Secker and Warburg: London, 1964).

HOENIGER, F. DAVID (ed.), *'Paul His Temple Triumphant'*, *Renaissance News*, XVI (1963), 181–200.

HOLMES, DAVID M., *The Art of Thomas Middleton* (OUP: London, 1970).

HOWAT, G. D. M., *Stuart and Cromwellian Foreign Policy* (Adam and Charles Black: London, 1974).

HOY, CYRUS, *Introductions, Notes, and Commentaries to Texts in 'The Dramatic Works of Thomas Dekker'* (4 vols.; CUP: Cambridge, 1980–1).

HUEBERT, RONALD, *John Ford: Baroque English Dramatist* (McGill-Queen's University Press: Montreal, 1977).

HUME, ANTHEA, 'Spenser, Puritanism, and the 'Maye' Eclogue', *Review of English Studies*, NS 20 (1969), 155–67.

HUNT, MARY LELAND, *Thomas Dekker* (Columbia University Press: NY, 1912).

HUNTER, G. K., 'Bourgeois Comedy: Shakespeare and Dekker', in *Shakespeare and His Contemporaries: Essays in Comparison*, ed. E. A. J. Honigman (The Revels Plays Companion Library; Manchester University Press: Manchester, 1986).

JENKINS, ELIZABETH, *Elizabeth the Great* (Victor Gollancz Ltd.: London, 1958; rpt. Book Club Associates: London, 1971).

JOHNSON, PAUL, *Elizabeth I: A Study in Power and Intellect* (Weidenfeld and Nicolson: London, 1973).

JONES-DAVIES, MARIE-THERESE, 'Note sur Thomas Dekker et les Marchands-Tailleurs', *Études Anglaises* (Feb. 1953).

—— *Un peintre de la vie londonienne: Thomas Dekker* (2 vols.; Collection des Études Anglaises; Librairie Marcel Didier: Paris, 1958).

—— 'Source du latin scolastique dans *The Whore of Babylon* de Thomas Dekker', *Études Anglaises* (May 1953).

KNIGHTS, L. C., *Drama and Society in the Age of Jonson* (Chatto and Windus: London, 1937).

LACEY, ROBERT, *Robert, Earl of Essex: An Elizabethan Icarus* (Weidenfeld and Nicolson: London, 1971).

LAWLESS, DONALD S., *Philip Massinger and His Associates* (Ball State Monographs, 10; Ball State University Press: Muncie, Ind., 1967).

LAWRENCE, W. J., 'The Problem of Lyly's Songs', TLS, 20 Dec. 1923, 894.

—— *Speeding up Shakespeare* (The Argonaut Press: London, 1937).

LEE, SIDNEY (ed.), *The Dictionary of National Biography* (63 vols.; Smith, Elder and Co.: London, 1899).

LEMON, ROBERT (ed.), *Calendar of State Papers Domestic, 1547–80* (Longman and Co.: London, 1856).

LIMON, JERZY, *Dangerous Matter: English Drama and Politics 1623–4* (CUP: Cambridge, 1986).

LOADES, D. M., *Two Tudor Conspiracies* (CUP: Cambridge, 1965).

LOCKYER, ROGER, *Buckingham: The Life and Political Career of George Villiers, First Duke of Buckingham* (Longman Group Ltd.: London, 1981).

MCCLURE, DONALD S., 'Versification and Master Hammon in *The Shoemakers' Holiday*', *Osaka Studies in the Humanities 1* (1969), 50–4.

MCGINN, BERNARD, *The Calabrian Abbot: Joachim of Fiore in the History of Western Thought* (Collier Macmillan: London, 1985).

MARTIN, MARY F., '*If You Know Not Mee You Know Nobodie*, and *The Famous History of Sir Thomas Wyatt*', *The Library*, 4th series, no. 13 (1932), 272–81.

—— 'Stow's *Annals* and *Sir Thomas Wyatt*', *Modern Language Revie*, LIII (1958), 75–7.

MORTENSEN, PETER, 'The Economics of Joy in *The Shoemakers' Holiday*', *Studies in English Literature*, 16 (1976), 241–52.

MULLANY, PETER F., 'Religion in Massinger and Dekker's *The Virgin Martyr*', *Komos*, II, no. 3 (March 1970), 89–97.

NEALE, J. E., *Queen Elizabeth* (Jonathan Cape: London, 1934).

NEW, JOHN H., *Anglican and Puritan: The Basis of Their Opposition 1558–1640* (Adam and Charles Black: London, 1964).

NICHOLS, JOHN (ed.), *Progresses of James I* (4 vols.; Society of Antiquaries, 1828).

NORBROOK, DAVID, 'The Masque of Truth: Court Entertainments and International Protestant Politics in the Early Stuart Period', article forthcoming in *Paideia*, Renaissance Issue.

—— *Poetry and Politics in the English Renaissance* (Routledge and Kegan Paul: London, 1984).

NORWOOD, F. A., 'The Strangers' "Model Churches" in Sixteenth Century England', in *Reformation Studies: Essays in Honor of Roland H. Bainton*, ed. Franklin B. Littell (John Knox Press: Richmond, Va., 1962).

NOVARR, DAVID, 'Dekker's Gentle Craft and the Lord Mayor of London', *Modern Philology*, LVII (1960), 233–9.

PATRIDES, C. A., and WITTREICH, JOSEPH (eds.), *The Apocalypse in English Renaissance Thought and Literature* (Manchester University Press: Manchester, 1984).

PECK, LINDA L., *Northampton: Patronage and Policy at the Court of James I* (George Allen & Unwin: London, 1982).

PENDRY, E. D., 'Thomas Dekker in the Magistrate's Court', *English Literary Renaissance*, 3 (1973), 53–9.

PETERSON, JOSEPH MARTIN, *The Dorothea Legend: Its Earliest Records, Middle English Versions, and Influence on Massinger's 'Virgin Martyr'*, Ph.D. thesis (University of Heidelberg, 1910).

PETTI, ANTHONY G., 'Beasts and Politics in Elizabethan Literature', *Essays and Studies*, 16 (1963), 68–90.

PIERCE, F. E., 'The Collaboration of Thomas Dekker and Ford: The Authorship of *The Sun's Darling*: The Authorship of *The Witch of Edmonton*', *Anglia*, XXXVI (1912), 289–312.

PINEAS, RAINIER, 'Biblical Allusions in *The Whore of Babylon*', *American Notes and Queries*, XI (1972), 22–4.

POLLARD, A. W. (ed.), *Shakespeare's Hand in 'Sir Thomas More'* (Shakespeare Problems Series, ed. A. W. Pollard and J. Dover Wilson; CUP: Cambridge, 1923).

PRICE, GEORGE R., *Thomas Dekker* (Twayne's English Authors Series, 71; Twayne Publishers Inc.: New York, 1969).

RAMSAY, G. D., 'The Foreign Policy of Elizabeth I', in *The Reign of Elizabeth I*, ed. C. Haigh (Macmillan: London, 1984).

RIBNER, IRVING, *The English History Play in the Age of Shakespeare* (Methuen and Co.: London, 1957; rev. edn. 1965).

RICH, E. E., and WILSON, C. H. (eds.), *The Economy of Expanding*

Europe in the 16th and 17th Centuries, Vol. IV of *The Cambridge Economic History* (CUP: Cambridge, 1967).

SAMSON, G. (ed.), *Concise Cambridge History of English Literature*, 3rd edn. rev. by R. C. Churchill (CUP: Cambridge, 1970).

SCHANZER, ERNEST, 'Justice and King James in *Measure for Measure*', in *Measure for Measure Casebook*, ed. C. K. Stead (Casebook Series, gen. ed. A. E. Dyson; Macmillan: London, 1971), 233–41.

SCHELLING, FELIX E., *Elizabethan Drama 1558–1642* (2 vols.; Houghton, Mifflin & Co.: Boston and NY, 1908).

SCOTT, MARY AUGUSTA, *Elizabethan Translations from the Italian* (Vassar Semi-Centennial Series; The Riverside Press: Cambridge, Mass., 1916).

SCRIBNER, R. W., *For the Sake of Simple Folk: Popular Propaganda for the German Reformation* (Cambridge Studies in Oral and Literate Culture, 2; CUP: Cambridge, 1981).

SHARPE, KEVIN (ed.), *Faction and Parliament: Essays on Early Stuart History* (OUP: Oxford, 1978).

SHEPHERD, SIMON, *Amazons and Warrior Women* (Harvester Press: Brighton, 1981).

SISSON, C. J., *Lost Plays of Shakespeare's Age* (CUP: Cambridge, 1936).

SPIKES, JUDITH DOOLIN, 'The Jacobean History Play and the Myth of the Elect Nation', *Renaissance Drama*, NS 8 (1977), 117–49.

STRONG, ROY C., *The Cult of Elizabeth* (Thames and Hudson: London, 1977).

—— 'Icons of Power and Prophecy: Portraits of Elizabeth I', in *Queen Elizabeth I: Most Politick Princess*, ed. Simon L. Adams (A History Today Production, series editor Juliet Gardiner, 1984).

—— *Portraits of Queen Elizabeth I* (OUP: London, 1963).

STRONG, ROY C., and VAN DORSTEN, J. (eds.), *Leicester's Triumph* (OUP: London, 1964).

TREVOR-ROPER, HUGH, *Renaissance Essays* (Secker and Warburg: London, 1985).

WARD, Sir ADOLPHUS WILLIAM, *A History of English Dramatic Literature to the Death of Queen Anne* (3 vols.; Macmillan and Co.: London, 1875; 2nd edn., rev. 1899).

WEDGWOOD, C. V., *The Thirty Years War* (Jonathan Cape: London, 1938).

WELLS, STANLEY, 'Mixed Humour', TLS, 26 June 1981, 727.

WHITE, HELEN C., *English Devotional Literature 1600–1640* (University of Wisconsin Studies in Language and Literature, 29; University of Wisconsin Press: Madison, 1931).

WILLSON, DAVID HARRIS, *King James VI and I* (Jonathan Cape: London, 1956; rpt. 1971).

WILSON, CHARLES, *Profit and Power: A Study of England and the Dutch Wars* (Longmans, Green and Co.: London, 1957).

WILSON, JOHN DOVER, Review of R. C. Bald's edition of *A Game of [sic] Chesse*, *The Library*, 4th series, no. 11 (1930), 105–16.

WORMALD, JENNY, 'James VI and I: Two Kings or One?', *History*, 68, no. 223 (June 1983), 187–209.

WORRINGER, W., *Lucas Cranach* (Klassische Illustratoren, III; R. Piper and Co., Verlag: Munich, 1908).

YATES, FRANCES A., *Astraea: The Imperial Theme in the Sixteenth Century* (Routledge and Kegan Paul: London, 1975).

—— *A Study of 'Love's Labour's Lost'* (CUP: Cambridge, 1936).

INDEX